UNDERSTANDING LITERACY

Personality Preference in Rhetorical and Psycholinguistic Contexts

edited by
Alice Horning
and
Ronald A. Sudol
Oakland University

 HAMPTON PRESS, INC.
CRESSKILL, NEW JERSEY

Printed in the United States of America

Library of Congress Cataloging-in-Publication Data

Understanding literacy : personality preference in rhetorical and psycholinguistic contexts / edited by Alice Horning and Ronald A. Sudol.
    p. cm.
   Includes bibliographical references and indexes.
   ISBN 1-57273-078-1 (cloth). -- ISBN 1-57273-079-X (pbk.)
   1. Language and languages--Study and teaching--Psychological aspects. 2. Literacy. 3. Rhetoric--Study and teaching--psychological aspects. 4. Personality. 5. Psycholinguistics.
I. Horning, Alice S. II. Sudol, Ronald A., 1943-
P99.U53 1997   96-40404
302.2'244'019---dc21   CIP

Hampton Press, Inc.
23 Broadway
Cresskill, NJ 07626

For Donald C. Hildum
(1930-1996)
Professor of Communication and Linguistics
Oakland University

His openness to theory and its applications exemplified one of the premier satisfactions of academic life. We appreciated his sharing of thoughtful commentaries on type theory and its use in helping us understand human development and promote literacy. On a more personal level, we are grateful to him for serving as an exemplary colleague over the years.

A. S. H.
R. A. S.

Contents

Preface   vii
Introduction   xi

PART ONE: PERSONALITY AND CULTURAL LITERACY

1. Finding a Way to Speak: Culture , Place, and Self in
    Heath's Ways With Words
        Shannon R. Wooden and George H. Jensen   3

2. Personality Preferences and the Concept of Audience
        Thomas Thompson   19

3. Self-Representation and Personality Type
    in "Letter From Birmingham Jail"
        Ronald A. Sudol   37

4. Writing Style, Personality Type and Brain Dominance:
    A New Model
        Sheila Davis   55

PART TWO: PERSONALITY AND STUDENT LITERACY

5. Collaborative Grouping and Personality Theory
        Angela Creech Green   91

6. Personality and Reading Response Journals
        Vicki Tolar Collins   105

7.   Personality Type and Revising by Student Writers
       Jane Bowman Smith   125

8.   Personality Type in the Foreign or Second Language
       Classroom: Theoretical and Empirical Perspectives
       Rebecca L. Oxford   153

PART THREE: PERSONALITY AND PROFESSIONAL LITERACY

9.   The Psycholinguistics of Revising
       Alice S. Horning   183

10.   Personality and Writing Process Preferences of
       Teachers Related to the Use of Computers
       Dianne Swenson Koehnecke   207

11.   Psychological Type and Extremes of Training
       Outcomes in Foreign Language Reading Proficiency
       Madeline E. Ehrman   231

Author Index   279
Subject Index   285

Preface

Literacy demands careful negotiation between the resistant poles of self and culture. Losing balance on the side of self leads to apathy and social fragmentation; losing balance on the side of culture leads to exclusion and separation. Until recently, literacy was defined in the monolithic terms of cultural hegemony. There was a clear sense of what sorts of functions were literate and illiterate and an equally clear determination to extend the advantages of literacy to those who did not possess it. The exclusions brought about by this imbalance on the side of culture have fueled considerable social and political debate. The central issue in the debate has been whether taking account of all the differences between classes of individuals restores balance or throws the scale out of balance on the side of self, thus contributing to fragmentation.

To what extent can literacy respect the full range of human difference (in terms of gender, race, ethnicity, language, and every kind of lifestyle classification) without losing the ability to provide a common basis for communication? One difficulty faced by those who wrestle with this question is that some of our differences involve deeply embedded alternative ways of viewing the world. Indeed, most contemporary discussion of literacy grapples with the ways in which gender, ethnic, racial, and lifestyle differences invoke alternative codes that confound monolithic views of literacy. These inquiries based on categorical differences inevitably become entangled with related social and political issues. The resulting conversation has been lively and productive.

The essays collected here under the title *Understanding Literacy: Personality Preference in Rhetorical and Psycholinguistic Contexts* take a different approach to the problem of balancing self and culture. Our contributors see difference defined not in terms of categories but in terms of personality. To a large extent, personality differences cut across categorical differences, but they are no less influential on how we read the world and engage in its human activities. Among educators, the Myers-Briggs Type Indicator, and the Jungian theory on which it is based, has provided an effective method for describing and understanding personality difference and its impact on human interaction. Accordingly, we invited contributors to employ this perspective in their explorations of some issues related to literacy and education. The Myers-Briggs theory, method, and instrument are at once elegantly simple and deeply complex. Professionals in education, government, counseling, business, and many other fields have found productive uses for the Myers-Briggs. At the same time, however, the eight variations of personality in four categories (extraversion/introversion, sensing/intuition, feeling/thinking, and judging/perceiving) are deceptively simple, sometimes leading to superficial analyses and false applications. Used with care and understanding, however, the Myers-Briggs method is highly potent, not least because of its positive view of difference—namely, that individual personality variations are not aberrations to be corrected but gifts to be well used.

We asked our contributors to place the Myers-Briggs theories and applications firmly within the contexts of existing theoretical frameworks in rhetoric and psycholinguistics so that readers would be able to see that the use of this method is not an alternative to existing frameworks but a way of understanding them differently. In order to assist readers who are unfamiliar with the Myers-Briggs system, we have included an introductory chapter that outlines its key concepts. The contributed essays that follow are divided into three sections: "Personality and Cultural Literacy," "Personality and Student Literacy," and "Personality and Professional Literacy."

In Part One, our contributors explore the effect of personality on several elements of rhetorical transactions—social context (Wooden and Jensen), audience (Thompson), persona (Sudol), and style (Davis). In "Finding a Way to Speak: Culture, Place, and Self in Heath's Ways with Words" Shannon Wooden and George H. Jensen take a fresh look at the contrasting discourse communities of Trackton and Roadville by way of the dominant personality preferences in the two communities. Thomas Thompson, in "Personality Preferences and the Concept of Audience," reviews the historical development of the concept of audience and finds correspondences between alternative theories and personality variations. In "Self-Representation and Personality Type in 'Letter From Birmingham

Jail,'" Ronald A. Sudol proposes using personality descriptions as a method for analyzing persona in public discourse. Finally, Sheila Davis, in "Writing Style, Personality Type, and Brain Dominance: A New Model," shows how personality type predicts writing style and how these preferences correspond with the master tropes identified by Giambattista Vico.

Part Two begins with Angela Green's discussion of the role of students' personality type in the transformation of a traditional classroom into a collaborative one. Vicki Collins examines students' reading response journals in a literature class and the ways that their choice of responses is consistent with their type. Jane Smith provides a in-depth comparative analysis of type and revising by novice and experienced student writers. The final chapter in Part Two by Rebecca Oxford reports on the role of personality type in the development of students' second language skills.

Part Three opens with Alice Horning's study of four students and two expert writers; results show that although all writers revise using preferred strategies, expert writers are able to shift to nonpreferred strategies when they work on tasks in which they are emotionally involved. In "Personality and Word Processing," Dianne Koehnecke presents a study of 90 teachers learning to use word processing in a professional development course; her findings show that type preferences influence responses to computer use. Finally, Madeline Ehrman's findings in a study of professional second language readers indicate that the sensing/intuition dimension of personality type is most significant for developing second language reading skills.

Introduction to Personality Type

This collection brings together current theoretical research concerning the uses of personality type in understanding human language behavior. Our particular focus is on the myriad aspects of language learning, literacy development, and critical ability in reading and writing. Personality type theory, as originally proposed by Carl Jung and developed by Katharine Briggs and Isabel Briggs Myers, offers significant insight into human behavior in general and language use in particular. This insight is particularly important now as we come to terms with the urgent need for critical literacy. In the United States, a recent survey of adult literacy shows that Americans are lacking in the critical literacy skills needed for full participation in our society (Kirsch, Jungeblut, Jenkins, & Kolstad, 1993). This collection contributes to our understanding of the complex nature of critical literacy and ways in which human beings interact with language consistent with their personality type. The chapters draw on basic concepts of personality preference, rhetoric and composition, linguistics, and psycholinguistics. This introductory chapter provides an overview of these concepts for those unfamiliar with the contributing areas of inquiry.

KEY CONCEPTS IN PERSONALITY TYPE THEORY

Jung's Theory of Personality

The patterns of human behavior and preferences among people have been analyzed by Carl Jung (1921/1971) and presented in his theory of personality type. There are a number of points on which Jung's analysis of personality compares favorably with views of linguists and psycholinguists, including the concept of innateness. Jung believed that personality type was innate just as many linguists believe that the capacity for language is innate in human beings. Jung defined personality type as follows:

> A type is a specimen or example which reproduces in a characteristic way the character of a species or class. In the narrower sense used in this particular work, a type is a characteristic specimen of a general *attitude* occurring in many individual forms. From a great number of existing or possible attitudes, I have singled out four; those, namely, that are primarily oriented by the four basic psychological *functions: thinking, feeling, sensation, intuition.* When any of these attitudes is habitual, thus setting a definite stamp on the character of an individual, I speak of a psychological type. (p. 482; emphasis in original)

Jung's theory, as interpreted by Isabel Briggs Myers (1980), claims that essential aspects of personality are innate, rather like the preference for using one hand or the other. However, full development of type is strongly influenced by environment, which may or may not be supportive. In this view, then, the environment is not the central determinant of type and its development, but can make an important contribution to it. Linguists who subscribe to a social interactionist view of language development would say much the same thing, and scholars in literacy development have provided research evidence of the impact of the environment on reading and writing acquisition. Jung also examines how psychologists can and/or should study type development in people. At the time he was living and working in the 1920s and 1930s, little was known about personality, and psychology was a new science. In "A Psychological Theory of Types," an essay within *Psychological Types* (1921/1971), he begins with a discussion of how to examine types, claiming that it is necessary to start with overt behavior and extrapolate from that to the internal mechanisms that drive people's choices. In a similar way, linguists examine the outcome of first language acquisition and propose from that the underlying mental mechanisms that drive language development. On these points, then, the understanding of personality preference and psycholinguistics have much in common.

FOUR DIMENSIONS OF PERSONALITY TYPE

Jung's analysis shows that people have preferences along four dimensions that bear on energy sources, preferred ways of taking in information, preferred bases for decision making, and preferred ways of interacting in the world. These preferences are established early in life and help account for the choices people make. Jung's work has been expanded and discussed by Katharine Briggs and Isabel Briggs Myers; their collaboration led to the development of a psychological instrument—the Myers-Briggs Type Indicator (MBTI)—to measure personality preferences and psychological type that characterizes those preferences (Myers & McCaulley, 1985).

The preferences Jung described, as expanded by Briggs and Myers, yield four dimensions of personality. The first dimension pertains to how people get energized. Those who get their energy principally from the outer world of people and things are characterized as extraverts (assigned letter E in Type Indicator results), whereas those whose preference draws energy from the inner world of ideas and concepts are introverts (I). Although individuals may at times appear to be at one or the other end of this and the other dimensions, both the Type Indicator and an analysis of behavior show that they have a preference for one side of this dimension or the other. Type preferences are related, as our collection will show, to strategies people use in approaching language, whether as readers or writers, as language learners or language interpreters.

A second preference dimension deals with how people take in information. The perceiving process may focus chiefly on information available through the five senses, yielding a sensing (S) preference on the MBTI. Or the perceiving process may focus less on the sensory data available and more on the possibilities and mental opportunities the information represents. If individuals choose to see more possibilities than facts, they are characterized as intuitive types (N). This second dimension of personality along with the third dimension have an added significance in Jung's theory as people choose one preference from these two dimensions as their dominant mental process, the one with which they feel most comfortable, the one most used, and the one most well developed in personality. The role of the dominant function in terms of language behavior is discussed later.

The third dimension of personality in which people show preferences is the dimension of decision making. Some people prefer to make most of their decisions based on facts, logic, and reason. If decisions are made this way, individuals are at the thinking end of this aspect of personality. Other individuals make decisions based on their feelings and human values, including consideration of how other people might feel or be influenced by the decision at hand. When decisions are made chiefly on human values rather than logic and reason, the result on the MBTI is a preference for feeling (F).

The fourth dimension of personality reflects characteristics Jung described only generally. Isabel Briggs Myers (1980) extended Jung's observations to this fourth dimension of personality development, having to do with preferences for lifestyle. Individuals may prefer a planned, orderly way of life in their interaction with the outside world, in which case they are said to be judging types (J). Those who have a more flexible, adaptable style of life and prefer a more spontaneous approach to life are perceiving types (P).

THE DOMINANT AND INFERIOR FUNCTIONS

This fourth dimension also helps explain the way in which the four aspects of personality interact such that the last dimension specifies which of the preceding two is an individual's most favorite or dominant function (Myers & McCaulley, 1985). A judging (J)type will have thinking or feeling dominant, whereas a perceiving type will have sensing or intuition dominant. Two additional concepts clarify this statement. Individuals deal with the outer world in different ways depending on their preference on the first dimension—extraversion or introversion. Jung's analysis shows that one's strongest preference or most developed dimension is either a perceiving function (sensing or intuition) or a judging function (thinking or feeling). This strongest preference is known in the theory as the dominant process. Naomi Quenk (1993) summarizes the dominant function this way:

> The *dominant function* represents what we want to devote our attention and activity to most of the time. This is either a person's preferred form of judgment (i.e., either thinking or feeling), or his or her preferred form of perception (either sensing or intuition). We tend to use our dominant function primarily in our preferred attitude or orientation of energy, either extraversion or introversion. (p. 29; emphasis in original)

The dominant is usually the most well-developed aspect of personality.

In addition to assigning one function a dominant role in the structure of personality, Jung described auxiliary, tertiary, and inferior functions. The auxiliary is always the other function, the one that is not the dominant, and always appears in the less preferred attitude (extraversion or introversion). Thus, a person whose dominant is extraverted thinking has introverted sensing or introverted intuition as the auxiliary (Quenk, 1993). The auxiliary is thought to work in the structure of the personality to support and complement the dominant function. The dominant and auxiliary work together, then, to provide a balanced personality. The tertiary, about which Jung said very little, is the opposite of the auxiliary.

The inferior function has been described in depth by both Jung and more recently by Quenk (1993). Simply put, the inferior function is the "polar opposite of the dominant" (p. 36). In the case of a person whose

MBTI result is ESTJ, the dominant is extraverted thinking and the inferior is introverted feeling (Quenk, 1993). That is, the inferior takes the opposite attitude and the opposite function on the same dimension as the dominant. The inferior plays an important role in the personality, although it is the least developed aspect. Quenk explains that although people can make conscious use of their tertiary and fourth functions and can become effective at doing so, this conscious use, particularly of the fourth or inferior function, does not preclude its eruption in its unconscious and poorly developed form (Quenk, 1993). Indeed, when the inferior erupts, according to Quenk, a person is not a positive exemplar of the opposite of the dominant, but shows all the worst traits of the opposite type. When individuals report being out of sorts or "not themselves," usually as a result of stress, illness, or fatigue (Quenk, 1993), they have probably had an eruption of the inferior function. The inferior may also play a role when a person is working with language and confronts the stress of trying to complete utterances in a new language or trying to write a difficult document.

Jung's theory focuses less on the auxiliary, tertiary, and inferior functions and more on normal human behavior because he was chiefly interested in describing healthy human interaction. Myers and Briggs drew on Jung's insights to fill out their understanding and observation of human behavior. Using their own observations and the theoretical base provided by *Psychological Types*, they were able to develop the Type Indicator as a personality instrument. The four dimensions of personality preference analyzed by the Indicator, together with Jung's proposals for dominant function and other features of his theory of psychological type, can help shed light on how people understand and use language in the ways explored in this collection.

APPLICATIONS IN RHETORIC AND COMPOSITION PEDAGOGY

The Jungian theory of personality, applied through the Myers-Briggs Type Indicator, enhances our understanding of certain features of rhetoric and composition pedagogy on two levels. First, it provides a fresh perspective on the nature of rhetorical transactions themselves. The difficulty of bridging the gulf between writers and readers in rhetorical situations is one part of the human condition that a knowledge of alternative personalities can at least marginally improve. Second, the MBTI can clarify the range of variation among writing and thinking processes and help students of various types discover and use an appropriate process. The most comprehensive study of these applications has been done by Jensen and DiTiberio (1989) in *Personality and the Teaching of Writing*. The following review of some of their findings should provide helpful background to readers of this collection of essays.

Extraversion and Introversion

Extraverted writers are distinguished by a clear sense of voice, probably because they prefer to develop their thoughts through dialogue. They make effective use of personal experience and write prose that has the vitality, immediacy, and informality of oral conversation. These strengths may be offset by corresponding weaknesses. The informality may not always be appropriate, and the writing of extraverts may become fragmentary and superficial. They benefit most from class discussion, collaborative groups, and oral feedback. Talking and writing are highly generative and productive activities for extraverts.

Introverts are less spontaneous, impulsive, and oral than extraverts. Introverts prefer to work from an agenda, follow plans and outlines, and use formal prewriting procedures. They prefer to think through a topic or problem before composing or speaking and may only need to transcribe what they have already composed mentally. As a result, their writing tends to be more intense, reflective, and abstract. At its best, it is concise and naturally formal, but the voice may lack vitality and a sense of connection with the audience. Their composing process is full of stops and starts as they try to find their way, in contrast to the flow of words that typifies the extravert's process. Furthermore, where the extravert prefers collaborative work, the introvert prefers to work alone, a preference variation that teachers of language and writing should take into account when they organize class activities.

Sensing and Intuition

Sensing types perceive the world through concrete, sensory data. They equate writing with reporting, and their reports are distinguished by accurate observation and clear details. They work well with complex data and can be relied on to get all the facts correct. Their preference for concreteness and precision may make dealing with the ideas and concepts behind the facts more difficult, and, as a result, they may treat concepts casually or superficially. They are most comfortable with a formulaic writing process in which the goals, and the steps by which those goals may be achieved, are clearly identified. Thus, sensing types respond well to specific directions, especially when the starting point of the writing process is direct experience and specific observation. Given their preference for facts and details, sensing types revise their writing by correcting errors. If teachers want to help students revise more globally, they should understand that this tendency toward equating revising with proofreading may be attributable to a personality preference and should be dealt with as such.

Intuitive types perceive the world through generalities and inferences. They feel comfortable with theories and concepts. As writers, they resist formulas and specific directives, preferring instead to set their own goals and find a unique approach to topic or task. Ideas come easily, and they write imaginatively. Nevertheless, their ideas may be nebulous and detached from facts and supporting examples. The writing may be excessively abstract and complex. Moreover, they may find following directions difficult. Teachers will appreciate their attempts at originality but will have to work at helping them understand the constraints of rhetorical situations.

Thinking and Feeling

Writers who use thinking judgment tend to distance themselves from topics and audiences. As a result, they excel at writing logically, objectively, and analytically. They prefer to frame their discourses within clear organizational patterns. These strengths have corresponding weaknesses—a tendency toward overly structured patterns, a dogmatic tone, and a dry and overly technical style. The writing process of thinking types is dominated by outlining, not only in the preliminary stages but in the composing itself. Their essays typically display the remains of the outline used to generate the content. Indeed, thinking writers are more focused on the content than the manner and effectiveness of its presentation to an audience. In revising, they may need to warm up to their readers.

Writers who use feeling judgment stay close to their topics and audiences. As a result, they excel at conveying deep conviction, making contact with the audience, and writing with expressive flair. They tend to organize the material around specific cases and personal examples or observation. These strengths have corresponding weaknesses—a slighting of critical and analytical modes, a tendency toward sentimentality, and a loose organization. The writing process of feeling types depends on the amount of personal involvement they can muster on behalf of the project. The topic and task will make sense if they can be understood in personal terms. Feeling writers are more focused on the effectiveness of the presentation than on the coherence of the content. In revising, they may need to clarify the content and tighten the organization.

Judging and Perceiving

A preference for either decisiveness or thoroughness characterizes the opposite tendencies of judging and perceiving writers. Judging writers seek closure and will stop the flow of data and ideas in order to complete a task. As a result, they write decisively, reach conclusions easily, state propositions forcefully, and conclude their work expeditiously. However, they may reach premature closure, arriving at conclusions arbitrarily and without qualification, denying ambiguity, and writing in an opinionated, overly condensed or underdeveloped style. Their writing process is characterized by expedient time management with decisions about content, organization, tone, and style arrived at early on the process. In revising, judging types need to reevaluate early decisions, consider modifying original conclusions, and develop ideas that may be presented cryptically and without adequate transitions.

In contrast, perceiving writers sacrifice decisiveness for thoroughness. On the one hand, they explore topics thoroughly, consider a broad range of possibilities, and present their ideas and conclusions prudently. Their writing will be fully developed, amply supported and illustrated, and presented with necessary qualifications. On the other hand, they may choose topics that are too broad—rambling on at tedious length, overgeneralizing issues, and digressing at every turn. The writing process of perceiving types is characterized by inclusiveness. They are somewhat more inclined to procrastination than judging types. They gather an immense amount of material and delay getting down to drafting until they feel comfortable with what they have. Then they try to include in their drafts all the material they have generated. In revising, they need to use focusing strategies to shape their material into discourse.

Personality Variation in the Classroom

These descriptions are not labels. They merely express the polar tendencies toward which all of us incline naturally. The strengths related to those preferences are offset by corresponding weaknesses, and human development involves making good use of strengths and compensating for weaknesses. Thus, for example, a judging type writer enjoys the benefits of decisiveness and expediency, but in order to write effectively he or she may have to develop some skills that come naturally to the perceiving type—such as thoroughness and prudence. The degree to which we may exploit our strengths or may need to compensate for weaknesses will vary according to conditions and circumstances.

For the classroom teacher, these eight categories of personality difference merely articulate what every teacher of writing and communication has no doubt already observed. The benefit of this particular way of organizing the range of human variation is that it is based on an enduring and coherent set of theories that provide a simple language we can use in our conversation about teaching and learning.

APPLICATIONS IN LINGUISTICS AND PSYCHOLINGUISTICS

Language and Linguistics

For most contemporary linguists, language is a subject of endless fascination. It is simply defined as a rule-governed system of symbolic communication in which the symbols (spoken, written, or gestural) are arbitrarily connected to the ideas they represent. The rules of language comprise what linguists call the grammar of a language, and the knowledge of these rules is largely unconscious. Human beings have, according to most linguists, an innate capacity to acquire the rules of their native language, and virtually all normal individuals do so early in life.

Linguistics is the scientific study of human language. That is, linguists draw on scientific method to make observations and propose hypotheses about the nature of language and human language behavior. These hypotheses can then be tested empirically. Theoretical linguists make proposals about the nature of various aspects of the grammar. They examine sounds, words, sentences, discourses, and meanings and suggest key features of a language or of languages generally. They may rely on data from a single language or cross-linguistic data from several languages or language families. There are a variety of current theories about the nature of language, including generative views such as that originally proposed by Chomsky (1965, 1982), cognitive views such as that originally proposed by Langacker (1987), functional views such as that proposed by Halliday (1985), and many others (Robins, 1990).

Psycholinguistics, Language Acquisition and Language Learning

Psycholinguistics is usually thought of as the area within the discipline in which the theoretical proposals of linguists are tested out. Psycholinguists attempt to design experiments to test the validity of theoretical proposals, with a focus on the brain mechanisms responsible for language. The experiments psycholinguists can conduct have become increasingly sophisticated as computer technology has improved and as devices such as C-T scans have made it easier to study brain activity in a noninvasive way. As the term suggests, psycholinguistics is the discipline in which linguistics and psychology cross, and the types of studies done are more focused on brain mechanisms in human language if psychologists conduct them and more focused on linguistic phenomena if linguists carry them out.

Two areas of particular importance in such testing are language acquisition and language learning. Theoretical developments in the 1960s and 1970s in linguistics raised many issues that warranted study from a developmental perspective. To account for theoretical proposals about how mature human beings use language, psycholinguists tested hypotheses about how such abilities might develop from birth. In the 1960s and early 1970s, much of the focus was on the development of sentence structure or syntax (Brown, 1973; Chomsky, 1969), whereas in the 1970s, more attention was paid to the development of meaning, or semantics (Berko Gleason, 1993; Bloom, 1973). Again, the studies rely on data from a particular language or on data drawn from a number of different languages (Slobin, 1985).

The major findings show that the capacity for language acquisition is innate in human beings and, at least for the time being, unique to human beings. In addition, the cross-linguistic studies show that all children acquire language in a similar fashion, passing through a series of stages that have been observed. The staged nature of language acquisition and the patterns of errors made by children have been documented in languages from different parts of the world, across different races, cultures, and socioeconomic classes. Virtually all normal individuals become fluent in at least one language, as do many individuals with disabilities.

Psycholinguists with an interest in second language acquisition do not find a similar consistency with regard to the successful acquisition of a second language. Although young children may acquire two languages (or more), if the environment provides them with the relevant language data, many individuals find it difficult or impossible to become fluent speakers of a second language in later childhood or adulthood. Much second language research has focused on why this is true, and scholars have looked at both successful and unsuccessful language learners in an attempt to account for the difficulty.

Although it is not yet clear why some second language learners succeed whereas others do not, there is research evidence to suggest that certain aspects of second language acquisition share features of first language development, and there is also research (some of which is presented or referred to in this collection) that supports the claim that language acquisition is influenced in various ways by psychological type. Second language acquisition among adults appears to proceed in stages that, although not as clearly defined or time-limited as the stages in L1, contain clearly marked features. Larry Selinker's (1972, 1992) proposals concerning the interlanguage hypothesis are a major theoretical contribution supporting this relationship between L1 and L2 . In addition, second language learners make errors that bear a resemblance to those made by children developing their first language (Brown, 1994), such as errors of overgeneralization (for example when children say "I have two foots" or "I falled down," extending regular endings to exceptional cases).

The psycholinguistic evidence suggests that the staged character of language development and the types of errors made by learners are two characteristics shared by first and second language acquisition.

Both processes seem clearly influenced by individuals' psychological type. There is more psycholinguistic research on the impact of personality type on second language learning than there is on its impact in L1 development (Brown, 1994; Oxford & Ehrman, 1990). However, psycholinguists may be capturing some fundamental differences in personality type when their findings reveal a difference in the lexical development of young children such that some children are described as "referential," preferring to learn nouns and names for things first, whereas others are "expressive," preferring to learn the words for social interaction (Nelson, 1973). The work of Oxford and Ehrman and other scholars in second language acquisition shows the importance of personality type in successful second language teaching and learning.

Psycholinguistic research in L1 and L2, then, shows the several characteristics shared by these processes. Among these are staged development, patterns of errors, and the influence of personality preferences as human beings develop language capabilities. These areas of inquiry share common ground in these observations, along with the view that both the capacity for language and individual personality preferences are present at birth, that is, innate.

Psycholinguistics, Literacy Development, and Critical Literacy

Psycholinguistic research has also addressed the development of literacy skills and more recently investigated the development of critical literacy. In terms of the development of literacy skills, there is evidence to suggest that, like L1 and L2 development, literacy too develops by stages (Chall, 1983; Teale & Sulzby, 1986). This is clear not only in reading development but also in the development of writing skills in early childhood. Similarly, psycholinguistic research on reading shows that there are important patterns in the errors readers make as they proceed through a text, and that errors can show how much information readers are getting from the text (Goodman & Burke, 1972). Error patterns among basic writers also show a developmental pattern that sheds light on writers' progress and growing mastery of written forms (Horning, 1987; Shaughnessy, 1977).

The work in critical literacy again draws together psycholinguistic findings and personality type theory. The seminal work of Jensen and DiTiberio (1989) shows the importance of personality type theory to our understanding of how adults become critically literate. Their discussion of both basic writers and graduate students shows how writing skills develop over time in ways consistent with writers' personality types. Their studies demonstrate the ways in which literacy instruction can be strengthened by an awareness of personality preferences for both writers and writing instructors. The relationship of personality to reading and to the interaction of reading and writing has also been explored directly (Horning, 1993; O'Hear, 1989) and indirectly (Sternglass, 1988). Psycholinguistic research that focuses on literacy development and critical literacy has increasingly focused on the ways in which personality type makes a difference to human language understanding and use.

Learning Style and Literacy

One way in which personality type is helpful in psycholinguistic research concerns our developing knowledge of individual variation in language acquisition, language learning and literacy development (Brown, 1994; Chall, 1983; Goldfield & Snow, 1993; Oxford & Ehrman, 1993; Skehan, 1989). Part of the reason for this lies in the expanding awareness of differences in learning style, a matter closely related to personality preferences. As Gordon Lawrence (1993) points out in *People Types and Tiger Stripes*, learning style and personality type are not the same, although they are related. In particular, with regard to literacy skills, Lawrence notes that reading is largely an introverted and intuitive activity that requires some different teaching strategies for students who are extraverted and sensing types.

Gordon Lawrence's (1993) work has focused chiefly on the importance of personality type in educational settings. In his discussion, Lawrence provided two key definitions of learning style. First, he notes that the sensing-intuition dimension is the one that has the greatest influence on learning style:

> In learning situations, sensing people attend most often to the literal meaning they find in concrete experiences. They learn best by moving step-by-step through a new experience, with their senses as engaged as possible. Intuitive learners' attention is drawn most often to things that stimulate imagination, to possibilities not found in sensory experience. Their minds work by skips and jumps, looking for patterns wherever the inspiration takes them. The other three dimensions of type also have learning style preferences associated with them, but the SN differences are the most basic. (p. 38)

Thus, in looking at learning style, the differences among learners on the perceiving dimension of sensing-intuition are most important. Because two thirds of the population has a reported preference for sensing (Myers & McCaulley, 1985), teachers, and especially teachers with intuitive preferences, need to be aware of the difference between their teaching styles and students' likely predominant learning style.

Lawrence (1993) further defines learning style as encompassing the following points: First, learning style has to do with cognitive preferences for information intake, forming ideas and judgments. Second, learning style accounts for what learners attend to based on their attitudes and interests. Third, learning style drives learners to choose learning environments that fit them and to avoid those that do not. Finally, learning style includes a preference for certain learning tools and success with those tools. There are any number of examples of the ways in which learning style and preference are related and can account for individual responses to different aspects of learning tasks.

For instance, extraverts will tend to prefer discussion to reading or individual research. Sensing types work best on step-by-step tasks, whereas students with a preference for intuition will prefer finding their own way and using imagination. Thinking types will follow a teacher's logical organization, whereas feeling types learn best through personal relationships with other learners and/or the teacher. Judging types will proceed in an orderly fashion through a task, seeking closure, whereas perceiving types like discovery and flexible, informal problem-solving work (Lawrence, 1993). Lawrence's work offers many other observations, but the main point is that the variations we see in how learners respond to and use language and literacy abilities are to some degree a function of their learning styles and personality preferences. These ideas are explored in more detail in the articles in this collection.

This brief overview of key concepts in personality type theory and their relevance to rhetoric and composition, linguistics, and psycholinguistics shows that these areas of inquiry share the domains of interest in human interaction with language, both written and spoken. Personality preferences are thought to shape how human beings get their energy, take in information, make decisions, and live their lives. Nowhere are these preferences displayed more clearly than in one of the most fundamental features of human behavior—language. The articles in this collection look at human language from diverse perspectives: language development and language learning, as well as the processing of written forms of language, whether through intake in reading or output in writing. Each chapter takes a different aspect of language but shows the variation in the psychology of personality type that accounts for how and why individuals develop, use, and understand language in their chosen ways.

REFERENCES

Berko Gleason, J. (Ed.). (1993). *The development of language* (3rd ed.). New York: Macmillan.

Bloom, L. (1973). *One word at a time.* The Hague: Mouton.

Brown, H. D. (1994). *Principles of language learning and teaching* (3rd ed.). Englewood Cliffs, NJ: Prentice-Hall.

Brown, R. (1973). *A first language.* Cambridge, MA: Harvard University Press.

Chall, J. S. (1983). *Stages of reading development.* New York: McGraw-Hill.

Chomsky, C. (1969). *The acquisition of syntax in children from five to ten.* Cambridge, MA: MIT Press.

Chomsky, N. (1965). *Aspects of the theory of syntax.* Cambridge, MA: MIT Press.

Chomsky, N. (1982). *Some concepts and consequences of the theory of government and binding.* Cambridge, MA: MIT Press.

Goldfield, B., & Snow, C. (1993). Individual differences in language acquisition. In J. Berko Gleason (Ed.), *The development of language* (pp. 299-324). New York: Macmillan.

Goodman, Y., & Burke, C. (1972). *Reading miscue inventory.* New York: Macmillan.

Halliday, M. A. K. (1985). *An introduction to functional grammar.* London: Edward Arnold.

Horning, A. S. (1987). *Teaching writing as a second language.* Carbondale: Southern Illinois University Press.

Horning, A. S. (1993). *The psycholinguistics of reading writing: A multidisciplinary exploration.* Norwood, NJ: Ablex.

Jensen, G., & DiTiberio, J. (1989). *Personality and the teaching of composition.* Norwood, NJ: Ablex.

Jung, C. G. (1971). *Psychological types* (H. G. Baynes, Trans., revised by R. F. C. Hull; Vol. 6 of *The collected works of C. G. Jung*). Princeton, NJ: Princeton University Press. (Original work published in 1921)

Kirsch, I. S., Jungeblut, A., Jenkins, L., & Kolstad, A. (1993). *Adult literacy in America.* National Center for Education Statistics. Office of Educational Research and Improvement, United States Department of Education, Washington, DC: Government Printing Office.

Langacker, R. (1987). *Foundations of cognitive grammar.* Stanford, CA: Stanford University Press.

Lawrence, G. (1993). *People types & tiger stripes* (3rd ed.). Gainesville, FL: Center for Applications of Psychological Type.

Myers, I. B. (1980). *Gifts differing.* Palo Alto, CA: Consulting Psychologists.

Myers, I. B., & McCaulley, M. H. (1985). *Manual: A guide to the development and use of the Myers-Briggs Type Indicator.* Palo Alto, CA: Consulting Psychologists.

Nelson, K. (1973). Structure and strategy in learning to talk. *Monographs of the Society for Research in Child Development,*38.

O'Hear, M. F. (1989). *Personality types and reading styles.* (ERIC Document Reproduction Service No. ED 303 778).

Oxford, R., & Ehrman, M. (1990). Adult language learning styles and strategies in an intensive training setting. *Modern Language Journal, 74*(3), 311-327.

Oxford, R., & Ehrman, M. (1993). Second language research on individual differences. *Annual Review of Applied Linguistics, 13,* 188-205.

Quenk, N. L. (1993). *Beside ourselves: Our hidden personality in everyday life.* Palo Alto, CA: Consulting Psychologists Press.

Robins, R. H. (1990). *A short history of linguistics* (3rd ed.). London: Longman.

Selinker, L. (1972). Interlanguage. *International Review of Applied Linguistics, 10,* 209-231.

Selinker, L. (1992). *Rediscovering interlanguage.* London: Longman.

Shaughnessy, M. (1977). *Errors and expectations: A guide for the teacher of basic writing.* New York: Oxford University Press.

Skehan, P. (1989). *Individual differences in second-language learning.* London: Edward Arnold.

Slobin, D. (Ed.). (1985). *The cross-linguistic study of language acquisition.* Hillsdale, NJ: Erlbaum.

Sternglass, M. S. (1988). *The presence of thought: Introspective accounts of reading and writing.* Norwood, NJ: Ablex.

Teale, W., & Sulzby, E. (Eds.). (1986). *Emergent literacy: Reading and writing.* Norwood, NJ: Ablex.

PART ONE

Personality and Cultural Literacy

Chapter 1

Finding a Way to Speak: Culture, Place, and Self in Heath's *Ways With Words*

Shannon R. Wooden
University of North Carolina-Chapel Hill
George H. Jensen
Southwest Missouri State University

In the Foreword to the Argentine edition of Psychological Types, written 13 years after the first edition, Carl Jung (1921) was able to reflect on the reception of his theory of personality differences. Typical of many original theorists, he felt that he had been misunderstood:

> Even in medical circles the opinion has got about that my method of treatment consists in fitting patients into this system and giving them corresponding "advice." This regrettable misunderstanding completely ignores the fact that this kind of classification is nothing but a childish parlour game, every bit as futile as the division of mankind into brachycephalics and dolichocephalics. My typology is for rather a critical apparatus serving to sort out and organize the welter of empirical material, but not in any sense to stick labels on people at first sight. (p. xiv)

For Jung (1961), analytical psychology was essentially a hermeneutic method by which the psychologist looks to "historical and literary parallels" to avoid "the crudest errors in judgment" (p. 200). And so, rather than begin *Psychological Types* with a description of the model or definitions of each preference, Jung begins by demonstrating the hermeneutic method that he has not yet explained. For 330 pages, he discusses how type theory can be used to analyze medieval thought, poetry, aesthetics, and biography. It is only after he has demonstrated the method that he provides, in Chapter 10, a description of its theory. He hoped this arrangement would prevent readers from thinking that his text was about labeling others. To his dismay, most readers skipped the early chapters. Even today, Chapter 10 remains the only section of *Psychological Types* that is frequently anthologized.

What do readers miss if they skip the early chapters? A hint can be found in Jung's stated intent in writing *Psychological Types*. In *Memories, Dreams, and Reflections*, his autobiography, Jung (1961) wrote that the book "was an effort to deal with the relationship of the individual to the world" (p. 207). As the reader moves through the generally neglected chapters of *Psychological Types*, he or she can sense that Jung was not writing about personality differences as if they operated apart from history or culture; rather he was writing about how our culture shapes who we are and about how we may feel at odds with our place in the world. Jung was saying, in short, that we cannot understand culture or individuals unless we look to the spots of tension that naturally develop between person and place.

In this chapter, we demonstrate this application of type theory to the study of literacy by revisiting Shirley Brice Heath's (1983) *Ways with Words*, her classic study of how two Piedmont communities in the Carolinas viewed literacy. We suggest that Trackton and Roadville, the two communities that Heath studied, each has its own collective personality (what Jung sometimes called a "national temperament"), and that applying type theory to the culture of these communities can allow us then to understand the points of tension between culture and individuals. We feel that such an analysis can provide a richer understanding of literacy in context and even suggest alternative forms of instruction.

HEATH'S ETHNOGRAPHY

Heath's (1983) *Ways with Words* is an ethnography of two Piedmont Carolina communities, Trackton and Roadville, that focuses on the literacy instruction occurring in the home and community. Although the two communities were just a few miles apart, Heath found startling differences, which we discuss in the next few sections. In this section, some general description about the region, the two communities, and Heath's methodology is in order.

When the study was conducted, from 1969 to 1978, the schools in the area were still adjusting to desegregation. The relative poverty of the area—over half the families received some kind of state aid, most of the families made between $8,000 and $10, 000 from two salaries, about the pay of a beginning school teacher—also influenced attitudes toward literacy. Both Trackton and Roadville are small mill towns of less than 150 residents.

As Heath began to study the two communities, she relied on her relationship with long-time residents to gain entree. She then began the painstaking and time-consuming work of learning about the community by, as much as possible, becoming one of its members:

> Detailed descriptions of what actually happens to children as they learn to use language and form their values about its structures and functions tell us what children do to become and remain acceptable members of their own community. Throughout the years of this study, parents, children, teachers and students pursued, to the extent possible in that period of history in that region, their normal priorities of meeting daily needs and sustaining their self-identities. . . . I spent many hours cooking, chopping wood, gardening, sewing, and minding children by the rules of the communities. (p. 8)

While in the communities (if possible) or shortly after leaving, Heath took detailed fieldnotes; when it was not intrusive, she audio- or videotaped the children's experiences in the classroom.

Heath's collection and reporting of data are meticulous. Certainly, one of the ways that ethnographers establish ethos is by presenting a "thick description," a narrative sufficiently detailed to allow readers to check the researcher's interpretations or formulate their own alternative interpretations (see Geertz, 1973). In the remainder of this chapter, we would like to rethink Heath's "thick description" through a different terministic screen. Kenneth Burke (1966) developed his idea of "terministic screens" by looking at a series of shots in a photography magazine, each of the same object but taken with a different lens or filter. Shifting from one set of terms or one theoretical perspective to another, Burke suggests, is like changing the lens or filter on a camera. We will see the same object in a different way.

When Heath analyzed her data, she, as an educational ethnographer, focused on the culture of each community. That is, she looked to areas of similarity among the residents of Trackton or Roadville. As we reinterpret her data through the lens of type theory (as we shift terministic screens), we attempt to determine both the "personality" of each community (as one way of describing *some* aspects of a culture) and the "personality" of individuals within each community. We hope that this perspective will not diminish in any way the importance of understanding the influence of culture on literacy learning or practice; rather, we hope that it will add a new dimension: an understanding of how individuals either feel generally at home within their community or have a persistent sense of working against its norms.

ROADVILLE

Roadville is a small community, exclusively Caucasian, on a curving street of single-family houses; it is separated from Laurence Mill by a small wooded area. At least one member of each family is working or has worked at the mill. As the reader moves through the early descriptions of Roadville, she is drawn to two central characters: Mrs. Macken, a school teacher, the most highly educated member of the community; and Mrs. Dee, whose family and extended family occupy four of the nine houses on the street. The community's personality is evidenced by the differences between the two women and the positioning of each to the community as a whole. What becomes evident in Heath's study of Roadville is not only that the community's cultural identity may make typical methods of communication or education more challenging for certain individuals, but that the cultural identity itself contributes to a schism between students and organized education, even as the community's citizens try to support the idea of education for their children.

One of the most important distinctions for Heath's purposes and ours in the philosophies of the women is between their attitudes about the value of education, and the manifestation of this conflict suggests the personality types of Mrs. Dee and Mrs. Macken. Mrs. Dee seems to be in Myers-Briggs terminology introverted and sensing. The community's attitude seems likewise introverted-sensing. This preference within the community (a tendency to equate "real" knowledge with "practical" knowledge) and the presence of the factory to generations of the residents (the decent jobs that come without much formal schooling) both contribute to the community's somewhat skeptical view of education. Mrs. Macken, who seems to be an extraverted-intuitive type, assuming a very public role and always looking to the future, is the self-appointed spokesperson for the benefits of education. The tension between her values and those of some of the residents of Roadville is most acute in her relationship with her husband:

> Everyone always speaks of the two Mackens by naming "Mrs. Macken, the schoolteacher," first. Mrs. Macken is a tall woman with a blonde bouffant hairdo who wears all store-bought clothes. She dislikes the "backwardness" of the mill life and continually tries to pull her husband away from the mill and interest him in other occupations. But he is a

loom fixer, has been for fifteen years, and wants no other job. He says he makes good money, "more'n my wife does," and he sees no reason to quit. . . . Mrs. Macken urges parents to get books for their children, to read to them when they are "li'l," and when they start school to make a certain they attend regularly. (pp. 34-35)

Mrs. Macken's message is heard by some of the parents in Roadville; however, when it is repeated in a public forum, her husband offers the opposing view: "When Roadville parents talk of their children going on to technical school or college to become secretaries, electricians, doctors, nurses, pilots, and to own their own businesses, Rob scoffs and reminds them 'that's further than any of you got'" (p. 35).

Mrs. Dee's voice, in similar opposition to Mrs. Macken's, represents Roadville's predominant lifestyle and personality type. Her prominence in the community is largely a result of her being the matriarch of such a large extended family. Three of her children currently work in the mill (her unmarried daughter works at her old station) as do seven of her grandchildren. Although Mrs. Macken seems to express the dreams of most residents of Roadville (the hope that their children can find a better life through education), Mrs. Dee seems to express what they really believe (one manages to make do by working hard). In a brief text that expresses the values of many sensing-judging types, Mrs. Dee stated:

My daddy was a Baptist preacher and a farmer, and they was seven of us chil'rn—five girls and two boys. And we worked, you know, in the fields in the summertime, just like boys—they wasn't any boys—the boys was the youngest, so the girls had to do the work. (p. 32)

Although storytelling like this occurs only on special occasions in Roadville (quite different, as we shall see, from the rich oral culture of Trackton), Heath indicates that the sentiment is something shared by the majority of Roadville. "For them," she says, "work equals money; if one works hard enough, there should be enough money, and if there is not enough money, someone is not working hard enough" (p. 41). The "oldtimers" value the ways of their own upbringing over formal schooling, remembering "a lot of lessons school can't teach" (p. 35), and the message to the young is clear: The kind of literacy that one learns at school will not make a significant difference in your life.

The concept of hard work is not all that the youth of Roadville gather from the stories of their parents and grandparents; the sensing and judging preferences are instilled in the children of Roadville from birth. Roadville seems to be a culture that is best suited for (and, perhaps, overrepresented by) Introverted-Sensing-Thinking-Judging types (ISTJs); teaching children language and preschool skills reflects similar values. Underlying much of the language instruction is the belief that children

8

should learn to play alone; teaching methods direct the child's attention to objects they can manipulate. Much attention is paid as well to unquestioned assumptions of right and wrong, as children are quizzed and either corrected or praised for their response. Consider, for example, Heath's description of the following scenario, a typical interaction between a Roadville parent and child:

> Beyond . . . games [like hide-and-seek] . . . , adults and older children require a toy, book, or ball to "play" with preschoolers. If a preschooler approaches them to try to gain attention, adults respond by saying "Go get you—[name of a toy, book, wooden puzzle, etc.]." Adults play with one-year-olds by taking all the rings off a teeter pole and beginning to replace them, sometimes in the right order to show the child how. Later, however, once the child can put the rings on in the correct order, the adult places the rings in an incorrect order to elicit correction from the child. Often adults play for a little while and then draw away, preferring the child to play alone once he has given his attention to the object and not to the social interaction with the adult. A purpose of adult play with children's toys seems to be to draw the attention of children to toys (or other stimuli) and encourage the child to practice by himself the skills called for in play with the particular object, e.g., matching colors, shapes, sizes, etc. (p. 136)

As we can view from the event described here, learning tends to be taught one on one (reflecting a preference for introversion), through tactile manipulation (sensing), through interacting with objects (thinking), and with the belief of one correct answer, even in playing (sensing and judging). One could certainly find much to praise about the ways of Roadville parents: They interact with their children, encourage independence, structure preschool learning, and create a learning environment with predictable expectations and rewards. Yet, one has to wonder, if viewing this scenario through the lens of type theory, how would those children whose learning style favors social interaction, talk, and spontaneity fare in Roadville?

Roadville children past the age of 3, to provide one example, are expected to "sit and listen to a story and not to participate—either verbally or physically—during the story" (p. 255). Heath recognizes the difficulty this can create in children with different preferences from those dominating the discourse community, saying "the children, many of whom have come to enjoy and relish active verbal and physical participation in the stories, find this shift to a new learning experience troublesome" (p. 266). Bedtime stories become a "struggle of wills" as the parents encourage the child toward introversion. Another, if minor, battle of preferences occurs between 2-year-old Sally and her Aunt Sue: When asked repeatedly "What is that?" about a tomato, Sally responds with a perception—"red"—and her aunt must assure her, displaying tendencies toward sensing and judging, she has not provided the "right answer."

That the social norms of the community are enforced is evident even in the "rules" of storytelling. Heath describes the "rules" as follows:

> Children in Roadville are not allowed to tell stories, unless an adult announces that something which happened to a child makes a good story and invites a retelling. When children are asked to retell such events, they are expected to tell non-fictive stories which "stick to the truth." Adults listen carefully and correct children if their facts are not as the adult remembers them. In contrast, fictive stories which are exaggerations of the real-life events, modeled on plots or characters children meet in storybooks, are not accepted as stories, but as "lies," without "a piece of truth." (p. 158)

As we said earlier, Roadville does not allow for many narrative texts. Language acts tend to be practical, direct and to the point, and often organized, as is typical of the discourse of sensing-thinking temperaments (STs), in spatial or enumerative patterns. When a narrative is allowed, it must adhere to the values that sensing types more typically anticipate: It must accurately reflect some event that actually happened, as it happened, within the experience of the members of the community. To use one's imagination to embellish a story is as severely admonished as "telling a fib" to cover up stealing another child's toy, and both acts are socially corrected in the same way: The offender is accused of lying. ISTJs, who naturally tell accurate stories, often without altering even minute details time after time, will find a sympathetic audience in Roadville; Extraverted-Intuitive-Feeling-Perceiving types (ENFPs), who naturally embellish their stories and alter even major components of the narrative each time it is retold, risk social censure whenever they speak.

We would suggest that Extraverted-Sensing-Feeling-Perceiving types (ESFPs) and Extraverted-Sensing-Thinking-Perceiving types (ESTPs), the kind of active and vocal learners who rarely fit into highly structured primary classes, might quickly be labeled as problem children in an ISTJ community such as Roadville, if no one will pay the sort of attention to differences Jung suggested. "Why is it," their parents might ask, "this child cannot learn to play by himself?" Or, "Why can't she be quiet?" Or, "Why does he have so much trouble concentrating on a single task for more than a few minutes?" Or, as Peggy, a young Roadville mother does say, describing her son Danny, "He talks all the time, why can't he learn to say the right thing?" (p. 142). Indeed, any child who demonstrated a preference for extraversion, intuition, feeling, or perceiving would probably be regarded, to some degree, as not fitting the norms of Roadville.

As great a difficulty in the predominantly ISTJ world of Roadville, however, is found when children trained in its cultural identity enter the largely intuitive world of public education. The children, typical of young sensing types, want knowledge to have immediate and practical applications. They are not convinced by teachers who speak abstractly of the "value of a diploma." The early school-aged children, even those in high school, lack this experience and often feel that mathematics, writing, and geography, at least as taught in their schools, have no practical value:

> The average, and even the good, students seem to do only minimally what is asked of them to conform. They do not engage themselves creatively in making use of school tasks, in plugging them into some activity where they might make a difference. They see no reason to use the word whose definition was learned in English class last week in either a conversation at home, or in an essay for this week's American History class. . . . By the time they reach high school, they have written off school as not making any difference for what they want. . . . The jobs they want seem unrelated to the tasks school sets up for them. They recognize no situational relevance; they do not see that the skills and attitudes their teachers promote make any difference in the jobs they seek: flying, nursing, selling, etc. They want to get out now, or as soon as possible, to get on with the business for which they feel prepared: setting up homes and families, working to make money, and planning to get ahead. (pp. 46-47)

The tension between education and aspirations for a better life, characteristic of intuitive types, and hard work and accepting one's position in life, classically sensing, is not easily resolved. Certainly, many of the parents do give voice to the importance of education, but even they tend to view the schoolhouse through the (sensing) lens of their experience in the mill, which impedes their involvement in their children's educations. The values of this community toward education express foremost a need for learning to have immediate and practical applications to the real world, and it is in this that school becomes daunting or unimportant to young people. Abstract expressions for the value of education (as expressed by Mrs. Macken, who seems to be an intuitive type) may be heard by the parents, but the generally intuitive world of school also seems beyond them. They do not know how to help their children succeed. Unless learning is made real and practical, the children will continue to feel that the secret to success in school is beyond them, or that what they are learning in a classroom has no practical application outside of it. Parents oftentimes cannot make the intuitive leap to practical application either:

> Their own expectation that hard work brings results, causes them to urge their children to "work hard" in school, and they ask for evidence of such hard work in practices familiar to them: spelling words, "learnin' lessons,"

and doing homework. Yet on those rare occasions when their children confront them with what they must do at school, they cannot grasp the ultimate purpose of the activities called for; as Lisa put it: "we have to look up definitions all the time, 'n when we have a test, we look up answers to questions in science, 'n such as that." These tasks always seem to point to something else, to suggest that they will have some purpose, some place to be put to use. But neither Roadville parents nor children see and participate in these ultimate occasions for use. (pp. 46-47)

What we would like to suggest here is that it is a combined influence of the culture of Roadville, the predominance of sensing types, and perhaps the rigidity of school curriculum that places the children of this community at risk for dropping out of high school. What these children need most, whether it come from their parents or teachers, is some sense of the practical value of schooling.

TRACKTON

As the reader is introduced to the exclusively African-American community of Trackton, a single street of rental duplexes, she is led by Allen Young, the self-appointed and generally acknowledged "mayor," as he makes his morning rounds to visit all the "respectable" residents. The "respectables"—those "who 'live right,' mind their own affairs and their children, and don't 'make no trouble' for others" (p. 52)—form a close-knit community within a community, largely held together by the charismatic "mayor" Young, apparently an extraverted feeling type who wants to bring the people together. Early in the first section devoted to Trackton, the "mayor" mediates between two boys who are arguing over a tricycle:

> You know what you oughta do? Ain't no good fightin' over sump'n you both want, jus' tear it up dat way. Lemme tell you sump'n 'bout dat. One time dere was a real smart man, knew everything, you know, and a woman, uh, two women, brought a child to 'im, each one sayin' it was hers. Dat ol' wise man, he rub his chin jus' so /putting his hand to his chin/ (long pause) and you know what he did? /looking from boy to boy, either of whom has looked at the mayor during his talk/ (long pause) He say he gonna chop dat baby in two (pause) //both boys look up briefly, then turn back to the tricycle// 'n give half to each one of dem mammas. Right quick like, one dem mamma say, now you give dat baby to dat woman, don't hurt dat baby. /looking intently at boys/ (pause) Now who you think got dat baby? Dat wise man give dat baby to dat mamma what didn't want de baby hurt. Now go 'bout yo' play and don't fight no more, you hear? (p. 50)

What we have here is not only a forceful person, who acts as a catalyst to bring the community together, but also a strong oral tradition, both of which seem to be absent from Roadville. It is interesting to conjecture as to why "mayor" Young is more influential in his community than Mrs. Macken is in hers.

A number of forces seem at work here, some related to type and some not. First, Trackton, at least those whom the "mayor" includes among the "respectables," does seem to be more highly represented by extraverted, intuitive, and feeling types. These preferences usually encourage more social interaction and might be, in part, a factor in the culture that evolved in Trackton. Second, given that residents live in two-family dwellings, in closer proximity to each other, they may be again more likely to develop a sense of community. Third, the residents of Trackton have a sense of their place in a moment of historical change, a transition between the past of limited opportunities, and a belief that things are getting better for African Americans, that the next generation will have new possibilities for education and careers. Finally, the community has a strong oral tradition. The older residents often tell stories of how things used to be, stories about struggles during the past, about kin and fictive kin who pulled together to survive and build a better life. In an oral history that reflects the tradition of these stories, Miss Bee stated:

> In my chil'hood, I kin remember when we live in a li'l log house, in de pasture—
> 'mong de cows (laughter) . . .
> we worked in de fiel', she worked in de fiel
> did, for 'bout (pause) thirty-five cents a day . . .
> 'n when I first started workin' out, li'l girl, I made one dollar a week,
> den I went to workin' for a sup'mtendent of a cotton mill, I'z makin'
> two dollar 'n a half a week . . . (p. 63)

Miss Bee's story about her struggles and progress, which in its entirety runs for two and a half pages of Heath's book, suggests an oral tradition that values language in a way that was not seen in Roadville. Heath describes it as a public performance, "often marked by varied repetitions and a lilting chant-like quality," that "brought out laughter about the past" as it "reflected pride in what had been accomplished" (p. 65).

The message of Trackton's orally recited stories seems to lead to a generally more positive view toward education. For example, Mrs. Young, "mayor" Young's 72-year old mother, said:

> Well, uh, I'm goin' (pauses) well, I'm goin' back to uh adult education hu uh school at night, 'n so I'm takin' (unintelligible) English 'n math, 'n so den I attend de Senior Citizen, 'n so I volunteer, 'n I mean do volunteer work, 'n so it's improve my education a good bit. (p. 59)

When tensions do arise within the community, they seem not to be about issues of education, as they are in Roadville; rather, they seem to come from jealousies about some resident acquiring a new possession or receiving a new governmental service. Here, also, the "mayor" is a positive force among residents. He stated: "We hep each other, but dere's a limit, and everybody know de other fellow's workin' hard to get ahead, and he ought not to pull 'im down" (p. 56).

Not surprisingly, Heath found that the assimilation of language and culture in childhood in Trackton is markedly different from that of Roadville. The two communities demonstrate very different notions of teaching their children to speak; indeed, they even have rather different ways of thinking about what it meant to be a child. As we saw in Roadville, parents instruct while playing with preschool children, providing them with objects, answers, and questions to teach and test. But whereas Roadville parents speak of "bringin' up" their children, "in Trackton, adults talk of children 'comin' up'. . . . In Trackton, all babies spend the first year of their lives swathed in human touch and verbal interactions; their lives flow with few spatial and time barriers imposed by their caregivers" (pp. 144-145).

In the extraverted-feeling environment of Trackton, children are perceived as being "born to the community" rather than to isolated families (p. 146). The parents of Trackton do not see children as "information-givers or question-answerers" (p. 103). Parents, as a result, rarely talk to infants; Heath stated, "Everyone talks about the baby, but rarely to the baby" (p. 75). Heath found that, as a result, even school-aged children in Trackton had difficulty answering "why" questions. Rather than dialogue with their parents, children learn to speak by repeating the tail end of adult utterances, almost as if they were their parents' chorus. The part of a baby's communication most valued by adults is nonverbal:

> When infants begin to utter sounds which can be interpreted as referring to items or events in the environment, these sounds receive no special attention. . . . Instead, [adults] praise the baby's nonverbal responses which seem to them appropriate to the circumstances: a coo and smile for Darett's new hat, and a grasp of Miss Lula's hand when she pokes at the baby. Held in the arms of an adult talking on the phone, a baby may jump up and down, and the adult interprets this as a response to a familiar voice on the phone: "Dis baby know you on de phone, Berta." (pp. 75-76)

This may seem to suggest that the child is encouraged toward introversion, as extraversion through language is unrewarded in early childhood. But once they are about 14 months old (this is more true for boys than girls), children are forced to become players in very public interactions; they must "break into adult conversation, making themselves part of the ongoing discourse," wrote Heath (p. 93). In the discourse of learning, energy is focused outward toward objects or audience members, and the learner seems to be expected to develop his or her extraversion. One example is in playing competitive verbal games, "talking junk," which requires quickness of response to what has been said and greater attention to oral word play than semantics. Children learn sound and rhythm patterns and the importance of obtaining the "highest response from the audience" (p. 176). Jump rope and hand-clap "playsongs" also require not only near-constant spoken language but attention to outside elements such as the equipment and the actions of others. In Trackton, language is perceived as inherently directed outward or else insignificant. As Annie Mae, an adult in the community, said: "Whatcha call it ain't so important as whatcha do with it" (p. 112).

True to the oral tradition among the adult community of Trackton, much of a child's early linguistic interactions with the external world are stories. Like "Mayor" Young's instructive story about the women fighting over the baby, much of talking in Trackton employs metaphor. Heath said:

> The most prevalent kind of question asked of preschoolers in Trackton is the analogy question, which calls for an open-ended answer which draws from the child's experiences. . . . When adults talk among themselves, they frequently use metaphors and similes in their conversations:
>
> Mayor: What you know 'bout him [a new black man in the area running for public office]? How do he take on [what is he like]?
>
> Transient: He nut'n but a low-down polecat, you know what he did to his own folks? Lemme tell ya, he so low he cain't git under dat rock yonder. (p. 105)

This tendency toward analogy, visible in habits of children, such as matching objects, and in the community's actions toward children, such as nicknaming, suggests Trackton's encouraging of the intuitive function.

From early childhood on we can see children being encouraged to develop as if they were thinking types, partly as a necessary component to reading one's audience. In Trackton, children are initiated into what is believed to be a harsh and constantly changing environment by being challenged, in a public arena, by adults:

> Preschoolers, especially boys, are always being presented with situations and being asked "Now what you gonna do?" The children must think before they respond, and as Annie Mae realized, must feel the motivations and intentions of other individuals. They are powerless to counter physically; they must outwit, outtalk, or outact their aggressors. (p. 84)

Heath relates the example of how the "mayor" took a bag of candy from Lem and demanded: "What you gonna do, I try to take dis? Let me keep it for you. Come on, I just be keepin' it" (p. 84). Through the repetition of this scenario, Lem eventually figures out that he can hide his candy in a hole between the boards in his porch, which is large enough for him to put his hand into but too small for "mayor" Young's hand. Young girls, although generally spared from these public challenges from adults, experience similar harsh interactions during "fussing" episodes, a female practice of making typically negative assertions about each other. Although Lem seems to learn how to stick up for himself and seems to feel some pride in being able to outwit an adult, we doubt that all children would thrive in a public drama marked by "feigned hostility, disrespect, and aggressive behavior" (p. 81). Trackton seems particularly well suited for ESTP, ENTP, ESTJ, and ENTJ children (Lem seems to be an ENTP), who respond well to social challenges, but not quite so well suited for children who are introverts and feeling types.

The "feigned" harshness of Trackton's culture might suggest that it is overrepresented by thinking types, even with the sensitivity to others required by Trackton social interaction, but harshness in this community is a quality quite different from what some might consider to be the aloofness or focus on rules that we found with the residents of Roadville. The social challenges and "fussing" seem to be ways that this exclusively African-American community, which we would argue is overrepresented by feeling types, teaches its children to deal with the emotional effects of racism. It appears, in other words, to be this community's adaptation to a long history of living in a racist culture. The learning that occurs through these kinds of social games is a knowledge that one comes to feel. As Annie Mae says of teaching her grandchild Teggie:

> He gotta learn to know 'bout dis world, can't nobody tell 'im. Now just how crazy is dat? White folks uh hear dey kids say sump'n, dey say it back to 'em, dey aks 'em 'gain 'n 'gain 'bout things, like they 'posed to be born knowin'. You think I kin tell Teggie all he gotta know to get along? *He just gotta be keen, keep his eyes open*, don't he be sorry. Gotta watch hisself by watchin' other folks. *Ain't no use me tellin' 'im:* 'Learn dis, learn dat. What's dis? What's dat?' He just gotta learn, gotta know; he see one thing one place one time, he know how it go, see sump'n like it again, maybe it be de same, maybe it won't. He hatta try it out. If he don't he be in trouble; he get lef' out. Gotta keep yo' eyes open, *gotta feel to know*. (p. 84; emphasis added)

It seems that Trackton trains children to expect unpredictability. The attention toward one consistently right answer we saw in Roadville, with adults only changing circumstances to elicit correction from their child, is virtually absent in Trackton. Adults instead see childhood instruction as preparation for a life that is seldom consistent:

Some residents of Trackton can talk about the fact that daily life in
Trackton brings many situations, and yet none can be faced each time
with a secure sense that a particular response will bring a specific result.
Annie Mae, the community cultural broker, who seems to know and be
able to explain many of the mainstream cultural practices as well as those
of Trackton, sees these shifting sands of reality as good training ground
for children. She considers such experiences the only way a child can
grow up without being set to be disappointed in life. Learning language is
a critical part of this process of "gettin' on in dis world." (p. 84)

The adults of Trackton believe that children must experience and feel to
learn how to live in what they consider to be a complex and changing
world, a world without clear rules.

Although the "training" of children in Trackton to expect
harshness in a changing world may very well prepare many of the children
to deal with a racist society, we wonder how some types (in particular,
introverted feeling types) might fare in this community. Would some of the
more sensitive children who need to be nurtured simply shut down? That
there are a number of "no-counts" in the community, some who are
children of the "respectibles," suggests that this form of cultural
preparation does not work for everyone.

CONCLUSION

All cultures, as Jung argues, are one-sided, and no culture is concerned
primarily about an individual's welfare and development. The "intent" of
culture is to encourage an adaptation to a particular view of reality. As we
have seen, the cultures of both Roadville and Trackton exert social
pressure of some kind to encourage the children to adapt to the norms of
the community; however, the norms, the very vision of reality, differ in
each community.

As we have argued, the norms and values of Roadville could be
described as those of ISTJs. The residents value independence and working
alone (I), the practical and useful (S), regularity and consistency (T), within
a structured and limited horizon (SJ). The norms and values of Trackton
could be described as those of ENFPs. The residents value social
interactions and learning through oral recitations (E) in a way that will
allow children to experience and feel (F) to be spontaneous (P) in a
constantly changing reality (NP). These two communities, just a few miles
apart, certainly demonstrate different cultural "temperaments."

That does not mean however, that all members of each
community feel at home with these generally shared values. The very fact
that Trackton is separated, largely through the personal judgments of the
"mayor," into the "respectables" and the "no-counts" points to the

exclusion or marginalization of those who do not fit in. It is, we would like to argue, those who do not fit into their community (like the "no-counts" in Trackton) or the communities that are at odds with the school system (as Roadville is, in many ways) who are at risk in the development of literacy, as it is culturally defined.

REFERENCES

Burke, K. (1966). Terministic screens. In *Language as symbolic action: Essays on life, literature, and method* (pp. 44-62). Berkeley: University of California Press.

Geertz, C. (1973). Thick description: Toward an interpretive theory of culture. In *The interpretation of cultures* (pp. 3-30). New York: Basic Books.

Heath, S. B. (1983). *Ways with words: Language, life, and work in communities and classrooms.* Cambridge: Cambridge University Press.

Jung, C. G. (1921). *Psychological types* (H. G. Baynes, Trans. Rev. ed. by R.F.C. Hull). Princeton, NJ: Princeton University Press.

Jung, C. G. (1961). *Memories, dreams, and reflections.* (A. Jaffé, Ed., R. & C. Winston, Trans.). New York: Vintage.

Chapter 2

Personality Preferences and the Concept of Audience

Thomas Thompson
The Citadel

Contemporary discussions of audience often seem to revolve around one or both of two questions: first, whether a writer should even be concerned with "the audience" in the first place; and second, whether "the audience" is located inside or outside the text—that is, whether the audience is a fiction created within the text or a reality that exists external to it. The way any individual formulates answers to those questions, I argue, may be influenced by that individual's personality preferences.

As far back as ancient Greece, rhetoricians described and discussed three key elements of any communicative act: a speaker, a subject, and an audience. More recent discussions include the text itself as a fourth element. Fulkerson (1979) describes four philosophies of composition, each of which emphasizes one of those four elements. He argues that "formalist" philosophies emphasize the text, valuing internal forms such as grammar, mechanics, and even penmanship; "expressivist" philosophies value acts of creation and discovery by the writer, as well as the writer's authentic voice; "mimetic" philosophies stress the connection between good writing and good thinking about the subject under consideration; and "rhetorical" philosophies focus on creating particular effects on particular audiences. As Fulkerson notes, the focus of each philosophy reflects the values of its adherents.

The notion that adherents to different philosophies should have shared values and interests *within* each group, but different values and interests *between* groups, is consistent with type theory. As Myers and McCaulley (1985) note, "People who have the same preferences tend to have in common . . . [t]he interests, values, needs, and habits of mind that naturally result [from the exercise of those preferences]" (p. 19). Through the lens of type theory, Fulkerson's categories suggest that expressivists have developed their interest in self-expression and self-discovery by exercising certain shared preferences, that mimeticists have developed their interest in clear thinking by exercising different shared preferences, and so on.

TYPE AND PHILOSOPHIES OF COMPOSITION

Two preferences that seem especially likely to have a bearing on one's philosophy of writing (and writing instruction) are extraversion/introversion (EI) and thinking/feeling (TF). The EI dimension describes a flow of energy and interest directed either outward or inward; the TF dimension, a decision-making process based on either principles or values. Combining these two sets of preferences in a two-by-two matrix produces four combinations that roughly correspond, I suggest, to Fulkerson's four philosophies, as illustrated in Figure 2.1.

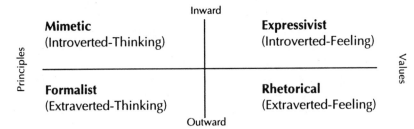

Figure 2.1. Type Preferences and Philosophies of Instruction

Introverted thinking types, with an inward flow of energy and a decision-making process that relies on absolutes and principles, seem most likely to be comfortable with a mimetic philosophy, with its emphasis on knowledge that is deeply considered, logically thought out, and clearly expressed. Extraverted thinking types, although also interested in logical thought and clear expression, seem more likely to focus their attention on the external expression of those ideas—that is, written texts—than on the ideas themselves or the internal processes by which they are worked out.

Introverted feeling types, whose energy flows inward, but whose decision-making process is more attuned to values and contexts than to absolute principles, seem most likely to align themselves with the expressivist camp, which emphasizes discovery—often self-discovery—and honest, authentic expression. Extraverted feeling types, similarly attuned to values and contexts, but with an outward flow of energy, seem most likely to be interested in rhetorical issues such as the writer's connection to the audience and the audience's response to the text.

Another way to consider these categories is in connection with the various elements Booth (1963) describes as components of the rhetorical situation, as shown in Figure 2.2.

In this scheme, introverted thinking types seem likely to be most interested in the subject at hand; extraverted thinking types, in the text itself; introverted feeling types, in the writer; and extraverted feeling types, in the audience. This alignment draws on the things/people distinction typically associated with the thinking/feeling dimension; namely, that thinking types tend to be interested in things (i.e., the subject or the text), whereas feeling types tend to be interested in people (i.e., the writer or the audience).

I offer these categories based on the EI and TF scales tentatively, mainly for the value they might have in helping to explain some of the literature on audience in composition studies. Numerous factors other than personality preferences alone affect teachers' philosophies and approaches

Emphasize **Subject** (Introverted-Thinking)	Emphasize **Writer** (Introverted-Feeling)
Emphasize **Text** (Extraverted-Thinking)	Emphasize **Audience** (Extraverted-Feeling)

Figure 2.2. Type Preferences and the Rhetorical Situation

to teaching, so conclusions based on these categories can be only partial at best. Still, the matrix based on the EI and TF dimensions offers some insights for understanding different views of the concept of audience.

TRADITIONAL VIEWS OF AUDIENCE[1]

Aristotle (1990) was one of the first rhetoricians to look systematically at the various kinds of argument that could be used to persuade an audience. In his *Rhetoric* he describes three kinds of appeals available to the rhetor: *ethical,* focusing on the character of the speaker; *pathetic,* focusing on the emotions of the audience; and *logical,* focusing on a logical analysis of the subject. Acknowledging that all three kinds of appeals are necessary for persuasion, because humans are emotional creatures who cannot be persuaded by logic alone, he nevertheless values logical appeals most highly. Still, he gives due attention to audience, offering a heuristic for audience analysis so rhetors can determine what kinds of arguments to use to persuade their listeners. Aristotle's observations about human nature are only gross stereotypes—for example, he describes young men as "changeable and fickle in their desires"; old men as "small-minded"; wealthy men as "ostentatious and vulgar"; and powerful men as "more ambitious and more manly in character than the wealthy" (pp. 2213-2216)—but his analysis at least represents an attempt to acknowledge that different audiences are likely to have different reactions to a given argument.

Aristotle's attempt to analyze rhetoric systematically should appeal to thinking types, as should his focus on *logos* as the most important element of persuasion. His apparent attitude toward *pathos,* too, seems consistent with thinking judgment: He acknowledges that rhetors must take the audience's affective responses into account, but he makes statements about large groups (i.e., "young men," "old men"), with little attention to individual variation. In the classroom, thinking types often teach to "the class" (as a group), whereas feeling types often try to teach to the individual students. Aristotle, like those thinking types, tends to describe "the audience" in monolithic terms rather than as a collection of individuals. Aristotle's rhetoric, therefore, is likely to hold more appeal for thinking types than for feeling types.

Aristotle remained the dominant influence in rhetorical theory until the advent of faculty psychology changed the view of audience from a collection of listeners to a collection of faculties, or powers, within the human mind. Bacon (1605/1990) saw the mind as composed of reason, memory, and imagination, as well as two faculties of a slightly different

---

[1]This section draws heavily from Bizzell and Herzberg (1990) and Golden and Corbett (1968).

order—appetite and will. The goal of rhetoric, he said, was to apply reason to the imagination to move the will. Hence, Bacon's rhetor could conceive of "audience" as uniform faculties of the mind, subject to logical rules of persuasion rather than to whims of human emotion.

Other thinkers followed Bacon's lead, although they divided the mind into other faculties. For example, Locke's (1690/1990) *Essay on Human Understanding* divides the mind into understanding and will, and Campbell's (1776/1990) *Philosophy of Rhetoric* describes two additional faculties, imagination and passion. Regardless of the specific ways the faculties were identified, however, the practical implication for rhetors was the same; namely, that the rhetor must present ideas clearly and vividly to the appropriate faculty of the mind to move the will. Hence, writers and speakers valued perspicuity (i.e., clarity) as a key element of persuasion.

Such a focus on clarity of thought and expression is consistent with philosophies Fulkerson labels "mimetic"—philosophies that tend to assume that a clear expression of well-thought-out ideas is most likely to be persuasive. (Note that "persuasive" in this sense seems to be a quality of the text or the ideas rather than a function of some interaction between the speaker and the audience.) Thus, rhetorical theory grounded in faculty psychology, like that grounded in Aristotle's *Rhetoric*, seems to favor thinking judgment over feeling judgment.

Perhaps one reason such theories remain popular today is that they are eminently teachable: Principles (i.e., rules) can be listed, memorized, and tested; and texts can be subjected to logical, objective analysis and graded accordingly. (The more "objective" a process is, the more "fairly" it can be taught and tested.)

CONTEMPORARY VIEWS OF AUDIENCE

Although Aristotelian rhetorics continue to flourish, other views have also begun to enjoy some popularity. For example, Moffett's (1968) hierarchy of forms of discourse illustrates the gradual removal, physically and temporally, of the audience (see Figure 2.3). In this hierarchy, the most basic form of discourse, reflection, occurs when one part of the speaker's self communicates with another part of the speaker's self. At this level, no physical distinction between speaker and audience exists. At the next level, conversation, the speaker and audience are within vocal range of each other. (This is the kind of communication addressed in speech textbooks: The speaker can usually both see and hear the reactions of the audience and can therefore adjust the speech while delivering it.) Moffett's next level, correspondence, reflects a shift from speaking to writing; the writer and reader are physically absent from one another but have some

Reflection------Conversation------Correspondence-------Publication
Directed to   Directed to a known,   Directed to a known,   Directed
oneself   present audience   absent audience   to an unknown,
                                                                            absent audience

Figure 2.3. Moffett's Forms of Discourse

personal knowledge of each other. (Because this kind of written communication most closely resembles oral communication of classical times, with the audience consisting of a relatively small gathering of listeners, and speaker and audience generally acquainted with each other to some degree, this is the situation in which classical forms of audience analysis seem likely to transfer to written texts with the greatest degree of success.) The final level, publication, involves communication to a wide, unknown readership extended over space and/or time. At this level, readers are likely to be so diverse as to render any but the broadest forms of analysis meaningless.

Speech classes typically focus on the kind of communication Moffett categorizes as conversation; composition classes more typically focus on reflection, correspondence, or publication—depending on the teacher's emphasis on the writer, the audience, or the subject, respectively. As the distance between writer and audience increases (or, in the case of reflection, collapses so that writer and audience are the same person), both the possibility of and the need for audience analysis diminish. At one end of the spectrum, someone writing to gain a better understanding of a problem, or perhaps to discover new knowledge, does not need to worry about analyzing the audience because the writer *is* the audience. At the other end of the spectrum, someone writing for unknown readers in an unknown context cannot engage in any meaningful "analysis" of that audience. Only when the audience is external to the writer, yet "known" to some degree, can it be subject to the Aristotelian kind of analysis.

Although Moffett's hierarchy discusses audiences as a function of their physical and temporal location with respect to the writer/speaker, the more common characteristic for discussing the concept of audience is its location with respect to the text. Park (1982) summarizes the two major positions succinctly:

> The meanings of "audience," then, tend to diverge in two general directions: one toward actual people external to a text, the audience whom the writer must accommodate; the other toward the text itself and the audience implied there, a set of suggested or evoked attitudes, interests, reactions, conditions of knowledge which may or may not fit with the qualities of actual readers or listeners. (p. 249)

The conceptualization of audience as either external or internal to the text profoundly affects the role of audience in pedagogy, because an external audience is subject to analysis, whereas an internal audience is simply created by textual features. The former concept equates "audience" to a greater or lesser degree with "readers," whereas the latter refers more to a set of conventions and relationships. The following examples illustrate the different pedagogical implications of those different views.

Mitchell and Taylor (1979) offer an "audience-response" model predicated on the existence of real readers as the audience. In this model, the writer engages in a process to create a written product for an audience, which, in turn, responds to that product and may (or may not) offer feedback to the writer, who then reengages in the process. In this model, the audience both evaluates and motivates the writing. Arguing from what Fulkerson would categorize as a rhetorical approach, they claim that "rational evaluation" is based not on "absolute qualities" (p. 269), but on the degree to which a piece accomplishes its purpose—a standard that is a function of audience response. In place of holistic scoring, which they see as arhetorical, they would have each piece evaluated (for its effectiveness) by the actual audience for whom it was intended.

In another argument that writers should write for "real" readers, Ede (1979) acknowledges that even though audience analysis "generally involves some consideration of demographic characteristics, . . . this is only a part of a more dynamic, fluid process" (p. 295). She would have students write for audiences to whom the written texts could actually be presented, such as through a letter, a memo, or publication in a journal. Practicing for, and completing, such "real life" assignments, she argues, helps train students to view their lives and their worlds in rhetorical terms.

Ong (1975), on the other hand, sees "audience" as a function of the text itself: The writer creates a role for the audience, then casts the audience in that role. Noting that "audience" is a collective term, initially used to describe a collection of listeners who were physically present to hear a speech, he points out that no such collection exists for written texts; "readers" necessarily read individually and in solitude, even if they are reading the same text at the same time. The writer therefore cannot *analyze* an audience and then write for that audience, but can only *create* a role for the readers to assume. The success of the text depends not on the match between the writer's analysis and the "actual" characteristics of the readers, but rather on their ability and willingness to assume the prescribed role.

Besides, notes Long (1980), attempts to "analyze" audience are doomed to failure because they rest on faulty assumptions. First, heuristics for audience analysis tend to assume that audience views are unified and readily apparent from such factors as education, sex, race, and age.

Second, they assume an adversarial relationship between the writer and audience. Neither assumption is valid, he claims, so writers would do better to spend their energy deciding the characteristics of the audiences they want to create, then generating texts that will create those audiences.

Pfister and Petrick (1980) try to synthesize the two views. They agree with Ong that students must fictionalize their audience, but suggest that, rather than fictionalizing the audience as *desired,* students "must construct in the imagination an audience that is as nearly a replica as is possible of those many readers who actually exist in the world of reality and who are reading the writer's words" (p. 214). That is, they would have students *fictionalize a real* audience. They offer a heuristic for such an analysis, basing their questions on the various relationships between writer, audience, subject, and text. Their questions also move from an audience of the self to a nebulous audience of the student's own choosing, roughly paralleling Moffett's progression from the self to absent others.

Ede and Lunsford (1984) also consider both real and imagined audiences, describing them respectively as "addressed" and "invoked." They critique both sides of the either/or question as being oversimplified and failing to consider the complexities of the writing and reading processes. In their attack on "real" audience models, for example, they claim that Mitchell and Taylor (1979) fail to consider the writer as a reader, underestimate the connection between style and substance, and encourage the writer to pander to the crowd. "Imagined" audience models fare no better: They claim that Ong (1975), for example, overemphasizes the writer and undervalues the reader, that he overemphasizes the distinctions between speech and writing, and that he fails to acknowledge that writers often create "imagined" readers based on models of "real" readers. They offer as an alternative a model in which "addressed" and "invoked" audiences are neither dichotomous nor contradictory, but instead are simply different perspectives from which to view relationships between writer and audience. They describe roles—self, friend, critic, mass audience, future audience—that can be either invoked *or* addressed, depending on the demands of the situation and the needs of the writer. Their model emphasizes the dynamic relationship between writing and reading, asserting that writers create readers, readers create writers, and communication results from the meeting of the two.

Responding to an increased interest in research on audience, and reacting in particular to Fulkerson's (1990) contention that rhetorical approaches to composition are supplanting expressivist, formalist, and mimetic approaches, Vandenberg (1992) argues that current composition scholarship and the textbooks informed by that scholarship overemphasize audience, thereby weighing down the writer unnecessarily with models for audience analysis. Furthermore, creating fictional audiences and fictional scenarios puts an additional burden on teachers, who must attempt to assume the persona of the assigned audience, often with inadequate experience to do so successfully. He challenges Ede and Lunsford's contention that "audience addressed" is somehow "outside the text," arguing that any audience actually addressed interacts with the text, so that audience members actually become co-authors (as Ede and Lunsford admit is the case with their addressed audience). Noting that writing requires the absence of a reader, and that reading requires the absence of a writer, he argues against classical audience analysis: "[T]he very idea of classical audience analysis assumes a kind of determinism that the separation of reader and writer, by the indeterminacy of the text, denies" (p. 93). In short, he argues that too much attention to audience distorts the rhetorical balance that Booth (1963) describes as characteristic of successful communication.

Kroll (1984), too, argues against too much emphasis on audience in his description of three perspectives on audience: rhetorical, informational, and social. He notes that the rhetorical perspective, which dates back to Aristotle, has been most frequently and carefully scrutinized and critiqued for its various limitations, one of which is its implication that all communication is persuasive in intent so that writer and audience are cast in adversarial roles. The informational perspective, which removes the element of persuasion, implies a reader struggling to extract meaning from a text and a writer trying to create a text that allows such extraction with minimal effort and minimal chance of error. The social perspective identifies the problem for novice writers as egocentrism—the inability to write with an awareness of an audience—but terms such as *sense of audience* can be so vague as to be useless; furthermore, some theorists question the degree to which writing is social *or* rhetorical, arguing instead that "the writer's task more centrally involves *creating* an audience with the text, largely by observing conventions which 'imply' or 'project' an audience with particular knowledge, assumptions, and attitudes toward the writer and subject matter" (p. 182; emphasis in original). Kroll closes with a warning: "If we focus too much attention on writing for an audience—whether conceived as a 'target receiver,' a 'needy reader,' or a 'constructive participant'—we may narrow our view of composing, forgetting that writing is also an exploration of ideas, a quest for purpose, and a projection of oneself" (p. 183). Kroll thus reminds readers that not all writing need be turned outward; it can remain focused inward on the world of ideas and still be valuable writing.

INTERNAL OR EXTERNAL?

When the question is whether internal or external concerns merit greater attention, one's preference for introversion or extraversion often supplies the answer. Introverts generally find the internal world of thoughts and ideas more interesting than the world around them, so they find external activity less important (and often of less value) than reflection. Extraverts, on the other hand, tend to direct their attention to the external world. As Jensen (1987) notes, they "rely on activity more than [i]ntroverts" (p. 183). They are thus more likely to need—and more likely to benefit from—the presence of a real or imagined audience with whom to engage in dialogue. Hence, extraverts seem more likely than introverts to turn to heuristics for audience analysis (which encourages them to engage in outward-directed activity) and to associate themselves with rhetorical pedagogies that attend more heavily to external concerns such as audience reaction and response.

Elbow (1987), however, argues that the presence of an audience—real or imagined—can be so overwhelming as to interfere with the writer's ability to find or express thoughts clearly; in such cases, he says, the best (and most natural) solution is to shut out the audience completely. The trick, he says, is to bring the appropriate audience to mind at the appropriate point in the writing process. Specifically, an inviting audience can be helpful to imagine during the generative stages of composing, whereas an inhibiting audience is best left alone until the final stages. Often, the best audience is *no* audience while the writer tries to think; only a writer with something to say is ready to try to say it to an audience.

Elbow's argument fits an introverted approach to writing, in the which the writer thinks first, then writes. (Extraverts, by contrast, tend to think "out loud"—either while talking or while writing.) In the following passage, Elbow reacts against the view that the ability to be aware of the audience is a higher-order skill:

> The ability to *turn off* audience awareness—especially when it confuses thinking or blocks discourse—is also a "higher" skill. I am talking about an ability to use language in "the desert island mode," an ability that tends to require learning, growth, and psychological development. Children, and even adults who have not learned the art of quiet, thoughtful, inner reflection, are often unable to get much cognitive action going in their heads unless there are other people present to have action *with*. They are dependent on live audience and the social dimension to get their discourse rolling or to get their thinking off the ground. (p. 56; emphasis in original)

Here he opposes the model of development that places social skills higher up the developmental ladder than reflective skills. His position is to acknowledge two models of development—one from Piaget, and another from Vygotsky, Bahktin, and Meade. In the former model, states Elbow, "we start out as private, egocentric little monads and grow up to be public and social," but in the latter model, "*we start out* social and plugged into others and only gradually, through learning and development, come to 'unplug' to any significant degree so as to function in a more private, individual and differentiated fashion" (p. 56; emphasis in original).

Through the lens of type theory, the former model seems to value the social skills associated with extraversion as being higher on the developmental hierarchy, whereas the latter model seems to value the reflective skills associated with introversion. In practical terms, these models affirm the validity of both orientations, but suggest that "audience awareness" might be of more interest, or maybe of more value, to extraverts than to introverts.

Kroll (1979) cites Moffett (1968) and others to argue that egocentricity accounts for lack of audience awareness—that is, that a self-oriented writer cannot recognize that a reader might not see things the same way the writer does. He notes that "at the high school and even college levels student writers appear to experience difficulties when adapting referential discourse to an audience" (pp. 8-9). For Kroll, such writers are developmentally stuck, unable to see beyond their own views. In effect, Kroll sees the inability to turn *on* audience awareness as a deficiency, whereas Elbow sees the inability to turn *off* audience awareness as a deficiency. These views do not necessarily conflict, but they do highlight different values: Kroll values the ability to look out (toward the audience), whereas Elbow values the ability to look in (toward the self).

As with other preferences, both introversion and extraversion have value. Elbow's reframing of the question as an issue of timing rather than an either/or choice (i.e., not "*Should* one look inward or outward?" but "*When* should one look inward, and *when* should one look outward?") offers a healthy synthesis of the two perspectives.

THINGS OR PEOPLE?

A decision to emphasize the subject, the text, the writer, or the audience is also a decision to emphasize *things* (i.e., subject and text) or *people* (i.e., writer and audience). Type theory suggests that a preference for thinking judgment could lead more naturally to an emphasis on things, whereas a preference for feeling judgment could lead more naturally to an emphasis on people.

Myers (1980) describes thinking judgment as "essentially impersonal. Its goal is objective truth, independent of the personality and wishes of the thinker or anyone else" (p. 65). Thinking judgment tends to be most effective when the problem under consideration is impersonal, and proposed solutions can accurately be judged as "true" or "false" in absolute terms. But, Myers continues, "the moment the subject is people instead of things or ideas—and some voluntary cooperation from those people is needed—the impersonal approach is less successful" (p. 65). With respect to the elements of a written text—the subject addressed, the text itself, the writer, and the audience— thinking judgment seems likely to be more effective when applied to the impersonal elements of subject and text than when applied to the personal elements of writer and audience. If people are drawn to philosophies or pedagogies that capitalize on their personal strengths, it follows that thinking types would be drawn to composition philosophies or pedagogies emphasizing impersonal elements: subject and text. Hence, to return to my earlier argument, it seems logical for thinking types to be drawn to the philosophies Fulkerson labels "mimetic" and "formal," as those philosophies are likely to be better served by thinking judgment.

The opposite attraction seems natural for feeling types. At their best when working with people-related problems, feeling types should be drawn to the philosophies Fulkerson labels as "expressivist" and "rhetorical," with their respective emphases on the writer and the audience. That is, feeling types should be drawn to approaches that value self-expression and self-discovery or that highlight the interrelatedness of the writer and audience through the text.

Jensen (1987) suggests that, as writers, thinking types tend to concentrate on the content of their message, with less concern for how (or whether) that message connects with the audience, whereas feeling types tend to concentrate more on how the message connects than on the message itself. Hirsch and Kummerow (1989) argue that, in questions of truth versus tact, thinking types tend to favor truth, whereas feeling types tend to favor tact. They also note that, with respect to communication styles, thinking types persuade with "cool, impersonal, logical reasoning," while feeling types rely on "personally meaningful information enthusiastically delivered" (p. 43). Thinking types tend to prefer "brief, concise communication . . . [noting] the pros and cons of each alternative," whereas feeling types prefer "sociable, friendly, and even time-consuming communication" with attention to "how a given alternative has value and how it affects people" (p. 42).

Jensen and DiTiberio (1989) claim that thinking types tend to start with structure, using it as a heuristic for developing ideas, whereas feeling types tend to begin with content, letting structure develop organically. They go on to note that "thinking types are most concerned about presenting the content clearly in a well-organized format. They are less concerned about the process of communication, about how they are relating to their audience. As a result, their essays may be clear and structured but also dull, similar to the archetypal dry, academic treatise" (pp. 61-62). For feeling types, however, the situation is different: "From early in the writing process, feeling types are concerned as much about the process of communication, that is, how they are connecting with their audience, as about the content" (p. 62). DiTiberio and Jensen (1995) say that thinking types "write from a distance," "focus on what they're saying," and "seek to be clear," whereas feeling types "write from what they value," "focus on how it's expressed," and "seek to stimulate and motivate" (p. 49). Maid (in press) suggests that thinking types tend to write "thing-centered discourse," and feeling types tend to write "people-centered discourse," so thinking types tend to depersonalize or objectify even personal topics, whereas feelings types create personally meaningful approaches when writing on impersonal topics. These observations all draw a picture of thinking types as more interested in what they say and how they say it than on any personal concerns of the writer or the audience, whereas feeling types seem more concerned with making connections, either for themselves or for the audience. Table 2.1 summarizes these differences.

Not surprisingly, an approach that favors one process—either thinking or feeling—could easily devalue the other. In their explanation of their audience-response model, for example, Mitchell and Taylor (1979) make the following observations:

> Writers, especially technical and amateur writers, respond to criticism with: "You can't dispute that—it's true." They appeal to the authority of the referent. But facts remain inert unless related to other facts by theory, explicit or implicit. They do not exist untouched by the medium or outside a context. "I'm just analyzing the facts and presenting my conclusions for the client," declares a management consultant. That facts

Table 2.1. Thinking Types and Feeling Types as Writers.

Thinking types	Feeling Types
Concentrate on content	Concentrate on connecting
Favor truth	Favor tact
Use impersonal reasoning	Use enthusiastic delivery
Are brief and concise	Are sociable and friendly
Start with structure	Develop ideas organically
Value clarity	Value communication
Write about things	Write about people

are as thick as leaves in Vallombrosa and must be selected—not to say
created—according to a perspective may be too heretical for such
writers. . . . The fact-centered writer approaches her task with fear and
contempt. Having gathered a fine collection of data, the researcher
despises the necessity of writing them up. Even more, she fears the
necessity of imposing an ordered relationship on her information. Facts
are unassailable, but a thesis is vulnerable. (pp. 257-258)

By lumping "technical and amateur writers" into a single group,
Mitchell and Taylor devalue the kinds of writing technical writers produce.
It makes sense that thinking judgment would serve technical writers well,
though, because one of the maxims of technical writing is that the writer
should write not so that everyone will understand, but so that no one will
misunderstand. That is, they should focus on the clarity of the text above
all other considerations. Rather than note the strengths of such writing,
however, Mitchell and Taylor focus on weaknesses, using those
weaknesses to build credibility for their audience-based model. They go
on to decry pedagogies that claim to "[teach] writing as if it could be
judged by universal standards" (p. 266). Clearly, they maintain that no
writing can be judged (in terms of its effectiveness) by universal standards
because *effectiveness* is necessarily a function of the audience that is
central to their model.

Technical writing—the "fact-centered writing" that Mitchell and
Taylor seem to disparage—is characterized by the clarity, brevity, and
logical presentation associated with thinking judgment. The technical
writer's distrust of a thesis mentioned by Mitchell and Taylor reflects a
distrust of the ambiguity that can result from overcontextualizing the facts.
In short, the aspects of technical writing devalued by Mitchell and Taylor
are the same aspects likely to be valued by thinking types. Hence, I
suspect that Mitchell and Taylor's model would be far more appealing to
feeling types than to thinking types.

PRACTICAL IMPLICATIONS

When, for whatever reason, one chooses to try to match a text to an
audience, an understanding of type concepts can make the process easier.
As DiTiberio and Jensen (1995) note, introverted-thinking types tend to
write naturally with a formal style, whereas extraverted-feeling types tend
to adopt a relatively informal style. Knowing these natural tendencies, IT
and EF writers can be prepared to shift their level of formality up or down
appropriately. DiTiberio and Jensen then use combinations of the SN and
TF preferences to describe other writing styles. They say that sensing-
thinking writers tend to write texts that are "factual, objective, clear,
realistic, unambiguous, logical, and to the point" (p. 188). Sensing-feeling

types, they suggest, also like clarity and details, but with a warmer, more personalized slant. Intuitive-thinking types tend to be emotionally neutral, but they tend toward the abstract and philosophical rather than the concrete and specific. Finally, intuitive-feeling types, with a concern for building "a communication bridge between and among human beings," often "seek to foster a general spirit of human growth and goodwill" (p. 192). Thus, DiTiberio and Jensen advise, writers need to be aware of the kinds of writing they are likely to produce naturally so they can learn to adjust it appropriately for readers with different preferences.

Teachers can use a knowledge of type theory to help understand their own approaches to writing and the teaching of writing. For example, the teacher who considers good writing to be the natural outgrowth of clear thinking will teach a different class from someone who considers good writing to be an act of self-discovery, and one who considers good writing to be effective communication from a particular writer to particular readers in a particular context to accomplish particular goals will teach a different class still. The questions of how, when, and even whether to discuss the concept of audience in a writing class is likely, as I have discussed here, to be influenced by the teacher's preferences; the way students respond to those discussions is likely to be influenced by the students' preferences as well. Inevitably, teachers' preferences will sometimes conflict with those of their students, or teachers' or students' preferences will conflict with the demands of the writing situation. At such times, type theory offers a way to understand, and perhaps resolve, those conflicts.

REFERENCES

Aristotle. (1990). Rhetoric. In P. Bizzell & B. Herzberg (Eds.), *The rhetorical tradition: Readings from classical times to the present* (pp. 151-194). Boston: Bedford Books. (Original work published c. 3rd century B.C.)

Bacon, F. (1990) The advancement of learning.In P. Bizzell & B. Herzberg (Eds.), *The rhetorical tradition: Readings from classical times to the present* (pp. 625-631). Boston: Bedford Books. (Original work published 1605)

Bizzell, P., & Herzberg, B. (Eds.). (1990). *The rhetorical tradition: Readings from classical times to the present.* Boston: Bedford Books.

Booth, W. (1963). The rhetorical stance. *College Composition and Communication, 14,* 139-145.

Campbell, G. (1990). The philosophy of rhetoric. In P. Bizzell & B. Herzberg (Eds.), *The rhetorical tradition: Readings from classical times to the present* (pp. 749-795). Boston: Bedford Books. (Original work published 1776)

DiTiberio, J. K., & Jensen, G. H. (1995). *Writing & personality: Finding your voice, your style, your way.* Palo Alto, CA: Davies-Black Publishing.

Ede, L.S. (1979). On audience and composition. *College Composition and Communication, 30*(3), 291-295.

Ede, L.S., & Lunsford, A. (1984). Audience addressed/audience invoked: The role of audience in composition theory and pedagogy. *College Composition and Communication, 35*(2), 155-171.

Elbow, P. (1987). Closing my eyes as I speak: An argument for ignoring audience. *College English, 49*(5), 50-69.

Fulkerson, R. (1979). Four philosophies of composition. *College Composition and Communication, 30,* 343-348.

Fulkerson, R. (1990). Composition theory in the eighties: Axiological consensus and paradigmatic diversity. *College Composition and Composition, 41*(4), 409-429.

Golden, J.L., & Corbett, E.P.J. (Eds.). (1968). *The rhetoric of Blair, Campbell, and Whately.* New York: Holt, Rinehart and Winston.

Hirsch, S., & Kummerow, J. (1989). *LIFETypes.* New York: Warner Books.

Jensen, G.H. (1987). Learning styles. In J. Provost & S. Anchors (Eds.), *Applications of the Myers-Briggs Type Indicator in higher education* (pp. 181-206). Palo Alto, CA: Consulting Psychologists Press.

Jensen, G.H., & DiTiberio, J.K. (1989). *Personality and the teaching of composition.* Norwood, NJ: Ablex .

Kroll, B.M. (1979, April). *Adapting a composition to the audience: The development of referential communication skills.* Paper presented at the annual meeting of the Conference on College Composition and Communication, Minneapolis, MN. (ERIC Document Reproduction Service No. ED 174 988)

Kroll, B.M. (1984). Writing for readers: Three perspectives on audience. *College Composition and Communication, 35*(2), 172-185.

Locke, J. (1990). An essay on human understanding. In P. Bizzell & B. Herzberg (Eds.), *The rhetorical tradition: Readings from classical times to the present* (pp. 699-710). Boston: Bedford Books. (Original work published 1690)

Long, R. C. (1980). Writer-audience relationships: Analysis or invention? *College Composition and Communication, 31*(2), 221-226.

Maid, B.M. (in press). The TF opposition in writing development. In T. Thompson (Ed.), *Most excellent differences.* Gainesville, FL: Center for Applications of Psychological Type.

Mitchell, R., & Taylor, M. (1979). The integrating perspective: An audience-response model for writing. *College English, 41*(3), 247-271.

Moffett, J. (1968). *Teaching the universe of discourse.* Portsmouth, NH: Boynton/Cook Publishers.

Myers, I.B. (with Myers, P. B.). (1980). *Gifts differing.* Palo Alto, CA: Consulting Psychologists Press.

Myers, I.B., & McCaulley, M.H. (1985). *Manual: A guide to the development and use of the Myers-Briggs Type Indicator.* Palo Alto, CA: Consulting Psychologists Press.

Ong, W. J. (1975). The writer's audience is always a fiction. *PMLA, 90*(1), 9-21.

Park, D. B. (1982). The meanings of "audience." *College English, 44*(7), 247-257.

Pfister, F. R., & Petrick, J. F. (1980). A heuristic model for creating a writer's audience. *College Composition and Communication, 31*(2), 213-220.

Vandenberg P. (1992). Pick up this cross and follow: (Ir)responsibility and the teaching of "Writing for Audience." *Composition Studies Freshman English News, 20*(2), 84-97.

Chapter 3

Self-Representation and Personality Type in "Letter From Birmingham Jail"

Ronald A. Sudol
Oakland University

In many rhetorical situations a speaker's or writer's manner of self-representation exhibits personality preferences strategically constructed for the occasion. In this chapter I examine this manner of self-representation in the context of ethos as a means of persuasion in the history of rhetoric and persona as a literary technique. As a form of discourse analysis, interpreting types in a text can be both productive and elegant. To illustrate this critical approach, I use descriptions of some of the 16 personality types identifiable by the Myers-Briggs Type Indicator to analyze a piece of public discourse, specifically a fragment of Martin Luther King, Jr.'s "Letter from Birmingham Jail."

The premise of this volume is that personality preferences have a discernible influence on making and communicating meaning. The processes and products of communication generally reflect preferences for either an extraverted or introverted orientation toward life, a sensing or intuitive way of acquiring knowledge, a feeling or thinking way of decision making, and a judging or perceiving way of getting things done. But preferences are not absolute and determinative. Situations frequently occur in which we override our preferences in light of other factors. A young person with introverted preferences faced with the need to sell vacuum cleaners door to door, for example, will have to develop some extraverted skills. Within the framework of that selling situation, the introvert may learn to play at being an extravert—a stressful bit of acting, to be sure, but the sort of thing we find ourselves doing all the time.

Writing is another type of situation in which we may need to temporarily modify our standard preferences. It is true, of course, that we rely on our natural preferences to see us through the complexities of generating information and ideas, of deciding what to include and how to organize it, and of simply getting the job done. The way these tasks are accomplished reflects the writer's personality as adapted for the task at hand. Within the framework of a discourse itself, however, the writer may invoke alternative qualities, reflecting the personality of the writer in only a residual way. The personality we encounter couched in the voice of the discourse is a simulation, a role, a mask, a persona. The writer invokes an alternative self in response to a rhetorical situation. Furthermore, as Ong (1975) has argued, the alternative self also creates a role for the audience to play in the discourse. Thus, in contemporary rhetoric we view discourse as strategically constructed and having a voice modulated according to the dynamics of purpose and audience.

The effort to achieve social cohesion through this process is what Kenneth Burke (1945) has called dramatism, a key concept in contemporary rhetorical study. Seeing rhetorical performance as an act in this Burkean sense means it is subject not to the certainty of natural law but to the uncertainty of nonempirical human motivation. The "magic" of theatrical illusion and technique is what we encounter in the drama of human communication. Writing is no more natural an activity than selling vacuum cleaners. We should not be surprised, then, if role playing complicates our understanding of how personality preferences influence literate performance: Despite its crafted and contrived character, the discourse itself is expected to seem a natural utterance of its author. Playing a role, assuming a voice, adopting a persona—these are self-conscious performative acts that must seem effortless and transparent. Indeed, success may be gauged by the degree to which an "identification," to cite another of Burke's key concepts, can be established between the persona and the audience. The method is artful but the outcome must be apparently natural.

The naturalness of personality types is expressed through the concept of preference. One prefers, for example, either the extraverted or introverted orientation toward life not by consciously considering these concepts as alternatives but by making countless unconscious choices between them. Over any given period of time, we will make more choices on one side than the other. This natural choosing is what gives us a personality. The standard analogy used to demonstrate the difference between a natural preference of this sort and a label is handedness. Everyone prefers to use one hand or the other. Preferring one does not disable the other. Although merely a preference, it plays a significant role in the way we do things. The preference is easy to test in any spontaneous situation. Imagine a criminal case in court. Physical evidence has established that the perpetrator was left-handed. In order to make a vivid point, the prosecutor tosses some object to the accused and watches him catch it with his left hand. It is a setback for the defense. Anyone who has ever had to sign a check with the wrong hand knows how difficult it would be to simulate otherhandedness on the spur of the moment. But suppose defense counsel anticipates the prosecution's trick, and she trains her client to catch an object with the nonpreferred hand. Doing so is well within human capacity. When the need arises, we can play a role that conceals the habitual preference. Or, to give the situation a more positive spin, we create a role that helps communicate a larger truth. In either case, the exact nature of the role is governed by the dynamics of purpose and audience, whether it is to beat a criminal charge before a judge and jury or to get a point across in a discourse.

ETHOS AND PERSONA

How are we to understand self-representation in a text? How much is "self," and how much is "representation"? The distinction between the person and the persona, between the self and the role, inevitably places rhetorical situations in an ethical framework. To what extent does the enacted role deceive the audience and corrupt the purity of the transaction? This has been one of the central questions in rhetoric from Plato's dispute with the Sophists to our contemporary efforts to distinguish between "mere rhetoric" and "reality." It is a problem primarily of ethos— the classical mode of persuasion based on the authority, character, and credibility of the speaker. How ethos is defined in any historical period is linked to the corresponding aims of persuasion and rhetorical education. Reviewing the connections between ethos and the aims of rhetoric will help set the historical context for this exploration of personality preference and persona (more fully articulated historical reviews may be found in Johnson, 1984, and Baumlin, 1994).

For Plato, the speaker must discover and identify ideal truth and provide moral instruction to the community. Only by being virtuous and using reason can we discover the truth. Without pandering to its whims, the speaker must lift an audience out of an inferior world of perception into the world of ideal goodness. Because the entire focus of rhetoric is the apprehension of truth, skillful rhetorical performance must be directed at revealing truth rather than moving an audience to action. It would be illogical, in the Platonic rhetorical system, for a speaker to adopt a role when the sole point of speaking in the first place is to discover truth by penetrating mere perceptions.

Aristotle is more pragmatic. He places rhetoric in the realm of human affairs in which persuasion is needed to guide and influence decision making. Truth consists not of ideal principles but of received opinion. Goodness is not absolute perfection but excellence. Using dialectical activity as a starting point, rhetorical performance also requires strategic skill in communicating values and opinions. In order to be persuasive the speaker may go beyond using reason (logos) and also use appeals to affections (pathos) and adjust the speech so that the audience may be persuaded by the speaker's authority (ethos). Because virtue and goodness become means rather than ends, we see in Aristotle the beginnings of a constructed role for the speaker.

The function of ethos in subsequent rhetorical theory and practice fluctuates between the idealism of Plato and the pragmatism of Aristotle and often incorporates both the desire to find objective truth and the desire to be effective. Among the Romans, Quintillian follows Plato in assigning a missionary role of spiritual edification to the speaker. Cicero, on the other hand, follows Aristotle by ascribing a strategic role to ethos— capturing the good will of the audience by creating in them a favorable impression of the speaker. But Cicero truncates Aristotle's conception of ethos by treating it as a stylistic device. Thus, the difference between the speaker and the role the speaker plays becomes more apparent because the latter must be a creation of the former. As Johnson (1984) states:

> It is Cicero's more narrow concept of strategy and pragmatism that colors later views of practical aims for rhetoric and definitions of the role of the speaker. Aristotle's notion of ethos as a major mode of persuasion based on a knowledge of received opinion is conspicuously absent in the rhetorics modeled on a Ciceronian framework. (p. 105)

In general, the rhetorics of Christian oratory, such as Augustine's *On Christian Doctrine*, follow Plato's idealism and assign to the speaker the role of offering testimony on the Christian life. The quality of that life itself should be more eloquent than the mere words used to describe it. Secular rhetorics, like handbooks on letter writing, follow the pragmatic Aristotelian tradition as truncated by Cicero. In these works, ethos is reduced to stylistic devices of diction and ordering.

The rhetorics of the 18th century attempt to accommodate both the ideal and pragmatic features of the classical and renaissance traditions by recognizing the complexity of human psychology. George Campbell, for example, tries to explain how certain rhetorical strategies affect innate faculties of the mind, how the separate faculties of reason, passion, and will may be invoked by appealing first to the passions, which in turn engage the will and affect persuasion. Thus, the role of ethos is both strategic and epistemic. In order to fulfill the role by which this sequence of mental faculties becomes activated, the speaker must understand not only the needs and dispositions of the audience at large but the nature of its mental functioning as well.

The role of the speaker or writer in contemporary rhetorical instruction clearly follows from the practical and strategic tradition of Aristotle, Cicero, and Campbell. It could hardly be otherwise in our image-saturated mass media environment. The mediated nature of communications in this environment favors perception. It is true, of course, that, as a matter of theoretical and ethical necessity, communications instruction admonishes us to use the instruments of perception to disclose truth. In practical application, however, the audience calls the shots. It will not be led where it has no predisposition to go. The speaker or writer acquires authority in the rhetorical situation by assuming a role that will provide access to that predisposition. Perelman and Olbrechts-Tyteca (1969) describe the speaker's positioning this way:

> Under normal circumstances, some quality is necessary in order to speak and be listened to. . . . This quality in a speaker, without which he will not be listened to, or even, in many cases, allowed to speak, will vary with the circumstances. Sometimes it will be enough for the speaker to appear as a human being with a decent suit of clothes, sometimes he must be a rank and file member of a particular group, sometimes the spokesman of this group. (p. 18)

Notice how between the first and second sentences the focus of "quality" shifts from a seemingly ethical consideration to one of strategic positioning. Furthermore such positioning vis-à-vis the audience continues with deeper refinement as a discourse continues.

The use of the term *persona* in this discussion reflects the influence of literary study on the classical concept of ethos. Adherents of the new criticism that emerged in the 1940s viewed literary works as objects of art susceptible to close examination. Because these critics opposed the expressive theories associated with romanticism, they were not interested in how authors expressed themselves in the text. Instead, they focused attention on the literary work itself, in which the authorial voice was to be distinguished from the author's voice. The notion of persona, apparently based on the actor's mask in classical theater, came to represent this disjunction between the author and the author's presence in the text. Booth (1961), as part of his highly influential theory of the rhetoric of fiction, added a layer of complexity by suggesting the existence of an "implied author" who creates the persona. Although the terms *ethos* and *persona* are used interchangeably, clearly ethos is associated with the mix of ideal and practical forms of self-representation in persuasive discourse, and persona is associated with the wholly artificial representation of the implied author in fiction. Cherry (1988) argues a clear distinction should be maintained between the terms, reserving persona for "identifying varying degrees of mimetic representation" and ethos for examining how writers define and portray rhetorical situations in nonliterary discourse. Ede and Lunsford (1984) urge a similar distinction by way of audience: Ethos is involved when the audience is addressed; persona is involved when the audience is invoked.

Abiding by these sensible distinctions, however, is easier said than done, especially in the realm of contemporary public discourse. It initially seems obvious that self-representation in a speech, for example, by Martin Luther King, Jr., should be a simple matter of examining how the speaker directs his moral authority in order to achieve a certain purpose with an identifiable audience. In such a context, self-representation would be a matter of ethos. But a public figure in an era of mass communications acts out the drama of a turbulent social movement mediated by countless outlets of information for a vaguely defined audience. Such a public figure needs to create and stabilize a persona, one subject to modification and refinement in every public appearance. The social and mythic dimensions of this role invite a mimetic form of self-representation to bridge the gulf between who the person really is and what role that person must play in the theater of public events.

Accordingly, it is only the constructed elements of personality that need concern us. As constructions, they are subject to the interpretive and critical scrutiny we would feel free to apply to any form of mimetic art. In addition, the moral neutrality inherent in the study of personality types demands that we view these constructions as elements of persona rather than ethos. The obvious connection between the words *ethos* and *ethics* reminds us that the study of ethos is grounded in values and beliefs. These considerations have no place in the study of personality difference, in which difference is merely difference and not a feature that can be fixed on a good/bad or positive/negative scale.

Understanding the 16 personality types requires cumulative experience and observation. We understand our own type best, and then we begin to understand the types of those people we know well, observing, in particular, similarities to and differences from ourselves. As a matter of daily observation and study, scholars, researchers, and practitioners develop deeper insights into the way the types differ from each other. This accumulated casework has created a kind of consensus that takes the form of personality sketches, including those by Myers (1980, 1987), Keirsey with Bates (1978), Kroeger and Thuesen (1988), and Jensen and DiTiberio (1989). Because they are based on the same theory, these sketches are essentially the same . They differ primarily in matters of emphasis and expression. For my analysis, I follow the sketches of Kroeger and Thuesen. Their descriptions are highly detailed and accessible, and they have handles that greatly facilitate the analytical task.

"LETTER FROM BIRMINGHAM JAIL"

The focus of that analytical task is the opening section of Martin Luther King, Jr.'s, "Letter from Birmingham Jail." In a recent study of the sources of King's language, Miller (1992) observed that King played the combined roles assigned by Black churches to their pastors—theologian, preacher, and activist. The pastor's authority depended on his expertise in combining these roles through public speaking. Miller shows how King borrowed liberally—as part of this traditional role—from the ideas and language of others. So a text such as "Letter from Birmingham Jail" is notable not for its originality of thought and word but for the way in which it synthesizes various oratorical traditions into an effective discourse in a larger public sphere. The homiletic tradition to which this text belongs, then, provides yet another reason to distinguish carefully between ethos and persona.

If we had to guess the personality type of Martin Luther King the historical figure, it would be ENFJ, and King is so identified by Kroeger and Thuesen. ENFJs are the "smooth-talking persuaders," skilled at understanding the needs and motivations of others (F) and able to inspire with an imaginative vision of reality (N). They are admired leaders whose grand designs for humanity attract many followers. Their search for peace and harmony may border on compulsiveness. They may become embittered if their ideas meet with resistance (J). They are natural teachers and preachers, although they may be criticized for being insincere and glib, and they may become frustrated by administrative details. To the extent that these and other personality preferences apply to King, they are elements of ethos because they exist in the minds of the audience prior to and outside of sermons, speeches, and letters. They need only be invoked and reinforced by the discourse in order to be effective. Persona, on the other hand, is an element of the discourse itself, constructed to serve its specific rhetorical ends. With this distinction in mind, I now turn to King's famous "Letter."

King landed in the Birmingham, AL, jail in the spring of 1963 as part of a well-organized campaign of nonviolent civil disobedience. Shortly after the incident, eight "fellow clergymen" published a critique of King's public involvement, providing him with a reason to defend his combined role of theologian, preacher, and activist by publishing a detailed reply. In an "Author's Note" he calls attention to the conditions of his imprisonment:

> [This letter] was composed under somewhat constricting circumstances. Begun on the margins of the newspaper in which the statement appeared while I was in jail, the letter was continued on scraps of writing paper supplied by a friendly Negro trusty, and concluded on a pad my attorneys were eventually permitted to leave me. Although the text remains in substance unaltered, I have indulged in the author's prerogative of polishing it for publication. (King, 1963)

In contrast to the extraversion of the King public personality of preacher and leader, the tone here, and in much of the "Letter," is more introverted. This introversion is suggested by the understatement ("somewhat constricting circumstances") and the aloofness (he attends to his important work while being served by a Negro trusty and a whole staff of "attorneys"). As is the case with most introverted writers, the text seems to exist in the writer's mind and needs merely to be transcribed on whatever small piece of paper is handy, and it requires only polishing in order to be ready for publication. These elements of voice and tone belong to a persona who finds the sources of energy within. This is certainly appropriate given the dominant imagery of incarceration, which itself serves to symbolize the enslavement of the Black race and its survival through inner strength.

The "Letter" begins:

MY DEAR FELLOW CLERGYMEN:

> While confined here in the Birmingham city jail, I came across your recent statement calling my present activities "unwise and untimely." Seldom do I pause to answer criticism of my work and ideas. If I sought to answer all the criticisms that cross my desk, my secretaries would have little time for anything other than such correspondence in the course of a day, and I would have no time for constructive work. But since I feel you are men of genuine good will and that your criticisms are sincerely set forth, I want to try to answer your statement in what I hope will be patient and reasonable terms.

The type of the persona here is ISTJ, to which Kroeger and Thuesen assign the handle "doing what should be done." ISTJs are motivated by a deep sense of duty and responsibility. Concrete, practical, and demanding, they expect things to be done their way and are prepared to be held responsible. Based on a sample of over 10,000 members of the U. S. military, from enlisted personnel to generals and admirals, the most common military personality is ISTJ (Kroeger & Theusen, 1988). The persona in the "Letter" continues the ironic understatement of the "Author's Note," except with an almost comic twist: How does one "come across" anything while confined to the city jail? These fellow clergymen are not going to be granted the satisfaction that their critique has been given any special attention. Instead, their letter is treated as a little mess the neat and tidy ISTJ has to clean up—an unpleasant task, but consistent with duty. The imagery of a productive office is superimposed on the jail image. There is the desk with its flow of paperwork and the staff of "secretaries" (to supplement the staff of "attorneys") barely able to keep up with the constructive output of this busy executive. Finally, there is a tone of parental authority in the last sentence, with its extravagant signs of impatience: ". . . since *I feel* that you are men of good will . . . , *I want to try to answer* your statement in what *I hope will be patient and reasonable terms.*" The parental tone is quite positive, actually, because it is based on love and kinship. It is important for unruly and inattentive children to be shown the proper way to behave, and a good ISTJ parent has just the right kind of clear-headed sense of duty to see it through: "I'm going to explain this one more time, so pay attention!"

In the second paragraph, we see a slight shift in the persona:

> I think I should indicate why I am here in Birmingham, since you have been influenced by the view which argues against "outsiders coming in." I have the honor of serving as president of the Southern Christian Leadership Conference, an organization operating in every southern state, with headquarters in Atlanta, Georgia. We have some eighty-five affiliated organizations across the South, and one of them is the Alabama Christian Movement for Human Rights. Frequently we share staff, educational and financial resources with our affiliates. Several months ago the affiliate here in Birmingham asked us to be on call to engage in a nonviolent direct-action program if such were deemed necessary. We readily consented, and when the hour came we lived up to our promise. So I, along with several members of my staff, am here because I was invited here. I am here because I have organizational ties here.

The persona has modulated from ISTJ to ISFJ ("a high sense of duty"), much the same personality except for a significant shift from thinking to feeling. Here we see the persona performing his duty not because that is the path he has chosen but because he feels obligated by the interdependency of a network of other people. He lays out the strands of that network in elaborate detail, using language brimming with the drama of human interaction: "honor," "share," "readily consented," "when the hour came," "lived up to our promise," "invited." In the first paragraph, his duty was imposed by the need to explain himself clearly (T); in the second, his duty is imposed by his obligations to others (F). In this instance, the modulation seems to be a shift in focus from what is right in an abstract sense to what is required in a social sense.

Another modulation takes us into the third paragraph:

> But more basically, I am in Birmingham because injustice is here. Just as the prophets of the eighth-century B. C. left their villages and carried their "thus saith the Lord" far beyond the boundaries of their home towns, and just as the Apostle Paul left his village of Tarsus and carried the gospel of Jesus Christ to the far corners of the Greco-Roman world, so am I compelled to carry the gospel of freedom beyond my own home town. Like Paul, I must constantly respond to the Macedonian call for aid.

Now the personality type looks like INTJ ("everything has room for improvement"), the major shift being from the sensing of the first two paragraphs to the intuitive thrust here. Enough of the details of the local situation, the city jail, the clergymen and their complaints, the network of organizations! King looks at the big picture: St. Paul, Jesus, the Greco-Roman world, the Macedonian call. The INTJ sees the patterns and connections invisible to others, and he may seem arrogant when he uses those abstractions to guide his large-scale repairs on whatever is wrong with the world. The second sentence is indicative of the INTJ style—long, complex, grand, inclusive, and putting heavy demands on the reader's short-term memory with its delayed subject and verb. One senses the writer's intellectual excitement with the vision of stepping into St. Paul's sandals, even if it means treading a dusty road in 20th-century Alabama.

This heady stuff cannot be kept up very long. It's time for another modulation:

> Moreover, I am cognizant of the interconnectedness of all communities and states. I cannot sit idly by in Atlanta and not be concerned about what happens in Birmingham. Injustice anywhere is a threat to justice everywhere. We are caught in an inescapable network of mutuality, tied in a single garment of destiny. Whatever affects one directly, affects all indirectly. Never again can we afford to live with the narrow, provincial "outside agitator" idea. Anyone who lives inside the United States can never be considered an outsider anywhere within its bounds.

This is the voice of the INFP ("performing noble service to aid society"). This type is an idealist who takes an easy-going approach to serving society. But despite this easygoing approach, he possesses a firm set of values and codes. The shift here from INTJ to INFP corresponds to the shift from ISTJ to ISFJ between the first and second paragraphs—that is, primarily from thinking to feeling. The persona offers an intellectual or imaginative framework in the T paragraphs and then humanizes it in the alternating F paragraphs. Between this paragraph and the one preceding, for example, we go from the St. Paul connection to the need for all of us to be insiders; from the wave-making, boat-rocking rabble-rouser to the weaver of the garment of destiny; from there to here; from "I" to "we."

In the next paragraph, King resumes the INTJ persona ("everything has room for improvement"), continuing the alternating T and F pattern by disclosing the logic (T) of his actions:

> You deplore the demonstrations taking place in Birmingham. But your statement, I am sorry to say, fails to express a similar concern for the conditions that brought about the demonstrations. I am sure that none of you would want to rest content with the superficial kind of social analysis that deals merely with effects and does not grapple with underlying causes. It is unfortunate that demonstrations are taking place in Birmingham, but it is even more unfortunate that the city's white power structure left the Negro community with no alternative.

He does not merely disagree with his critics. (And with a perfunctory and somewhat haughty "I am sorry to say" at that!) He and they are not even seeing the same things. Where they focus on the unpleasant "effects" of the local demonstrations (S), he focuses on intangible historical "causes" embedded in social history (N). Where they seem alarmed by the prospect of upsetting decent White folks (F), he presses forward with the inexorable logic that the White power structure has left "no alternative" (T). It is time for justice (T), not mercy (F). The oppositions of S/N and of F/T undergird the contrapuntal structure of the paragraph.

In these early paragraphs, King creates a broader frame of reference than that of his critics. They have not been seeing the bigger picture. Now, in the next two paragraphs, he is ready to deal with the specifics of their critique by attacking the problem at hand. Thus, we see another modulation, this time from intuition to sensing:

> In any non-violent campaign there are four basic steps: collection of the facts to determine whether injustices exist; negotiation; self-purification; and direct action. We have gone through all of these steps in Birmingham. There can be no gainsaying the fact that racial injustice engulfs this community. Birmingham is probably the most thoroughly segregated city in the United States. Its ugly record of brutality is widely known. Negroes have experienced grossly unjust treatment in the courts. There have been more unsolved bombings of Negro homes and churches in Birmingham than in any other city in the nation. These are the hard, brutal facts of the case. On the basis of these conditions, Negro leaders sought to negotiate with the city fathers. But the latter consistently refused to engage in good-faith negotiation.

> Then, last September, came the opportunity to talk with the leaders of Birmingham's economic community. In the course of the negotiations, certain promises were made by the merchants—for example, to remove the stores' humiliating racial signs. On the basis of these promises, the Reverend Fred Shuttlesworth and the leaders of the Alabama Christian Movement for Human Rights agreed to a moratorium on all demonstrations. As the weeks and months went by, we realized that we were the victims of a broken promise. A few signs, briefly removed, returned; the others remained.

Here we see a return to the personality with which the "Letter" opened: ISTJ ("doing what should be done"). Framing a complex problem by a series of simple steps is highly characteristic of the ISTJ. He is saying, in effect, "Let's get the facts straight." This was the attitude at the beginning, in which he patiently justified taking time out of his busy schedule to explain reality to his critics. Now he goes a step deeper into history to establish the factual basis for the march itself. The language is objective and concrete ("hard, brutal facts"), and the focus is on the tangible and pragmatic (S). At the same time, there are checklists of criteria against which the facts of the case are measured (T). One checklist is specified (the four steps of a nonviolent campaign), and the other is implied (the steps in the process of negotiation). Moreover, the checklists are not there merely to generate data but to provide a basis for judgment. With an unambiguous sense of right and wrong, King finds the city fathers wrong (J). Yet the sense of right and wrong here is not abstract but concrete; it is not so much a matter of *being* right or wrong but of *doing* things the right or wrong way (S). The ISTJ sensibility is particularly offended by broken promises. For the ISTJ, after all, actions speak louder than words. Words are nothing but abstractions unless they have tangible referents.

The sensing and judging now gives way to intuition and perception:

> As in so many past experiences, our hopes had been blasted, and the shadow of deep disappointment settled upon us. We had no alternative except to prepare for direct action, whereby we would present our very bodies as a means of laying our case before the conscience of the local and the national community. Mindful of the difficulties involved, we decided to undertake a process of self-purification. We began a series of workshops on nonviolence, and we repeatedly asked ourselves: "Are you able to endure the ordeal of jail?" We decided to schedule our direct-action program for the Easter season, realizing that except for Christmas, this is the main shopping period of the year. Knowing that a strong economic-withdrawal program would be the by-product of direct action, we felt that this would be the best time to bring pressure to bear on the merchants for the needed change.

Then it occurred to us that Birmingham's mayoral election was coming up in March, and we speedily decided to postpone action until after election day. When we discovered that the Commissioner of Public Safety, Eugene "Bull" O'Connor, had piled up enough votes to be in the run-off, we decided again to postpone action until the day after the run-off so that demonstrations could not be used to cloud the issues. Like many others, we waited to see Mr. O'Connor defeated, and to this end we endured postponement after postponement. Having aided in this community need, we felt that our direct-action program could be delayed no longer.

Although the last phrase implies the closure of a decision made (J), the dominant personality of these two paragraphs is INTP ("a love of problem solving"). The narrative details are important chiefly for what they tell us about the underlying process of organizing a successful demonstration. What is conveyed is not information so much as a reflective attitude about what to do with information (IN). What happens when your hopes get blasted? How do you prepare for jail? When is the best time to make an economic boycott work? The series of contingencies that affect the potential outcome of the demonstration is fully analyzed (T). In doing so, King emphasizes how imaginatively the organizers considered all possibilities (P)—the difficulty of using bodies in a nonviolent way, the highs and lows of the merchandising cycle, the possible outcome of an election, the anticipation of public reaction and potential misunderstanding. The INTP is absorbed by the excitement of fitting together the many pieces of a puzzle. He understands that any small piece of the whole is provisional and subject to correction. Thus, apart from the narrative background that these two paragraphs provide, the personality here conveys a subtext message: "Before you criticize, you should understand how complex and contingent these things are."

Despite its strategic shifts between sensing and intuition, feeling and thinking, and judging and perceiving, the personality in this discourse has so far been consistently introverted. At this point in the "Letter," however, a more extraverted personality emerges:

You may well ask "Why direct action? Why sit-ins, marches, and so forth? Isn't negotiation a better path?" You are quite right in calling for negotiation. Indeed, this is the very purpose of direct action. Nonviolent direct action seeks to create such a crisis and foster such a tension that a community that has consistently refused to negotiate is forced to confront the issue. It seeks so to dramatize the issue that it can no longer be ignored. My citing the creation of tension as part of the work of the nonviolent-resister may sound rather shocking. But I must confess that I am not afraid of the word "tension." I have earnestly opposed violent tension, but there is a type of constructive, non-violent tension which is necessary for growth. Just as Socrates felt that it was necessary to create a tension in the mind so that individuals could rise from the bondage of myths and half-truths to the unfettered realm of creative analysis and objective appraisal, so must we see the need for nonviolent gadflies to create the kind of tension in society that will help men rise from the dark depths of prejudice and racism to the majestic heights of understanding and brotherhood.

The purpose of our direct-action program is to create a situation so crisis-packed that it will inevitably open the door to negotiation. I therefore concur with you in your call for negotiation. Too long has our beloved Southland been bogged down in a tragic effort to live in monologue rather than dialogue.

The shift from introversion to extraversion supports several transitions at this point in the text. The introspective critical analysis gives way to an expansive homily. No longer confined with his own thoughts, the speaker is now reaching out to encourage collective action. Whereas before he emphasized the critical differences between himself and the fellow clergymen, he now emphasizes the connections and similarities between them ("you are quite right," "I therefore concur with you in your call for negotiation"). He shows he understands what they are thinking and feeling ("You may well ask"; his ideas "may sound rather shocking," he acknowledges). The personality here is ENTJ—"life's natural leaders." They are natural leaders not only because they are excellent communicators, able to connect effectively with audiences and publics (E), but also because they are purposeful and argumentative, knowing where they and others should be going (TJ). Their goals are informed by large patterns of meaning and possibility (N). The communicative style of ENTJs is hearty, robust, and impatient. The prose in the earlier part of the "Letter" was relatively spare, but here it becomes elaborate in the manner of a rousing sermon. In the sentence in which Socrates is mentioned, for example, notice the complexity, delayed closure, and florid diction—nearly to the point of overloading. Prejudice and racism must be sunk to "dark depths," and understanding and brotherhood must be elevated to "majestic heights." There is obviously no shortage of paper once we have emerged rhetorically from the confinement of Birmingham jail. Indeed, the oratorical flourishes suggest the words are no longer even confined to paper.

The extraversion continues in the next paragraph, with some modulations:

One of the basic points in your statement is that the action that I and my associates have taken in Birmingham is untimely. Some have asked: "Why didn't you give the new city administration time to act?" The only answer that I can give this query is that the new Birmingham administration must be prodded about as much as the outgoing one, before it will act. We are sadly mistaken if we feel that the election of

Albert Boutwell as mayor will bring the millennium to Birmingham. While Mr. Boutwell is a much more gentle person than Mr. Connor, they are both segregationists, dedicated to maintenance of the status quo. I have hope that Mr. Boutwell will be reasonable enough to see the futility of massive resistance to desegregation. But he will not see this without pressure from devotees of civil rights. My friends, I must say to you that we have not made a single gain in civil rights without determined legal and nonviolent pressure. Lamentably, it is an historical fact that privileged groups seldom give up their privileges voluntarily. Individuals may see the moral light and voluntarily give up their unjust posture; but, as Reinhold Niebuhr has reminded us, groups tend to be more immoral than individuals.

The grand and single-minded gestures of the intuitive and judging personality (ENTJ) in the paragraphs previous to this one give way here to the action-oriented sensing and perceiving personality of the ESTP—"the ultimate realist." These are the people who firmly distinguish between the ideal and the real, the ones who are restless to get things done in the real world. They are impatient with tried and true methods that somehow do not work. An ironic style fits the ESTP's concern with whatever obstructs a clear view of reality, as in this sentence: "We are sadly mistaken if we feel that the election of Albert Boutwell as mayor will bring the millennium to Birmingham." The focus on human relations (E) continues: King adopts a respectful and understanding attitude toward his critics' question about timely action. His response encourages collective action. Moreover, the "fellow clergymen" of the more introverted "Author's Note" are here embraced in an extraverted greeting as "my friends." He is also grounded in factual reality (S), especially when reality is obscured by appearances. He shows, for example, that his critics should not be deceived by the gentle demeanor of Mr. Boutwell. In addition, they should grasp the political efficacy of public pressure, citing the "historical fact" that privileged groups do not easily shed their privileges. His assessment of the situation continues to be highly analytical (T). He refutes the argument that his actions are untimely by referring to historical patterns of defeat, in contrast to the feeling approach of his critics who do not want to offend the authorities. His distinction between the morality of individuals and of groups creates a clear thinking-type alternative to the more feeling-type attitude through which someone might be deceived by the apparent good will of individuals. Finally, he encourages openness to alternatives (P). The facts, the causes, the predictions—these elements of the presentation demand new approaches to solving the problem.

These 12 paragraphs constitute barely a quarter of the whole "Letter," but perhaps they are enough to demonstrate this approach to discourse analysis. The pattern of personality shifts looks like this, with the changes identified in bold print: ISTJ —> ISFJ —> **INTJ** —> **INFP** —> **INTJ** —> **ISTJ** —>

INTP —> ENTJ —> ESTP. The sense of a continuous line of discourse animated by contrastive and modulating elements is reminiscent of musical composition, especially if we are thinking in terms of final effect. Our understanding of personality preference can help us understand the function and effect of a writer's or speaker's manner of self-representation. In this instance, we see a highly protean persona, shifting and modulating through a complex series of rhetorical maneuvers. We find strategic shifts in attitude, in perspective, in the manner of argument, and in the discourse style.

CONCLUSION

The general characterizations of personality types can be useful probes in the process of interpretation. The personality descriptions, such as those of Kroeger and Thuesen that I have used here, usually guide our understanding of real people interacting in genuine social and learning situations. Applying these descriptions to real people is risky (although often highly productive) because the complex mental functioning of real people will always confound the relative simplicity of these eight categories. But the representation of self in a text is not a real person but an artful contrivance, conceived in broad strokes to meet a very particular need, and stabilized in a text where it cannot change. Applying personality descriptions to these self-representations is interpretive in the manner of literary or rhetorical criticism, subject to argument and revision, but utterly without clinical significance. So, for example, where I have talked about King doing this or that, I have meant King's persona was doing this or that. The distinction between author and persona is easy enough to make in literary works but more difficult in a public document like "Letter From Birmingham Jail," which seems to all outward appearances to be the pure expression of its author's ideas. And so it is— but the expression is very much shaped and formed by the devices of self-representation analyzed here.

The distinction between the central self and the rhetorical self proposed by Lanham (1976) may be useful in connection with this discussion of how the self is represented in a public text. The central self, in Lanham's analysis, is the serious self, the self we seek to understand through philosophy and meditation. It is the self Plato was interested in. The rhetorical self, in contrast, is the social and represented self, attentive to verbal surfaces, dramatically manipulating reality (rather than trying to discover it), concerned with what is *accepted* as reality (rather than what is real). This is the self of the Sophists, specializing in the way knowledge is held. The competing selves are sometimes reconciled (as in Aristotle), and this fragile reconciliation is one way of comprehending the duality that runs through Western civilization. At one time, the rhetorical self held a respectable place in schooling, and the revival of rhetoric in our media age has to some degree revived interest in understanding the rhetorical self. Schooling the rhetorical self should enhance literate performance by disclosing the mechanisms of communicative acts, one of which certainly must be how the self is represented in a text.

That representation is rhetorical (as distinct from central) because it is constrained by contexts such as audience and purpose. The personality preferences implied in the represented self are adaptations to those constraints. So, for example, certain rhetorical purposes invite the creation of roles dominated by certain personality preferences. Table 3.1 shows some examples of the personality preferences a writer might adopt in order to be particularly effective in various kinds of discourse situations. For each adopted manner of self-representation there is a corresponding role for the audience.

As the example of King's "Letter" illustrates, there may be a multitude of rhetorical situations within a discourse, each inviting a different manner of self-representation. The deployment of multiple personalities—competing, contrasting, and modulating in sequence—signifies highly literate performance because it embraces a broad range of personality preferences.

Table 3.1. Personality and Rhetorical Roles.

Discourse Situation	Persona Role	Audience Role
Argumentative	Thinking (T): be logical, objective, analytical	Follow a reasoned train of thought, tolerate abstraction
Persuasive	Feeling (F): express beliefs, feeling, sympathy, connect with audiences	Be willing to be moved by expressive conviction, tolerate personal involvement
Thesis-centered	Judging (J): be conclusive definite, expedient, focused	Expect finality, respect firm judgment, tolerate closure
Topic-centered	Perceiving (P): be open, thorough, cautious	Expect the unexpected, tolerate ambiguity and inconclusiveness

REFERENCES

Baumlin, J. S. (1994). Introduction: Positioning ethos in historical and contemporary theory. In J. S. Baumlin & T. F. Baumlin (Eds.), *Ethos: New essays in rhetorical and critical theory* (pp. xi-xxxi). Dallas: Southern Methodist University Press.

Booth, W. C. (1961). *The rhetoric of fiction.* Chicago: University of Chicago Press.

Burke, K. E. (1945). *A grammar of motives.* Berkeley: University of California Press.

Cherry, R. D. (1988). Ethos versus persona: Self-representation in written discourse. *Written Communication, 5,* 251-276.

Ede, L., & Lunsford, A. (1984). Audience addressed /audience invoked: The role of audience in composition theory and pedagogy. *College Composition and Communication, 35,* 155-171.

Jensen, G. H., & DiTiberio, J. K. (1989). *Personality and the teaching of writing.* Norwood, NJ: Ablex.

Johnson, N. (1984). Ethos and the aims of rhetoric. In R. J. Connors, L. S. Ede, & A. A. Lunsford (Eds.), *Essays on classical rhetoric and modern discourse* (pp. 98-114). Carbondale: Southern Illinois University Press.

Keirsey, D., with Bates, M. (1978). *Please understand me: An essay on temperament styles.* Del Mar, CA: Prometheus Nemesis Books.

King, Martin Luther, Jr. (1963). Letter from Birmingham Jail, April 19, 1963. *Why we can't wait.* New York: Harper and Row.

Kroeger, O., & Thuesen, J. M. (1988). *Type talk: The 16 personality types that determine how we live, love, and work.* New York: Delta.

Lanham, R. A. (1976). *The motives of eloquence: Literary rhetoric in the renaissance.* New Haven, CT: Yale University Press.

Miller, K. D. (1992). *Voice of deliverance: The language of Martin Luther King, Jr. and its sources.* New York: Free Press.

Myers, I. B. (1980). *Gifts differing.* Palo Alto, CA: Consulting Psychologists Press.

Myers, I. B. (1987). *Introduction to type.* Palo Alto, CA: Consulting Psychologists Press.

Ong, W. J. (1975). The writer's audience is always a fiction. *Publications of the Modern Language Association, 90,* 9-21.

Perelman, C., & Olbrechts-Tyteca, L. (1969). *The new rhetoric: A treatise on argumentation.* Notre Dame, IN: Notre Dame University Press.

Chapter 4

Writing Style, Personality Type, and Brain Dominance: A New Model

Sheila Davis
The New School for Social Research, New York

Teaching lyric writing from the triple perspectives of personality type, figurative language preference, and neuropsychological processing has produced evidence of an affinity between writing style, Jungian typology, and brain function.

Although the lyric, with its musical purpose and emphasis on rhythm and rhyme, falls outside the general college creative writing curriculum, it can clearly illustrate the writing style/type/brain relationship (rhythm and rhyme aside). We will see why the work of one writer tends to be poetic, another satiric, yet another symbolic irrespective of literary form—lyric, essay, or novel.

POLARITY, BIPOLES, AND THE QUATERNITY

Like Jung's theory of psychological types, the theory of literary style advanced here is grounded in the ancient psychological law espoused by Heraclitus that all energy involves the play of opposites—on-off, hot-cold, beginning-end, and so on. Such bipoles embodying two extremes are often arranged in a quaternity, that is, they form a cross of two related pairs of adjacently harmonious opposites; for example, the four cardinal directions north-south, east-west. Converging research implies that the brain may be organized as such a quaternity.

The Quaternary Brain

Roger Sperry's split-brain studies in the 1960s, for which he was awarded the Nobel Prize, established that the Left Hemisphere (LH) and the Right Hemisphere (RH) function in a complementary manner, with the LH specializing in analytic, logical, sequential, focal processing and the RH in visual, synthetic, holistic, diffuse processing (Burns et al., 1985). More recent research data suggest that the frontal lobes and posterior area, like the RH and LH, also function in a complementary manner, with the frontal lobes concerned with processing abstract thinking, future planning, and "novel" material, whereas the posterior area subserves the processing of concrete thinking, stored memory, and routinized tasks (Mesulam, 1986). Accumulated neurological findings thus imply that the brain operates in a quaternary manner: We might say that the LH and RH act as a horizontal axis that functions at right angles to a vertical anterior-posterior axis. Together they appear to form an invisible cross of polar-opposite cortical regions that serve as four prime processing centers.

The Quaternity of Cognitive Styles

Jung (1968) proposed that the four fundamental psychological functions form a cross with a rational axis (thinking-feeling) at right angles to an irrational axis (sensation-intuition), which together serve as the psychological compass by which the psyche takes its bearings. Brain research supports the attribution of the four functions to the following general cortical/subcortical areas: thinking to the left frontal lobe (Springer & Deutsch, 1989), feeling to the right posterior area (Burns et al., 1985) intuition to the right frontal lobe (Ornstein, 1986), and sensation to the left posterior area (Springer & Deutsch,1989). Jung's function cross can thus he said to, in effect, "straddle" the hemispheres and operate in the X-position.

    In discussing the dynamics of cognitive styles, Jung (1989) modeled the functions in a circle to illustrate the manner in which the most differentiated function, the dominant, pairs up with an adjacent complementary auxiliary function to create the four major cognitive styles that are identified by the Myers-Briggs Type Indicator (MBTI): intuitive thinking (NT), intuitive feeling (NF), sensing feeling (SF), and sensing thinking (ST).

Figure 4.1 models the manner in which each cognitive style appears to be processed by a major cerebral area, making apparent why we can consider the ST to be a "Left-brain Dominant," the NT a "Frontal (or Cerebral) Dominant," the NF a "Right-brain Dominant," and the SF a "Posterior (or Limbic) Dominant."

THE MBTI SCALES AND THE BRAIN

The second quaternity of related bipoles identified by the MBTI—the two orientations, extraversion and introversions and two attitudes, perception

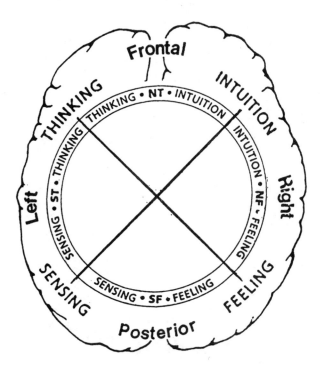

Figure 4.1. The model proposes the manner in which Jung's Cross of the Functions is mediated by four discrete, overlapping cortical areas, thereby producing the four cognitive styles—NT, NF, SF, and ST

and judgment—appears to be mediated cortically in a similar cross-like manner: Data have linked extraversion and perception with the RH (Eimas & Galaburda, 1990), and introversion and judgment with the LH (Burns et al., 1985). Figure 4.2 incorporates all four polar-opposite MBTI scales, indicating their relative relationship to RH and LH processing. Although every day we commonly need to access all eight functions and attitudes, our four-letter type represents those cerebral areas that we are inclined to use with more frequency. Neurolinguistic studies suggest that, like personality type, the language system is similarly composed of interconnected quaternities of related bipoles.

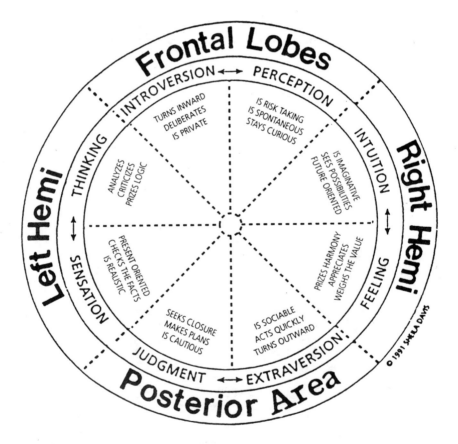

Figure 4.2. The four pairs of polarities measured by the MBTI and their symbolic relation to right- and left-hemispheric processing

LANGUAGE AND THE BRAIN

I start with the two basic pairs of word types abstract-concrete and literal-figurative, which I have termed the Lexical Cross. The LH is associated with literal language and RH with figurative language (Burns et al., 1985), thereby acting as the horizontal axis of the cross; the frontal lobes have been linked to the processing of abstract language (Calvin & Ojemann, 1994) and the posterior areas to concrete language (Mesulam, 1986), thereby forming the vertical axis of the cross (see Figure 4.3).

Just as Jung's function cross produces four distinct cognitive types, the lexical cross produces four distinct semantic types: *abstract/literal, abstract/figurative, concrete/figurative, concrete/literal.* To illustrate, I use the words *weather* (abstract) and *rain* (concrete) and start in the left frontal lobe and move clockwise: An example of abstract/literal language is expressed in the prediction by a newscaster of "stormy weather tomorrow"; the lyric to the song "Stormy Weather," however, which invokes the common metaphor, *emotional states = weather,* expresses

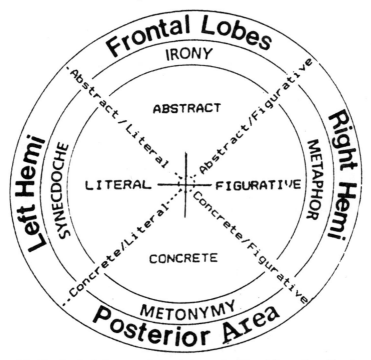

Figure 4.3. The Lexical Cross—*abstract-concrete, literal-figurative;* The Semantic Cross—*abstract/literal-concrete/figurative, abstract/figurative-concrete/literal.* The master tropes, *synecdoche-metaphor* and *irony-metonymy*

abstract/figurative language; the song title "I Made It Through the Rain," although again invoking the weather metaphor, employs concrete/figurative language; finally, a headline forecasting "heavy rain tomorrow" expresses concrete/literal language.

The Four Master Tropes

The realm of figurative language has for centuries been beset by contradictory terms and overlapping categories. It was illustrious Italian philosopher and rhetorician Giambattista Vico who offered the first clarifying identification of the significant figures of speech or *tropes* from the Latin *tropus* "to turn a phrase." In his seminal work *The New Science*, published in 1744 (/1991), Vico proposed that four major *tropes*— *metaphor, metonymy, synecdoche*, and *irony* (to which all others could be reduced)—acted not as mere decorations to writing but rather as four "necessary modes of expression" (para. 4, p. 131). Although Vico did not suggest an inherent polarity in the tropes, a close look at their functioning reveals that one exists.

The Tropic Cross and Four Thinking Styles

Figure 4.3 models the manner in which I propose that the four tropes form two pairs of polar-opposite thinking styles that appear to be mediated by the same four processing centers as the lexical cross: synecdoche, a vertical, reductionist form of thinking, LH; metaphor, a lateral, holistic form of thinking, RH; irony, a divergent form of thinking, frontal lobes; and metonymy, a convergent form of thinking, posterior area. Now I examine the innately antithetical qualities of the metaphor-synecdoche and irony-metonymy bipoles.

The Metaphor-Synecdoche Bipole

Metaphor is a lateral thought process that enlists the RH attributes of noting similarities, synthesizing, and the processing of figurative language. It acts to compare two unlike realms and unite their similarities as in "All the world's a stage"; it thereby creates a new (third) concept, *life = a play* (one of our core metaphors). Simile, the simplest form of metaphor, makes the comparison explicit by using *like, as,* or *than*: "(Like a) Bridge Over Troubled Water (I will lay me down)," or "Younger Than Springtime (am I)."

What I have termed the *compact simile* employs the compared realm as an attributive noun: "Coal black," "razor-sharp tongue." A major subtype of metaphor, *personification*, further extends a fanciful comparison by attributing human emotions and actions to nonhuman things: "the sun smiled," or "the wind whistled." *Apostrophe*, an extension of personification, addresses a nonhuman quality as if alive, exemplified by such song titles as "Willow, Weep For Me" and "Luck, Be a Lady." Metaphor, by figuratively uniting two distant domains, produces expansion of meaning.

Synecdoche, in direct opposition to metaphor, is a vertical/linear thought process that enlists the LH's small, focused semantic fields and its skill of breaking into parts. As a figure of reductive substitution (Davis, 1996), synecdoche comes in two inverse forms: It represents the part for the whole ("all hands [sailors] on deck") or represents the whole for the part(s) ("America is collapsing and buckling [its bridges and highways]"). A synecdoche always forms a whole with the subject it represents (Du Marsais, 1988).1t comes in such additional forms as *general for particular* ("the law [police] just arrived"), *raw material for finished product* ("Where the rubber meets the road"), *place for event* ("Remember the Alamo"), and *attribute for possessor* ("The ponytail is at the bar"). Synecdoche also subsumes the contraction of the beginning, middle, and end syllables of a word—*'em* for them, *s'pose* for suppose, *ope'* for open—as well as the contraction of two words into one—*wannabe* for want to be. Other subtypes include acronyms (AIDS) and nicknames ("I like Ike [Eisenhower]"). Synecdoche thus produces contraction of meaning.

The Irony-Metonymy Bipole

Irony is a divergent thought process that points up some kind of disparity between the way something is and the way it might have been, or used to be, or was expected to be. For example, "The more things change, the more they stay the same." Ironic subtypes represent forms of purposeful paradox in the service of truth: *hyperbole*, an overstating of something, often trivial ("You could have knocked me over with a feather"); *understatement*, a minimizing of something, often serious ("We lost a little thing called love"); *litotes*, expressing an affirmative by the negation of its opposite ("It's not unlikely"); *oxymoron*, a compact paradox ("idiot savant"); *pun*, a figure contrasting a similarity of sound with a disparity of meaning as in the headline, "Caffeine, Any Grounds for Concern?"; *zeugma*, a form of pun in which a verb is used in two senses ("she hid her wallet and her fear"); *paragram*, a figure of alteration that amends a word, expression, or allusion for purposeful effect ("Friends in Low Places"); and *sarcasm*, saying the opposite of what is meant as in the frequently heard comment on a rainy day, "Lovely weather we're having." Forms of extended irony include *parody*, a literary or artistic work that imitates the characteristic style of an author or a work for comic effect, and *satire*, which holds up human vices or follies to scorn or ridicule. Processing irony enlists both hemispheres of the frontal lobes: the literal, analytic, difference-detecting attributes of the LH; and the figurative, similarity-detecting, synthesizing properties of the RH. By juxtaposing incongruities, irony produces dissolution of meaning.

Metonymy, in direct opposition to irony, is a convergent thought process, a figure of symbolic substitution that represents an abstraction with a related concrete symbol (Davis, 1996): "From the cradle to the grave." In distinction to synecdoche—with which it is often confused—the metonymic substitution always entails an *external* image, which remains independent of the subject meant. Metonymy comprises such common forms of substitution as *symbol for thing symbolized* ("Bernstein gives up baton"), *cause for effect* ("Retin-A, the face cream that erases the years"), *controller for controlled* ("Bush Bombs Iraq"), *place for industry* ("Hollywood On Strike"), *container for contained,* ("Brown bag lunch"), and *apparel for wearer* ("The blue suit gets the hamburger"). As a master trope, metonymy subsumes all lesser figures of substitution; *euphemism* is a less blunt way to express an unpleasant subject ("passed away [died]); *doublespeak* uses deliberately inflated language to mislead ("transportation manager [elevator operator]"); *antonomasia* substitutes the name of a famous person or literary character to symbolize a particular quality ("your Romeo called"). Metonymy also comprises an expanded subtype, the *symbolic enactment* ("they walked down the aisle"). The literary forms of *fable* and *parable* can both be considered as extended symbolic enactments. Metonymy, which enlists the visuospatial, symbol-making properties of the bilateral posterior area, produces solidification of meaning (Davis,1996).

The Four Literary Modes

Forms of creative writing can also embody one final quaternity—two pairs of polar-opposite archetypal literary modes—*satire-romance* and *fantasy-realism*. Because the four literary modes also reflect their creators' worldview, a relationship between the modes and the four functions will be made evident as indicated in Figure 4.4: satire with thinking, romance with feeling, fantasy with intuition, and realism with sensation.

The Type/Trope/Literary Mode Relationship

Extensive evidence from typed students in the form of writing examples collected over a period of years makes apparent that writers sharing the same cognitive styles exhibit a preference for the same master trope in its many forms over the other three in this manner: the intuitive thinking (NT) type with irony, the intuitive feeling (NF) type with metaphor, the sensing feeling (SF) type with metonymy, and the sensing thinking (ST) type with synecdoche (see Figure 4.4). In addition, a key characterizing attribute applied by type/temperament theorists to each cognitive type—NT/Philosophic, NF/Idealistic, SF/Realistic, or ST/Pragmatic—will be seen mirrored in the recurring themes and philosophical perspective of the four types.

The following four lyric-writing profiles exemplify the work of adults who represent a range of ages (mid-20s to late 50s) and professions—not only the expected singers and musicians, but also accountants, lawyers, and surgeons (among others). Students, whose lyric excerpts help to illustrate the interplay of cognitive type to writing style, graciously granted permission for such quotations.

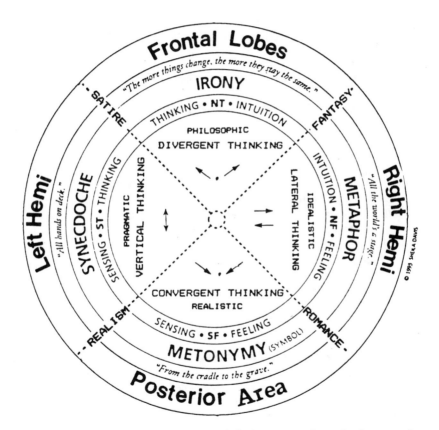

Figure 4.4. The four cognitive types and their proposed cerebral processing center, dominant trope, and thinking style: NT, frontal lobes, irony, divergent thinking; NF, right hemisphere, metaphor, lateral thinking; SF, posterior area, metonymy, convergent thinking; and ST, left hemisphere, synecdoche, vertical thinking. The four literary modes: *satire-romance, fantasy-realism.*

A SENSING THINKING (ST) LYRIC WRITING PROFILE

The ST Style: An Overview

The sensing thinking lyricist tends to portray the actions of particular characters in specific places with an emphasis on sensate details such as names, colors, numbers, and dates. These features accord with type theory, which attributes to the ST a tendency to focus on facts that can be verified by the senses (Lawrence, 1982). The first draft is usually clear, linear, logical, and grammatical, reflecting the LH skills of syntax, discriminating thinking, step-by-step sequencing, and the processing of closely related semantic fields.

The opening verse of a lyric about a shopaholic by an ISTJ illustrates the literal, detailed, and linear thinking style:

> "She makes the rounds of beauty stands
> Testing lipsticks and eye shadows on her hands.
> She scurries to the second floor
> Where there're dresses, skirts and blouses galore."

Sensing types—both ST and SF—tend to be anecdotal, spinning stories with a beginning, middle, and end. Here are a few isolated phrases from a lyric by the same ISTJ that underscore the emphasis on the discrete detail: "After five years in Ethiopia . . . he signed a two-year contract . . . just 20-minutes more to wait . . . chocolate cake . . . a little evergreen he'd planted . . . the hands of two small children." The STJ tends to focus not only on the facts, but on the parts ("the hands of two small children") rather than the whole. One ISTJ title underscored the inclination, "All the Right Parts in All the Wrong Places."

The STJ as "Guardian"

Lyrics of ST types with the SJ temperament often reflect the tendency of the SJ to act as the "guardian" of society, with plots that offer advice, articulate the rules, give ultimatums, or "scold" perpetrators of unreasonable, uncouth, or immoral behavior. One ESTJ lyric, noting the phenomenon that today's fads can become tomorrow's collectibles, offered this useful advice:

> Hang on to your clutter
> Throw nothing away.
> My Superman comics,
> My Jack Armstrong knife,
> Could have set me up for life.
> So hang on to your clutter
> And you'll find in time it will pay.

Extraverted ST writers often directly address either the *collective you,* that is, the listening audience (as in the foregoing excerpt), or a particular "singee." An ESTJ writer of a lyric about a woman confronting an unfaithful mate characteristically chose second-person singular to give the order: "Tell Your Story Walkin'!"

The ST and Satire

The sensing thinking type is known for its dry, understated wit and sometimes mocking tone. Because STJs may be especially critical of society, they quite naturally lean toward satire: One ISTJ, in "The Touchtone Blues," bemoaned telephone technology:

> "My phone gives me orders I can't refuse:
> 'Press 1 now . . . press 2 now . . . press 3 now.'
> I'd like to answer back but how?
> And I'm getting prematurely old
> From spending all that time on hold."

Another ISTJ folk song writer mocked such social/political issues as: the ubiquitous expression "Have a Nice Day!," unethical practices in the recording industry in "It Ain't Over Till Milli Vanilli Sings," and presidential decisions in "What I Did During George Bush's Summer Vacation" subtitled, "Dear Mom, Here I am in Saudi Arabia."

Satirizing can also lead to giving a cliché a new twist as in the paragram title "As the Caviar Hits the Fan," a song that mocked millionaire Donald Trump. With another paragram, "Kill and Tell," an ESTJ pointed a finger at both the public's appetite for the sordid and the media's glamorization of crime. The following is an excerpt:

> Then there was the feller
> Who got tired of his wife
> And laced her wine with arsenic
> Thus cutting short her life.
> While out on bail awaiting trial
> He made a pile of dough
> Giving interviews on Donahue
> And the Oprah Winfrey show.
> 'Cause when you kill and tell
> You're flashbulbed and recorded
> When you kill and tell
> No crime goes unrewarded.

The ST-Synecdoche Relationship

As already noted, the ST, as the most matter-of-fact and pragmatic of the four cognitive styles, prefers the most matter-of-fact and pragmatic of the four tropes—synecdoche. The varied forms of this reductive thinking style appear in such substitutions as *trade name for general product* ("The Bics in the banks are all on chains," "My U.S. Keds had worn clear thru") and *raw material for finished product* ("The Grape [wine] and the Grain [whiskey]," "When the leather [baseball] hits the pine [bat]"). ST writing abounds with all forms of abbreviations ("down at the V.F.W. Hall") and contractions ('bout, 'em, gov, zines, mem'ry, flow'r, nothin'). Occasionally, an STJ lyric will make a feature of abbreviations: "He's no Ph.D. from M.I.T./But that's O.K. with me./'Cause A.M and P.M./His kisses are T.N.T."

Partitio. Sometimes an ST draws on *partitio,* a form of synecdoche that breaks a subject into its parts. This excerpt from a lyric for children by an ESTJ mocks a highly mockable aspect of the English language:

If b-o-u-g-h spells "bow,"
Shouldn't c-o-u-g-h spell "cow"?
But c-o-u-g-h spells "koff."
'That's enough,' I say, 'to turn me off.'
T-h-r-o-u-g-h spells "thru,"
So shouldn't d-o-u-g-h spell "do"?
But my teacher says by now I oughta know
That d-o-u-g-h spells "doe."

In another lyric by the same writer, the singer complains about the kinds of disgrunted, disheveled, and uncouth men she had encountered. Then, by synecdochically lopping off the prefixes to those words, she anticipated a happier day:

The man of my dreams, I can picture him now
Just the way that I have since my youth.
Though we still haven't met,
It's a pretty safe bet
He'll be "gruntled" and "sheveled" and "couth.

The ST and the Nondominant Tropes

ST writing rarely contains forms of metaphor—the trope polar-opposite to synecdoche; when such examples do appear, they generally exhibit a somewhat caustic nature. In a lyric by an ESTJ, which employs apostrophe in the form of a letter addressed to Mr. Murphy (of the infamous Murphy's Law), we hear, among her list of literal complaints, a single rueful metaphor linked to a pun: "Every time a dreamboat sails into my life/I find that he is anchored to a very stubborn wife."

Neurophysiologists have observed that activities within a hemisphere tend to suppress or inhibit activity in the opposite hemisphere (Laughlin, McManus, & d'Aquili, 1990). This offers a likely cause for the rare instances in ST and STJ writing of metaphor or fantasy, both of which are attributed to the RH—polar-opposite to their dominant LH. And when a metonymy makes an appearance, it is likely to be in its compact form ("his well-capped grin").

Potential First-Draft Problems and Revisioning

Some first drafts may stress small details that lack a larger implication; others may reflect characters who lack credibility. These flaws will require the writer to draw on the RH functions of insight (N) and of genuine feeling (F) respectively, which will usually produce a successful second draft.

Revisioning: An ESTJ Example. An ESTJ first draft, "Sick of Health Food," exhibited many (expected) noteworthy points: sensate detail, perfect rhyme, logical sequence, good syntax, and playful puns:

> When I'm eating beansprouts and tofu,
> I'm biting off more than I can chew.
> That's a lot for a person to have to do,
> And I'm getting sick of health food!
> Herbal tea, I have found, is not my bag.
> It makes my dejected spirits sag.
> It's a bore, it's the pits, it's a grade-A drag,
> And I'm getting sick of health food!

Subsequent verses displayed the same craft and wit but lacked a motivation for a woman to eat food she does not like. The writer was encouraged to imagine a believable motive for her character's behavior (that is, to access both her feeling and intuiting functions). In the revision, she made the singer a male, wrote a new (motivating) introduction, and replaced the final verse with a more amusing and climactic one. The following is the introduction that now supplies the required emotional connection:

> The girl I adore is a health-food nut,
> But she's thoughtful, and caring, and sweet.
> She wants me to share in her way of life,

So whatever she's eating I eat.
I wish I could say that our meals are fun,
But if I said that, I'd be lying;
Of all the foods I have ever tried,
Health food is by far the most trying.

Summing Up the Sensing Thinking Style

It would appear that teachers of creative writing should not expect from the sensing thinking type subjective, confessional, or poetic writing. For STs to develop their primary gifts as social commentators, humorists, and satirists, they may require becoming more aware of the implications of their (lists of) sensate details and the motivations of their sometimes stereotyped characters.

AN INTUITIVE FEELING (NF) LYRIC WRITING PROFILE

The NF Style: An Overview

Type theory holds that intuitive feeling types are typically interested in the complexities of communication, especially in personal relationships (Myers & McCaulley, 1987). The theory is born out by the subject matter that the NF frequently chooses: interpersonal concerns with an emphasis on romantic involvements and plots centered on aspects of breaking up/making up, evidenced by titles such as "First You Cry," "Every Aching Hour," and "I Can't Get Over You."

In contrast to the literal, concrete vocabulary of the ST, that of the NF is more figurative and abstract as in the INFP title, "He Takes Me to Paradise." Lyrics by intuitive feeling types are frequently infused with the words *love, feelings, heart,* and *dream*; in fact, it is not uncommon for a single lyric to contain all those words.

The Fantasy Connection

An emphasis on possibilities, characteristic of the intuitive function, is particularly evident in the writing style of the intuitive dominants, the ENFP and INFJ: Both types manifest a tendency toward magical thinking and fantasy, which perhaps is what frequently leads them to write for children. An ENFP wrote this excerpt from a song for the toddler set "Make a face, a monkey face/It's easy as can be./Now erase it and replace it/With another magic'ly" In a musicalized update of Puss 'n Boots by an INFJ, we find: "Here's a magic lamp/That I have brought for you./If you rub and make a wish/Your dreams will all come true."

The NF-Metaphor Relationship

Type theory has long noted the affinity between NFs and the use of metaphor. It is a rare NF lyric that lacks some instance of metaphoric expression, such as "I was born with a fire burning inside of me," "Your touch was a bolt of lightning," or "There's a wall around your heart." Metaphor often serves as a lyric's central device and title: This chorus by an ENFP typifies the inclination of the intuitive feeling types toward metaphoric expression, while it also reflects their desire for harmonious relationships:

> I wanna give you oceans of love
> Waves of pleasure,
> Waves of pleasure,
> Oceans of love.
> You gona feel the rhythm,
> You gotta feel the motion,
> And the oceans and oceans of love.

The lyrics of NF students tend to be infused with all the metaphoric subtypes: *simile,* "Dreams are like feathers in the wind"; *compact simile* titles, "Lightning Love" and "Paper-Thin Lies"; *apostrophe,* "Wind, you fooled my heart again"; and *personification,* "The sky is frowning on my day." Not surprisingly, forms of the polar-opposite (nonemotional) trope synecdoche are rare in NF lyrics—other than instances of common contractions such as 'neath and mem'ry.

Some First-Draft Problems

Given the NF-RH affinity, it is not surprising that first drafts of the intuitive feeling type may contain problems whose revisions will require left-brain skills such as proper syntax, linear sequencing, and logical thinking. I now examine the most common.

Conflicting Time Frame and Viewpoint. In view of the RH's "time-independent" nature (Burns et al., 1985), it becomes understandable why NF first drafts are sometimes rendered confusing by murky time frames and/or conflicting viewpoints A mixed time frame (present/past) was evidenced in a lyric about a phone call from an old friend which began, "You called [past tense] today and it made me feel good," thereby establishing that the action was over and the singer was recollecting the call. In the lyric's chorus, however, the phone conversation is clearly in progress and the singer is talking to the caller: "What's happening [present tense] in your life?/How are things with you?" In the revision, the writer successfully unified the time frame in the present tense so that the whole lyric became a phone conversation.

One ENFP lyric inadvertently alternated between second person (directly addressing her lover as "you") and third person (talking about him as "him"). NF writers are encouraged to prevent such first-draft problems by spending longer in the prewriting process to clarify the "facts" of the plot, that is, to decide on a precise time frame and setting in which the singer's feelings take place—even if those facts are never actually stated in the lyric.

Putting Ideas in Sequential Order. Because of their right-brain dominance, NF writers sometimes bypass the sequencing function of the left brain. This may manifest in specific grammatical errors or in a general need to reorganize ideas. Dangling modifiers are not uncommon: "Like the crash of the waves/I hear you say/Your heart is gone far away." What was meant, of course, was "Like the crash of the waves, your words. . . . " First drafts of the ENFP, the most right-brain dominant of the 16 types, frequently require a resequencing of events. In the following first-draft excerpt, an ENFP reflects on the pleasures of fatherhood:

> I never dreamed my life would be so full
> But it has been since the day I saw you.
> With hardly a murmer or a cry
> You were born into my life.
> Everyday brings a new surprise
> When I look into your big brown eyes.
> The first words you ever said
> Are still ringing in my head.
>
> You could be pointing at your toes
> Or wrinkling up your funny nose.
> You might be trying to comb your hair
> Or waving your arms around in the air.
> You make a gesture for me to pick you up
> Or give you a drink from your cup.
> Or just look at me and smile
> And make me feel my life's worthwhile.

All the genuine feeling was there, but the lyric could be enhanced by a more chronological ordering of images. The following revision embodies the writer's successful accessing of his left-brain's sequencing skills:

> I remember the night you were born
> What a thrill it was for me:
> When I heard your cry
> I'd never heard a sound so sweet.
> I remember the first time you stood
> And the look that was in your eyes.
> Since the moment you walked across the room
> Every day's brought a new surprise.

I love the funny games you play
When you re sittin' on my knee,
Like coverin' up your eyes
And sayin' peek-a-boo to me.
And at night when I tuck you in,
And you smile that magic smile
And hug me with a kiss,
It makes my life worthwhile.

Practicing Parallel Construction. The writing of dominant feeling types can often be made more memorable by recasting a nonparallel phrase in a parallel construction, as, for example, this line about a molested child: "She was too young to grasp the meaning/But she knew she felt ashamed." The revision made the second half of the thought parallel to the first: "She was too young to grasp the meaning/But not too young to feel the shame."

The Right Hemisphere and the Multiproblematic Metaphor

Given the diffuse nature of the RH with its horizontal and overlapping cell structure and thus its sensitivity to semantic overlap (Beeman et al., 1994), it becomes clear why many intuitive feeling types produce problematic metaphors. Traditionally, a coherent metaphor suggests a potential reality and thus requires internal consistency, visual clarity, and semantic truth. I now identify some of the main metaphoric anomalies and suggest ways to correct or, better still, prevent them.

The Mixed Metaphor. Mixed metaphors generally submit readily to revision; for example, this from an ENFP about a troubled relationship, "Last night we were flying at supersonic speed/But today we screeched to a halt." Although it conveys the idea of a troubled relationship, it lacks both internal consistency and visual clarity: The initial comparison of a relationship to a flight inadvertently slipped into another (although somewhat related) semantic field—a car ride. When students are encouraged to practice picturing what they feel, they revise with ease. The writer was asked to unify his original statement two ways; first to complete the plane metaphor, then to introduce the car metaphor. He responded with these two coherent statements: "Last night we were flying at supersonic speed/But today we took a nosedive"; then, "Last night we were speeding down the highway of love/But today we screeched to a halt."

The "Malaphor". Other flawed metaphors are not so much mixed as they are false. Picture this: "Like the restless sea/You've drifted far from me." Here is a case of misrepresentation of reality: It is not the sea that drifts but rather a boat on the sea. Attributing to a subject/object an inappropriate or untrue element or function creates what I have termed a "malaphor," that is, a figurative comparison that falsifies reality.

Here is another example from a lyric about a woman in a problematic relationship: "I feel your love is like a trap/Holding me, stifling my freedom./I'm like a hawk, and I need to fly." There are two problems here: A trap, of course, cannot stifle; Additionally, a hawk is a bird of prey, not at all an appropriate image for the feeling the INFP wanted to convey. Here is her revision: "I feel your love is a cage/Locking me in, barring my escape./And like any bird, I need to fly."

The Unrelated Series of Metaphors. Some NF writing is made ineffective by multiple unrelated metaphors Often a lyric could be vastly improved by linking the most related images and eliminating the others. To illustrate a successful revision, first, here is the initial verse of metaphoric thoughts linked more by rhyme than reason:

When the fog rolls in,
When you take it on the chin
Say a prayer,
A prayer will clear the air.
When you've lost the way,
When your world has turned to gray,
Reach inside,
You can turn the tide

It was suggested to the writer that the verse would benefit from regrouping the weather images and eliminating unrelated metaphors. Here is the revision:

When the sky's turned gray
And you feel you've lost your way,
Then a fog rolls in,
And your view keeps growing dimmer
Say a prayer,
A prayer will clear the air.

By removing the unrelated body metaphor ("take in on the chin") and the unrelated water metaphor ("turn the tide") and uniting the lines relating to poor visibility, a coherent figurative statement results: bad weather = troubled times.

The Inapt Literal-Figurative Link. Another form of incoherent metaphor results from alternating between a literal and a figurative use of a single image. The following is the opening of a lyric that introduces the common metaphoric concept *rain = sadness* with an inappropriate *literal* use of rain:

It's another rainy Friday night
The ocean is rough, no calm in sight.
We came to the sea for a holiday
But now I see it won't work out that way
As I hold you near, it becomes so clear
Your love is gone for evermore.
It's rained on me before,
I guess it's gonna rain on me some more.

The writer misperceived that the way to set up a metaphoric concept was to introduce it (and mix it) with words from the same semantic field used literally. That, of course, does not make coherent metaphors—although it can lead to amusing puns. Another NF had similarly introduced her figurative concept—*lovemaking = a trip to paradise* (titled "He Takes Me to Paradise")—with a literal image from the same semantic field (travel). Here is the original opening verse: "I can't wait till he meets me at the station/Won't be late, feels like a New Year's celebration./Oh my heart is beating stronger/Can't hold out much longer." Of course, a trip to paradise does not leave from a train station. Here is her revision: "My desire is building to elation/I'm afire with hot anticipation./Oh my heart is beating stronger/Can't hold out much longer." The new opening treats the singer's escalating emotions in an appropriately figurative manner (*passionate feelings = fire*) and now coherently expresses the concept that lovemaking = a trip to paradise.

Summing Up the Intuitive Feeling Style

Just as the literary modes of realism and satire may scaffold the writing of the sensing thinking types, fantasy and romance often animate the lyrics of intuitive feeling types. The overview of potential first-draft problems encountered in the writing of NFs suggests that exercises to access left brain functions such as sequencing, discriminating small differences, and finding the flaw (Burns et al., 1985) will enhance the clarity of the natural metaphoric style of those with the intuitive feeling preference.

A SENSATE FEELING (SF) LYRIC WRITING PROFILE

The SF Style: An Overview

Like the first drafts of the ST, those of the SF generally embody well defined song forms, rhythmic patterns, and rhyme schemes reflecting the structural attributes of the left brain. As sensing types, the vocabulary again features concrete sensate details. Their preference for feeling, however, puts the emphasis not on *things,* but rather on people; as a consequence, the details tend to be more sensuous in nature. References to individual body parts abound in SF (and especially SFJ) lyrics in such titles as "Give Me Your Hand," "In An Open Palm," and "Wrapped Around Your Finger." In individual lines, we also hear a focus on discrete parts: "Rub my back," "he has sashayin' hips," "talkin' to me with your thighs," and "nibbling my earlobes."

Articles of clothing are frequently noted: "the green and white cape," "blue jeans on the bedpost," and "a peek at my black lace brassiere." The pleasure of food and drink looms large in SF lyrics: "the perfume of fresh croissants," "a ham and Swiss," "beef en brochette," "your half-full can of Stroh's."

Far more often than the other three cognitive types, SF lyricists tend to be tellers of tales. The stories of SFJs often center on family life ("Watching My Daughter Grow") and express appreciation ("Thank You, Mama"). Anecdotes honoring traditional values frequently span three generations as evidenced in the titles of two ISFJ writers, "Grandmother's Ring," "Grandfather's Watch," and "Grandmother's Rocking Chair."

The SJ and SP Temperaments and Writing Style

Although both ISFJ and ESFP types share the SF cognitive style, their value systems—as evidenced by their lyrics—could not be more different. David Keirsey's temperament theory (Keirsey & Bates, 1984) proposes that sensing judging (SJ) types and sensing perceptive (SP) types represent two of the four archetypal personalities (the other two being the NF and NT). Keirsey characterizes SJs as conservatives who live by "oughts" and "shoulds", honor traditions, rites, and rituals; are pillars of the church and belong to meaningful institutions. The following is an excerpt from an anecdotal ISFJ lyric that reflects such values:

> At her office desk in Phoenix,
> A typist breathes a prayer.
> She's fed up with the corp'rate life;
> She finds no future there,
> Then she comes across a listing
> For a job in Santa Fe.
> She sees the leading of the Lord—
> She'll follow; she'll obey.
>
> On his bus in downtown Boston,
> A driver's thoughts burn slow.
> He recalls his godly promises—
> All broken, years ago.
> He wonders, can he still turn back

And walk the "narrow way"?
He sees the leading of the Lord—
He'll follow; he'll obey.

In a church outside of Nashville,
Two children hear a plea,
A missionary challenge,
And rise for all to see.
They say that they can change the world.
(And with God's help, they may!)
They see the leading of the lord—
They'll follow; they'll obey.

In contrast to the SFJ values noted earlier, SFPs are fun-loving, chance-taking optimists who avoid dull routine and are skilled at seizing opportunities. This introductory verse and chorus to a ESFP list song reflects the SP temperament:

When some women end a love affair
They frequently go to pot,
And pills, and gin, and Haagen Dazs,
And lie around a lot.
But when this heart of mine's about to break
It's not uppers or downers or fudge carmel ripple I take:

Between men, I take French conversation,
How to roll sushi, or unroll a tent.
Between men, I've learned reincarnation
And sexual styles of the Orient
Plus real estate, belly dance, scuba, ceramics (but not sten),
When? Between men.

Both the SJ and SP lyrics exhibit the literal and concrete details we have come to expect from the sensing type. But the contrast in philosophy expressed by the two writers points to how a preference for either the J (left brain) or P (right brain) attitude imbues one's writing.

The SF-Metonymy Relationship

The SF type's attraction to the physical world and people-centered values quite naturally manifests in forms of metonymy, that is, the substitution of a concrete attribute or symbol for an abstraction. The following is a sampling of metonymic thinking of SFs in titles and single lines:

> *Symbol for the symbolized:*
> "It's the Red and Green Season Again"
> "At work I got a pink slip/The day you packed to leave"

Possession for possessor:
   "A sharkskin suit is coming up the street"
Container for contained:
   "I haven't lost a pound/But my wallet has slimmed a lot"
Effect for cause:
   "With both names on the mailbox and the door"
   "I've a tan without one strapmark"
Attribute for subject:
   "Soon you'll take off in that silver shell"
   "I've traded in the highway for the backyard barbeque"
Antonomasia:
   "Dreaming dreams of Walter Mitty"
   "I meet another Don Juan and the story repeats"
Euphemism:
   "The angels took my mama home"
   "I've a friend [condom] in my pocket"
Symbolic enactment:
   "In just a few moments, a woman, a man
   Will place golden circles on each others' hands
   And promise to love as long as they live.
   More precious than gold is the promise they'll give."

The Compact Metonym. The compact form of metonym lends itself to distinctive titles. Several by an ISFJ writer reflect her spiritual orientation: "Subway Sermons," "Bibleland," and "Jerusalem Whisper." In contrast, those by an ESFP feature more down-to-earth concerns: "Prime-Time Lover," "Diaper City," and "Hardhat Woman."

Potential Metonymic Problems. Unlike the multiproblematic metaphor, metonymic usage is pretty much fail safe with one key caveats: The listener/reader needs to be prepared for a shift from literal to metonymic language. Here, from an ISFJ lyric, is an illustration of a potential pitfall:

You thought you got it all
When you got rid of me.
But you missed a thing or two.
You didn't get happiness
You didn't get peace of mind
All you got was you.
You forgot your knees
Until they hit the ground.
Funny, how life comes back around.

I am referring, of course, to the jarring image, "You forgot your knees. . . . " Prior to that line, the language had been literal and abstract (happiness, peace of mind). Because the brain anticipates more of what it has been hearing or reading, the expectation is for more literal language. "Knees," of course, was not being used literally but figuratively in a metonymic substitution for apologize, as in the idiom, "to get down on one's knees" to ask forgiveness. To prepare the listener/reader for the shift from abstract/literal to metonymic requires a preparatory phrase; for example, "You never said you were sorry then/Now it's too late to drop to your knees." Writers may need to become conscious of the necessity to make a smooth transition from literal to metonymic language.

The SF and the Nondominant Tropes

Because metaphor arises from a felt need to bypass literal language and more expressively convey a particular experience, it is not surprising that the SF, sharing the feeling function with the NF, also frequently employs metaphor. Also not uncommon in SF writing are synecdoches and occasional puns. A look at Figure 4.4 offers a biological reason that the SF, a "split-dominant" with a preferred function in the posterior region of each hemisphere, can readily "reach up" to metaphor in the right hemisphere and to synecdoche in the left. Not surprisingly, the puns of the SF ("When some women end a love affair/They frequently go to pot") exhibit a playful tone in contrast to those of the NT, which tend to have a more ironic bite.

The SF and Metaphor. As we might expect, the metaphors of SFs often exhibit a symbolic nature. Here is a chorus by an ISFP in which he employs apostrophe to address an abstraction—an impending hailstorm, the symbol of his father's failed cotton crop: "Hailstorm, Hailstorm, go away/Change your icy hail to rain./If the good Lord's willin'/And you leave us alone,/We can pick enough cotton/To save our home."

The following is the opening of an ISFJ's lyric that takes the metaphoric subtype of personification to its ultimate: A house acquires human characteristics as it addresses its new owners:

I've been cold, dark and empty
Since my old owners divorced.
But I used to be the house of their dreams—
With my modern country kitchen
And sunken living room
And my ornamental plants and evergreens.
Then you brightened up my morning
With an orange moving van.
I'm glad you and your wife are here to stay.
'Cause I'd almost forgotten

The warmth of family
You gave me a new lease on life today.

Potential Problems with Figurative Language. We have seen that the NF may seesaw between literal rain and metaphoric rain (as trouble). The sensate feeling writer may also inappropriately alternate between literal and figurative language or ineffectively link the two—but in a different manner. Here, for example, is a line from an ISFJ that gives one pause: "The cold March winds still blow/To remind me how my heart felt frozen in the snow." The surreal image of a disembodied heart "*in* the snow" results from a tendency by some SFs to unconsciously concretize the figurative; in this case, the fusion of a figurative use of "heart" (a metonym for feelings) with a literal use of "snow." The writer took the suggestion to modify the false metonym to a true simile: "my heart [feelings] felt frozen like the snow."

"Concretistic" Thinking. An SF may also inappropriately interlace concrete literal language with multiple forms of figurative language (metaphor, pun, and metonym) from the same semantic field, resulting in a semantic jumble. For example, I recall a student lyric about a male auto racer who was attracted to a successful female racer and was beaten by her at the Indianapolis 500; literal lines, however, were juxtaposed with both synthetic metaphors ("there are hearts all over the asphalt") and puns ("a faster woman you just won't meet"). The writer was trying to use auto racing as symbolic of dangerous (fast) loving. By blurring the distinction between literal and figurative, the lyric lacked both a convincing character and a credible situation.

That kind of literal-figurative fusion appears to result from what Jung (1976) called "concretistic thinking," manifest by the inability of a sensing type to discriminate between subjective feeling and the sensed object. Lyricists who switch back and forth between literal and figurative aspects of the same semantic field often believe that they have produced a symbolic work, and thus they cannot grasp the need for revision. As a result, some promising first drafts remain unfulfilled.

The Literal Foundation of Symbolic Writing

I have seen many such instances in which the writer appears to be aspiring to symbolism. *But a symbol is not a figure of speech: Symbolism is achieved via literal language.* A true symbolic work consistently represents a real situation in a literal manner as it simultaneously suggests (symbolizes) a larger meaning. For example, "April Showers," "Bein' Green" and "September Song" are symbolic songs. In each, the lyric's central image—*rainy spring weather, a frog's greenness,* and *autumn,* respectively—is used in a consistently literal manner. The message that each image tacitly conveys, however, represents something of greater significance: "our troubles will pass," "self-acceptance is the requisite of happiness," and "time moves more quickly as we age." The paucity of symbolic songs in the popular repertoire suggests that, of all literary forms, the symbolic work might well be the most daunting.

Summing Up the Sensate Feeling Style

In the lyrics of the SF, we again find the interplay of the literary modes: This time it is the terrain between realism and romance. With the exception of the concretistic thinking noted earlier, most first-draft problems of the SF—a list of sensate details lacking significance or a character who behaves illogically—are likely to be readily remedied with some insightful intuition and/or discriminating thinking. In contrast to the unilateral NF and ST types, the bilateral sensing feeling type—having one preferred function in each hemisphere—may have an innate ability for more rapid interhemispheric processing.

AN INTUITIVE THINKING (NT) LYRIC WRITING PROFILE

The NT Style: An Overview

The first drafts of the intuitive thinking type tend to manifest clear, logical writing usually requiring only minor revisions. The NT gift for innovation may be shown by the inventive modification of a classic song form for purposeful effect.

As we might expect, the lyric vocabulary of the intuitive thinking type has a more objective style than that of the two feeling types. For example, this comment on living in the age of AIDS, "Here's to the days that were full of why not?/Before they got full of what if?" Instead of a predominance of the words *heart, feel,* or *love,* we are more likely to hear the words *mind, think,* or *know* as in these lines from an INTP woman, "I'm gonna dance him out of my mind" and "I'm thinkin' fool if I don't/Fool if I do." When the word heart does appear, it may take on a more philosophical cast as in this rueful complaint from another INTP that her former lover had become "A Habit of the Heart"; note *the* heart, as opposed to *my* heart. It is not surprising that an INTJ (a dominant intuitive) wrote a lyric entitled "Intuition (tells me beware)."

The INT and Structuring Devices

NT types are given to strengthening the structure of their writing through forms of repetition, especially the INTP and INTJ. *Anaphora*, a frequently employed device, repeats a word or phrase either at the beginning of successive lines or of successive verses, as in these examples: "I can't give/I can't promise/I can't swear"; "You got me thinking/You got me wishing/You got me hoping"; "Don't just lie there/Don't just sit there/Don't just stand there." INTs also exploit the power of *polyptoton* by repeating, for emphasis, forms of the same root words "My ticker just stopped tickin'" or "I've got an indecent proposition/That I'd like to propose to you."

The Questioning NT

In contrast to the SF type's focus on observable facts, which tends to result in concrete statements, the NT type's desire to solve enigmas (Keirsey & Bates, 1984) often manifests in abstract questions, whether about personal relationships or social issues: "What Do I Need/To make it sink in/To show me it's over/With no way to win?" One INTJ asks a more cosmic question: "What are we doing here?/Is there a god?/Why do we rise and then fall?/What would you give as the reason we live?/Is there a reason at all?"

The NT and the Ironic Viewpoint

NT types have a natural bent for analyzing the objective situation and noting patterns in complexities (Giovannoni, Berens, & Cooper, 1988). This naturally leads them to point out any incongruity or inconsistency between the real and the ideal—that is, to irony. Ironic thinking calls on faculties associated with functions of the frontal lobe (Grattan et al., 1995)—detecting discrepancies (LH) and synthesizing (RH).

 Irony in lyrics, as in any literary form, manifests in two ways—paradoxical themes and situations, and the use of figures of irony, in particular, the *pun* and the *paragram*. One INTJ lyric offers this incongruous situation, which has been compressed here to offer the gist:

"Grandma plans to escape from the nursing home tonight.
She'll be gone by the time the doors are locked up tight.
She cooked up the coup with her best friends Beth and Ann.
But you know who forgot the plan
An hour after the plan began.
But dreams will do if there's no coup in sight:
It's where Grandma escapes from the nursing home each night."

For a musical revue based on the AIDS quilt, another INTJ underscored life's ironic twists in a dramatic piece, "A Victim of AIDS," sung by the mother of a gay man: She had gotten a call that he had tested HIV negative, and she was relieved he would not become a "A Victim of AIDS." But when out celebrating the good news with his partner, the two men are attacked by a gang of gay bashers, and the son is beaten to death: Ironically, he became a victim of another kind of acquired deficiency syndrome—homophobia.

The Ironic Pun. In NT lyrics, ironic puns make frequent appearances, for example, "He never got the hang of hangin' on," or "When you let yourself let yourself go." Many NT lyric plots pivot on a pun title—either instant or sequential. A lyric by an INTJ about a failed marriage began, "When I woke up this morning, you were on my mind," and ended with the line, "When I woke up this morning, I woke up too late." The same writer also conceived the punning titles "The Higher I Get, the Lower I Feel," and "I Can't Get Over How She Got Over Me."

The pun can also be effective in making a serious point. One INTP found a pun the ideal trope to send a message about gun control: A lyrical phone call to a congressman pleading for a tougher law opens with the song's title, "I'm Calling With a Grave Concern." Near the song's end, the caller discloses that earlier that morning he had buried his only son who had been killed in the school playground by a classmate. In the lyric's final line, the title resonates with the added meaning of a graveside.

The Paragram. The NT qualities of an ironic perspective and a desire for originality coalesce in a fondness for paragram, a subtype of irony that puts a twist on a colloquialism. Here is a sampling of NT paragram titles: "Flattery Will Get You Everywhere," "Living on Borrowed Love," "It's All Over But the Leaving," "Everything You Don't Say Will Be Held Against You," and "If It Ain't One Thing It's a Lover."

Paragrams, both thoughtful and humorous, also thread themselves through NT lyrics: "'Neath the spreading mushroom tree/The world revolves in apathy"; "She who doesn't hesitate is lost"; and "I never met a manicotti I didn't like." In a satirical lyric by an INTP, one phrase wittily links two aspects of the same semantic field (food) by combining a paragram with a pun on a idiom: "Gimme pizza on earth, not pie in the sky."

The Oxymoron and Zeugma. NTs also favor two other ironic subtypes: The *oxymoron,* a compact form of irony, is exemplified in the titles, "Hard Flab," "Together Apart," and "Dying to Live." The zeugma, a subtype of pun, is evidenced in the lines, "The waitress wore an apron and a smile," "The way I spend an hour or a dime," and "His love words and the surf were whisp'ring in my ear."

The Character of the Nondominant Tropes

As noted with the other three cognitive styles, when a nondominant trope appears, it usually takes on the character of the dominant trope. Similarly with NT lyrics, forms of metaphor, synecdoche, and metonymy often have a ironic cast. An ENTJ's metaphoric title lacks the usual romantic tone: "Love is a Strange, Strange Poison." An INTJ offered a rather philosophical simile: "We're like snowflakes/Drifting from the sky/Here today and gone tomorrow/Hello life—and then—goodbye."

Unlike the subjective style of metonymic substitutions favored by the SF ("I've been dreaming of wearing white"), those by the NT tend to express a more objective or philosophical observation: "Finding solace in a chalice," and this one about drug addiction, "Trading gold dust [cocaine] in for mushrooms [psilocybin]/No deposit, no return." Compact simile titles by NTs, although featuring "heart," often bear the thinker's critical observations about the singee: "Hard-headed Heart," "Rawhide Heart," and "Turnstile Heart."

When an NT character's thinking and feeling functions conflict, metaphor and pun may overlap. To illustrate, here is an extract from a lyric by an INTP woman:

> It's hard to leave while the music's playing
> 'Cause I love how you play me like you do.
> It's hard to leave while the music's playing
> So my feet won't move when I tell them to.
> Though we've only met tonight, maestro,
> The song in my heart is singing for more.
> But staying this late is not very smart
> 'Cause I already know the score:
> A voice inside my brain is sayin'
> Refrain, grab your coat and go
> Tomorrow I'll regret this casual duet,
> But the music is tempting me so.

Potential First-Draft Problems

Type theory has noted that intuitives sometimes get the facts wrong. One INTP, lacking a knowledge of chess wrote: "Checkmate/Your move/Time to make your mind up about me./Are you livin' with or without me from this day hence?" The writer failed to check that checkmate means that one's opponent *cannot* move.

Problems may also arise from the intuitive's tendency to "leap ahead," rather than to put ideas in linear order. As a consequence, an unidentified pronoun—some *he, she, it, them, they*—may arrive before it has been identified: "A little after daybreak he'd gone over there/Before the clinic opened—no one anywhere." The word *there* struck the ear without proper preparation. The revision made the action easy to follow: "Before the clinic opened, he'd gone over there;/It was six in the morning—not a soul anywhere." In his revision, note that the INTJ, in accessing his sensing function, transformed the abstract "after daybreak" into the concrete "six in the morning."

The Versatile NT

Teaching experience has produced evidence that the writing of NTs displays great diversity of both subject matter and style. Space constraints do not permit examples of the NTs' frequent and competent use of their three nondominant tropes or of their successful forays into comedy, satire, parody, and children's songs, which have been detailed elsewhere (Davis, 1992). To illustrate is an example by an INTP woman who has written on such societal concerns as gun control, teen suicide, and drug addiction; now she accesses her two less-favored functions:

I'll be dressed in gold lamé
Gardenias in my hair
He'll be partly Schwarzenegger,
Partly Fred Astaire—
Our eyes will meet and wordlessly
We'll start the big affair
That's the scene I see
The way it all will be
The Ultimate Night

He'll glide across a ballroom floor
And sweep me off my feet
Whisk me to a limousine
And never miss a beat
A private plane will take us
To his St. Tropez retreat:
There'll be a balcony
That overlooks the sea
The Ultimate Night.

We'll light the lemon candlesticks
And when I count to ten,
He'll rub me down with jasmine oil—
Won~t stop till I say, "When!"
I'll give him my best *femme fatale*;
Then we'll do it all again.
We'll be so high on love
That we could fly on love
The Ultimate Night.

> But meanwhile there are rooms to dust
> And dishes in the sink—
> A button off, a cavity—
> A TV on the blink.
> And meanwhile, there's a fellow
> Who'd supply the missing link;
> But I'm unconvinced he's it
> And unwilling to commit,
> 'Cause there's still a part of me
> That's holding out to see
> What may be waiting slightly out of sight
> On some magical, glamorous, fairytale, amorous,
> Starlit Ultimate Night.

The lyric, with its multisensory details antonomasian metonyms, and romantic fantasy, seems to mirror an ESFP sensibility. But the ironic ending suggests the NT worldview that points up life's underlying dichotomies.

Summing up the Intuitive Thinking Style

The intuitive thinking types' evident competence with all forms of figurative language might be attributable to the hypothesized NT-frontal lobe relationship: Neuroscientists have identified the frontal lobes as the "executive" part of the brain because of their subcortical connections that allow for rapid access to distant areas (Calvin & Ojemann, 1994). So it might be that the NT has a neurological advantage that results in stylistic versatility.

THE IMPLICATIONS OF THE TYPE/TROPE/BRAIN AFFINITY

The foregoing writing profiles resonate with multiple implications for understanding literacy and teaching language arts. Initially, they reveal that, given a fundamental understanding of the theory of Jungian personality type and a comprehensive knowledge of the four tropes and their subtypes, writing style can be seen to predict cognitive style and vice versa.

Cognitive Style as Cerebral Process

The profiles also reveal that a writer's creative process tends to be type related. The first- and final-draft examples by each style underscore two significant points (a) that the first draft will probably be produced by the writer's two dominant functions, and (b) that the revision will require the writer's incorporating aspects of the two less-favored functions. This suggests that literacy—or what has been called "whole-brain thinking and writing"—ultimately requires the accessing of all four major processing centers of the brain, or, to put it in type talk, accessing all four functions. This leads to the inevitable proposal that type and brain function represent an effect-cause relationship.

Not Two, But Four Thinking Styles

The four profiles also imply that we need to revise our understanding of thinking styles. The popular view of hemisphericity tends to emphasize LH-RH dichotomies, thereby recognizing only two major thinking styles— left-brain vertical/reductionist thinking and right-brain lateral/holistic thinking. The Myers-Briggs Type Indicator, based on Jung's quaternary theory, implicitly recognizes two pairs of polar-opposite cognitive types— NT-SF and ST-NF—without formally acknowledging that this implies a corresponding pattern of cortical activity.

The Archetype of the Quaternity. It would appear that Vico and Jung shared an awareness of the quaternity as a structural archetype: Jung's four cognitive styles represent four archetypal modes of apprehending reality; Vico's four master tropes represent four archetypal modes of expressing that reality. Together they represent two pairs of polar-opposite thinking styles. In addition to the vertical/reductive left-brain style of the ST characterized by synecdoche and the lateral/holistic right-brain style of the NF characterized by metaphor, there is the divergent frontal-lobe style of the NT characterized by irony and the convergent posterior-area style of the SF characterized by metonymy (see Figure 4.4).

The four lyric writing profiles illustrate the manner in which the worldview of each cognitive style depicted by type/temperament literature is subserved by its linked trope: The NF, a seeker of harmony, strives to "harmonize" disparate domains through metaphor in service to idealism; the SF, the implementor, tends to concretize the abstract with symbolic metonyms in service to realism; the ST, the most matter-of-fact of the types, prefers the time- and space-saving device, synecdoche, in service to pragmatism; and finally, the philosophic NT requires forms of irony to express life's complexities in service to truth.

Cognitive Style as a Window on the World. Figure 4.4 proposes the way in which each wedge-shaped cerebral area, with its dominant thinking style, acts as one's main window on the world Yet, as the writing profiles reveal, each type can and does move around the cerebral circle to experience other perspectives as evidenced by a writer's use of nondominant tropes: When appropriate, an NT can mellow into metaphor; a romantic NF can concretize with a symbolic statement; the SF can tersely reduce a concept to an essential part; and the ST can playfully create an oxymoron. In fact, when the occasion demands, every type can and does express all four thinking styles.

The Case of the Three Invisible Tropes

The evidence strongly indicates that the thinking process of each cognitive style exhibits an affinity for a particular trope in its multiple aspects. Type/temperament literature, however, has recognized only the NF metaphor relationship (Berens & Cooper, 1988; Keirsey & Bates, 1984; Myers & McCaulley,1987). Keirsey and Bates have also observed the NT's fondness for paradox and satire, but without noting that these constitute aspects of irony. It should come as no surprise then that the terms for the two most subtle forms of figurative thought, metonomy and synecdoche—despite their widespread use by sensing dominants—lack recognition by the type community.

More relevant here is the virtual absence of the tropes from the college curriculum: Where is "Figurative Language 101"? The relative unfamiliarity of teachers with everyday forms of metonymy, synecdoche, and irony and their relationship to cognitive type would seem to send a message to curriculum designers: Teachers can best help students to develop their individual thinking and writing styles when they themselves possess a sound knowledge of the four tropes and their subtypes. It would seem essential for a teacher of language arts to be able to readily distinguish a metonym from a synecdoche, a symbol from a metaphor (Davis, 1996), and to quickly identify the ineffective mental process that leads to such anomalies as mixed metaphors and malaphors.

Practicing the Tropes. I hope that the definitions and examples of the tropes given earlier will encourage teachers to devise exercises to stimulate thinking in diverse ways. Readily available source material such as newspaper headlines, advertising copy, and cartoons can provide lively examples of well-conceived figurative usage for emulation and poorly conceived usage for critical analysis.

My experience in teaching classes in figurative language confirms that the purposeful practice of the four master tropes tends to expand one's repertoire of thinking styles. Making original metaphors and apt puns, transforming an abstraction into a metonym, or creating new *portmanteau* words each acts to access a different cortical region. By exercising less-used brain areas and practicing less-favored functions, we become more whole-brained thinkers and writers.

SUMMING UP

An editorial in the *Consortium for Whole Brain Learning*, a periodical for educators, observed (Ellison. 1995, p. 4): "In all of the calls for improving education, few teachers, administrators, or citizens recognize that the brain has anything to do with learning." To that I add, "and with personality type and writing style." Teachers with a understanding of the logical, linear nature of the LH, the diffuse, random nature of the RH, the abstract thinking and novel-material processing of the frontal lobes, and the concrete thinking and routinized processing of the posterior area greatly enhance their ability to provide practical guidance to their typed students to help develop their less-favored functions in service to their natural cognitive style.

REFERENCES

Beeman, M., Freiedman, R.B., Grafman, J., Perez, E., Diamond, S., & Lindsay, M.B. (1994). Summation priming and coarse semantic coding in the right hemisphere. *Journal of Cognitive Neuroscience, 6*,1.

Burns, M.S., Cummings, J.L., Halper, A.S., Kozy, M.C., Mogil, S.I., & Tarvin, G.A. (1985). *Clinical management of right hemisphere dysfunction.* Rockville, MD: Aspen Publishers.

Calvin, W.H., & Ojemann, G.A. (1994). *Conversations with Neil's brain.* Reading, PA: Addison-Wesley.

Davis, S. (1992). *The songwriters idea book.* Cincinnati: Writer's Digest Books.

Davis, S. (1996). 'Metonymy' and 'synecdoche.' In T. Enos (Ed.), *Encyclopedia of rhetoric.* New York: Garland.

Du Marsais, C.C. (1988). *Des tropes ou des differents sens.* Paris: Flammarion.

Eimas, P.D., & Galaburda, A.M. (Eds.). (1990). *Neurobiology of cognition.* Cambridge, MA: MIT Press.

Ellison, L. (1995). Editorial. *Consortium for Whole Brain Learning, 10*, 4.

Giovannoni, L.C., Berens, L.V., & Cooper, S.A. (1988). *Introduction to temperament.* Huntington Beach, CA: Telos Publications.

Grattan, L.M., Eslinger, P.J., Price, T., & Aldrich, F. (1995). Recall of contextually congruent and contextually incongruent information after frontal lobe lesions. *Journal of the International Neuropsychological Society,1, 2,* 174.

Jung, C.G. (1968). *Analytical psychology, its theory and practice.* New York: Random House.

Jung, C.G. (1976). *Psychological types.* Princeton, NJ: Princeton University Press.

Jung, C.G. (1989). *Analytic psychology.* Princeton, NJ: Princeton University Press.

Keirsey, D., & Bates, M. (1984). *Please understand me.* Del Mar, CA: Prometheus Nemesis Book Co.

Laughlin, C.D., Jr., McManus, J., & D'Aquili, E.G. (1990). *Brain, symbol & experience.* Boston: New Science Library.

Lawrence, G. (1982). *People types & tiger stripes* (2nd ed.). Gainesville, FL: Center for Applications of Psychological Type.

Mesulam, M.-M. (1986). Frontal cortex and behavior. *Annals of Neurology, 19,* 320-325 .

Myers, I.B., & McCaulley, M.H. (1987). *Manual: A guide to the development and use of the Myers-Briggs type indicator.* Palo Alto, CA: Consulting Psychologists Press.

Ornstein, R. (1986). *Psychology of consciousness.* New York: Viking Press.

Springer, S.P., & Deutsch, G. (1989). *Left brain, right brain.* New York: W.H. Freeman.

Vico, G. (1991). *The new science of Giambattista Vico* (T.G. Bergin & M.H. Fisch, Trans.). Ithaca, NY: Cornell University Press. (Original work published in 1744)

PART TWO

Personality and Student Literacy

Chapter 5

Collaborative Grouping and Personality Theory

Angela Creech Green
Lee College

Consider the following classroom situation: You have divided your class into several groups trying to apply the collaborative grouping strategies you have heard and read so much about in the last few years. Everyone has spoken positively about it, but it is not working for you. While you are trying hard to make this a positive learning experience, Myra and Becky are chatting away about the ball game last night. Scott will not speak to anyone as he looks down at the floor and finally lays his head on the desk. Only after several requests does John finally move over with his group, and then he stares at the floor. In a second group, all of the students are staring at their books, but no one is speaking. They all have their hands over their foreheads or their arms crossed over their chests. Nothing is happening there, whereas another group is busy addressing the lesson with great zeal and excitement. You wonder why every group cannot be like this last group. You feel frustrated and defeated and then decide not to try collaborative grouping again.

This scenario is not uncommon. What works so well in theory often does not work in the classroom. Sometimes what works well with one class of students will not work one hour later with another.

Although many writing teachers have only considered collaboration in the past 10 to 20 years, collaboration is not a new concept in the field of composition. Writing groups, literary societies, and women's groups have met since colonial days to share their writing with others. It was only later in the century that writing instruction and practice was considered an "individually creative act" (Ede & Lunsford, 1990, p. 109), with the writer or poet locked into a room feverishly searching his or her soul to find the right words. Mara Holt studied professional educational journals from 1911 to 1986 researching the emphasis of collaborative pedagogies throughout those years. She found that the call for collaboration depended on the often changing social trends of the day (Ede & Lunsford, 1990).

Early in the 20th century, education experts such as Piaget and Dewey called for collaborative teaching strategies. Piaget demonstrated often that children learn best through social interactions. Dewey urged a new and "progressive" education, insisting that

> learning occurs in interaction, that social context is of utmost importance in the classroom, and that we should reform our traditional model by enhancing "the moving spirit of the whole group . . . held together by participation in common activities." (Ede & Lunsford, 1990, p. 110)

Dewey's influence changed the way British educator Edwin Mason taught, and it was Mason who actually coined the term *collaborative learning* in the 1970s. He urged drastic educational reform in British schools, calling for a change in the educational system he described as "competitive, authoritarian, overly specialized, departmentalized, and alienated" with a system emphasizing "interdisciplinary study, small group work, collaboration and dialogue" (Ede & Lunsford, 1990, p. 112). Nevertheless, applying these progressive ideas to classrooms should not be done without an understanding of personality differences, especially considering techniques involving interpersonal relations.

DIFFERENCES BETWEEN EXTRAVERTS AND INTROVERTS

Psychologist Carl Jung invented the terms *introversion* and *extraversion* to describe the two patterns that determine individuals' preferred responses to life. In his observations, Jung suggested that human behavior was not random but was, in fact, predictable and, therefore, classifiable. Jung believed that extraversion and introversion are simply different "orientations to life," both equally valuable. Extraverts focus on outward aspects of life and are very comfortable working actively with people or things. Introverts focus inward and are more interested and comfortable when they are permitted to think or concentrate on ideas alone (Lawrence, 1984). According to Jung, the division between extraverts and introverts is the most important difference between people because it is the distinction that determines the "source, direction and focus for one's energy" (Kroeger & Thuesen, 1988, p. 33).

According to type theory, everyone develops preferences for dealing with life's experiences, including writing. Over the years, individuals learn to depend on and trust these preferences. Introverts prefer one way to confront life, whereas extraverts prefer the opposite. Students become more comfortable and confident when they are able to react to life according to these preferences.

Lawrence (1984) observes in *People Types and Tiger Stripes: A Practical Guide for Learning Style* that students who are introverted tend to choose the following mannerisms in class:

1. Like time to consider things
2. Are slow to act without thinking first
3. Want to set their own standards
4. Spend time in thought

Conversely, extraverts:

1. Like action and variety
2. Act quickly, often without reflection
3. Are enthusiastic about activities involving action
4. Readily offer opinions
5. Dislike complicated procedures
6. Get impatient with slow jobs

If we review conflicting expert advice about writing strategies from the experts, in light of the specific characteristics of extraversion and introversion, an interesting parallel becomes evident. One group of experts encourages journal writing, meditating, and thinking, which are specifically introvert preferences, whereas a second group urges talking, peer group collaborating, and feedback interacting, which are extravert preferences. Even the experts are swayed by their own personality types when determining how they believe writing should be taught (Jensen & DiTiberio, 1989). Thus, we organize classroom activities and include teaching strategies that seem to value the learning preferences of one type over the other, often according to the individual teacher's preference.

INTROVERTS AND THE COLLABORATIVE EXPERIENCE

It is my contention that in the writing classroom of the 1990s, the introverted student is at a disadvantage, especially under the demands of group collaboration. Sometimes these students are so uncomfortable in certain classroom settings that they refuse to comply with the instructor's directions, even if the result is failure. To demonstrate this recalcitrance, I tested several of my classes using the Myers-Briggs Type Indicator. I then observed introverted students in small group discussion. Although these students may prefer not to participate orally in groups, they speak loudly and clearly with their body language. I observed the following physical behaviors repeated regularly and consistently from the introverts in group situations:

1. Avoided eye contact;
2. Read and reread papers without responding to other group members;
3. Avoided conversation until compelled and only then with great hesitation;
4. Pulled knees up to their chests, locked arms around their knees;
5. Refused to move into the group until repeatedly requested; and
6. Used some part of their body as a screen or shield (placed hands over chin and mouth; covered face from forehead down).

The introverts were clearly uncomfortable in the small group settings. At the completion of the collaborative activities, the students were asked to describe how they felt about the groups and how these feelings compared to the actual writing of the assignment. Almost unanimously, the students responded that only later, when they were in their rooms or library, could they even begin to regroup and reorganize their thoughts. They said the groups were "too distracting," "too loud," and "nerve wracking." The extraverts, on the other hand, commented that "the group was the best part of the assignment," "a lot of fun," and "a neat way to make friends."

The irony of the writing classroom is that when left alone to write individually, the introvert students tend to have less difficulty writing than extroverts. Sides (1990) stated, "Type theory, in fact, suggests that particular types are better suited to writing. It requires introspection and concentration, abilities associated with introversion" (p. 36). Introverts want to write alone, usually doing much of it in their heads. According to Jensen and DiTiberio (1989), introverts actually think better when they are alone and have a continuous span of time in which to work. When forced into a group setting, introverts are working against their natural tendencies.

Their thinking process is disturbed, their need for quiet contemplation is eliminated, and they are expected to speak quickly without ample time for reflection. To further complicate matters, they appear to be uncooperative as they close themselves off from the classroom activity. If instructors do not understand the differences in personality, they may, as one writer does, group these students into negative categories. Diana George (1984) described as a "dysfunctional" group what sounds like several introverts:

> My initial impression of this kind of group was that I had somehow, at random, gathered the five most alienated individuals in the room into one space, and now I was asking from them the impossible—collaboration. They made a statement [by physical arrangement in the group] that "this is some kind of game, and I am not playing any games for you."(p. 321)

If we really understand introverts, we will realize that they are not necessarily "alienated individuals" but simply prefer not to study in group settings. Jung (1921) observed this action in his studies, noting, "his [introvert's] retreat into himself is not a final renunciation of the world, but a search for quietude. . . . This type of person is the victim of numerous misunderstandings" (quoted in Storr, 1983, p. 143). When forcing introverts into group settings, opposite forces are at work, sharply reducing the likelihood of a successful classroom activity. When a student prefers to work alone and is forced to work in groups, he or she is affected both intellectually and emotionally, creating the basis for the misunderstandings Jung describes.

Introverts are often negatively affected by the misunderstandings created by collaborative grouping. Their peers may view them as shy, conceited, difficult to get along with, unfriendly, and sometimes stupid or unprepared for class. These attitudes can be devastating for the introvert, especially if he or she has a combination of other personality types such as sensing or feeling. Introverts may in fact not be shy or withdrawn. They may be very confident and comfortable in social settings but simply more quiet and reserved. Nor are they necessarily any more self-centered or conceited than extraverts. Introverts like to think and consider before answering. They may be slow to act, hesitant, or even distrustful. Jung wrote that the introvert values the inward side of experience more than the outward: "In a large gathering, he feels lonely and lost. . . . He is not a good mixer. . . . He is apt to appear awkward . . . glum, unapproachable . . . causing unwitting offense to people (quoted in Storr, 1983, p. 142). These behaviors should not be misread as a form of tuning out.

As one of my introverted students said: "Why don't they let me be quiet? I've tried to talk in groups but I hate it. I can't do it. I've got to have my own train of thought going first." Collaborative grouping for this introverted student is a reason to miss class, break out in hives, and "throw up" as another of my students so eloquently stated.

Furthermore, according to Storr (1983), introverts may be suspicious of the motives behind a colleague's actions. Kroeger and Thuesen (1988) noted that this tendency is probably the greatest hindrance when trying to get extraverts and introverts to work together. All too often, the introverts have thought, planned, and organized a project, whereas the verbal extrovert gains the recognition. The extroverts spend class time "proving" their understanding of the issue at hand, whereas the introverts fade into the background, drained of emotional energy and longing for the solitude of their own thoughts. Thus, grouping can alienate introverts from the mental processes with which they are most comfortable. In the discourse required in grouping, if the introverts do not speak, they are viewed as nonparticipating. If they do speak, they may be interrupted by an extravert, for whom, according to Jensen and DiTiberio (1989), interruption is a necessary part of the conversation. For extraverts, speaking is thinking, and they give themselves the liberty to change their minds in the middle of discussion. Speaking their ideas is a trial and error method of discovering what they ultimately accept as true.

This extraverted process frustrates the introvert, who would prefer to think it through in solitude. Collaboration stimulates and energizes the gregarious extraverts while draining and depleting the energies of the introverts. To the introverts, the actions of the extraverts are an invasion of both physical and intellectual space.

The difficulty introverts have with the collaborative process is reflected in these student comments:

Student 1:   "I wish they would just be quiet, just for a second."
Student 2:   "Yeah, they don't even know what they think. They just start talking like the answers are going to just fall out of the sky into their minds."
Student 1:   "It gets on my nerves so bad. I'd rather get a zero on daily work than have to participate in peer review."
Student 3:   "I'd rather just write down what I think than have to talk about it. You know what I mean.
Student 1:   "Yeah. Exactly."

Therefore, before incorporating collaborative activities into the classroom, teachers need to figure out how to make them useful to introverted students.

IMPACT OF PERSONALITY TYPE ON
FACULTY-STUDENT RELATIONSHIPS

The manner in which students respond in the classroom is not determined by logic or intellectual capabilities but on differences in thinking styles. Problems arise in the classroom when teachers reward one response type over another. Teachers who are introverts may emphasize individual work, whereas extraverted teachers may emphasize group work. Furthermore, both types of teachers tend to be impatient with students whose preferences are contrary to their own or who seem resistant to working in a classroom arrangement unsuited to their preferences (Fontana, 1986).

Dave Kalsbeek at St. Louis University developed a longitudinal eight-year study to provide educators with data on student characteristics in relation to academic performance and attrition. The study called TRAILS (Tracking Retention and Academic Integration of Learning Styles) found no difference in the intelligence level of extraverts to introverts. It did note, however, that faculty viewed students with different types than their own as deficient (Schroeder, 1993).

Teaching strategies that consider different personality types create a diversity that would offer success to all students. Therefore, personality type should be considered when implementing teaching strategies. According to Sides (1990),"It is not always the student who fails to follow directions or successfully complete assignments"; sometimes "the failure was forcing a particular invention strategy or writing process, onto someone for whom it was inappropriate" (p. 24).

Many studies have come to the same conclusion. Based on these studies, Jensen and DiTiberio (1989) asserts that there is not even one single activity that teachers can say is necessary when teaching writing. Britton, Burgess, Martin, et al. (1975) stated in *The Development of Writing Abilities* (11-18): "We found that there were some irreconcilable differences between the way writers work and the way many teachers and composition textbooks are constantly advising their pupils to set about their tasks" (p. 20).

DEVELOPING AS A COLLABORATIVE TEACHER

Incorporating new strategies in the classroom can be difficult for both students and teachers, especially if the goal is to change from traditional learning to collaborative learning. First, students have not been taught to collaborate because collaboration has often been viewed as cheating. Traditionally, students wrote alone, studied alone, and tested alone.

According to Bruffee (1973), if students reject or mistrust collaborative learning, it is because "they are being asked to do something their whole education has not only left them unequipped to do, but has actually militated against" (p. 642). Furthermore, instructors will have to change their ideas about teaching in order to incorporate collaborative learning: "This will mean putting aside previous images of university faculty as people with all the information and answers while acknowledging that they also have questions" (Gomez, 1991, p. 41).

Collaboration changes the traditional relationship between teacher and student. In collaborative learning, students are in dialogue with each other as well as the instructor. Students are not passive receivers of knowledge but instead are interactive. They become "knowledge-makers not knowledge memorizers" (Strasma & Gavin, 1992, p. 119). Therefore, students realize they can learn without the constant intervention of the instructor, which is very empowering. Many instructors, however, have trouble surrendering this power.

Several researchers address this issue. Clark and Connelly (1993) wrote in "Collaboration: Mutual Empowerment/Silencing?" that in the "competitive, patriarchal model of education . . . any collaboration would be the student being forced to collaborate with the professor. Therefore, instead of genuine collaboration, there is an authority figure and a subordinate population" (p. 8). In response to those who challenge statements like those of Clark and Connelly, Bruffee (1972) wrote the following in "The Way Out: A Critical Survey of Innovation in College Teaching":

> We are likely to hear the rationalization that we have so much to "give" our students. But the concept of teaching as a kind of intellectual and informational philanthropy is at best dated, it seems to me, and at worst condescending and perhaps corrupt. . . . Instead of being an intellectual "donor," he finds his purpose as a teacher in helping people discover, accept and develop their own intelligence and talent. (p. 470)

Ultimately, developing a collaborative model means one must change him- or herself first. Having confidence that the change is a positive one and having confidence in one's self are crucial elements in changing from a traditional classroom to a collaborative classroom:

> To shift responsibility (and its concomitant power) from one who clutches it to himself for the sense of security it provides, to those who must experience it in order to grow is not to abrogate responsibility but to redefine it. It is not to drop the burden, but to lift it into a more rewarding and helpful place. (Bruffee, 1972, p. 469)

INCORPORATING COLLABORATIVE
LEARNING INTO THE CLASSROOM

The objective of the traditional and collaborative models is to see that the students learn. The difference is not content but social context. Students collaborate, thus learn for themselves while helping each other (Bruffee, 1984). The foremost position of the collaborative teacher is to structure the class as a community of learners (Bruffee, 1973). John Dewey stated: "Community life does not organize itself in an enduring way purely spontaneously. It requires thought and planning ahead" (quoted in Bruffee, 1973, p. 637).

John Clifford wrote in "Toward an Ethical Community of Writers" that it is much easier for students to lose their way in a collaborative classroom than in a traditional setting (quoted in Clark, 1993). Any teacher who has tried collaborative learning has probably observed this to be true. The first consideration for avoiding failure in collaborative learning must be personality fit within the group. The instructor should choose the group members. There should be both extravert and introvert students in each group. Then there must be time allotted for bonding and trust to build (Bruffee,1973; Ede & Lunsford,1990; Gomez,1991). Because there is often conflict between introverted and extraverted learners, there must be time for them to learn to work together.

I think it is good to explain the differences between personality types and group dynamics and assure them that conflict is often a productive part of collaboration. I share the goal I have for my students, which is to produce the best possible assignment while caring enough for the other group members to want to see them succeed. Bruffee (1973) encourages keeping the same groups for a period of time so that "they bond, become settled and even loyal to each other" (p. 637). Ede and Lunsford (1990) also call for this time together to allow for group cohesion. They wrote in *Singular Texts/Plural Authors* that instructors should "allow for evolution of group norms and the negotiation of authority and responsibility" (p. 125). As a group, the final joining together must be a collective agreement to work together for the successful completion of the project (Gomez, 1991).

The second consideration in collaborative learning is to have a specific text. There are several ways to incorporate this into the classroom. Bruffee (1984) suggests gradually introducing the groups to collaborative activities. First, he encourages the instructor to pose the problems to be solved, then to pose broader problems with the goal of eventually having the students find their own problems or questions. In this way, Bruffee believes the instructor can gradually "demythogize" him- or herself from the traditional all-knowing figure in the classroom. He further warns teachers to avoid the tendency to fall back into this figure by helping correct the problems in the groups.

Reither and Vipond (1989) also encourage the use of text. According to them, collaboration should be a long-range activity of "knowledge making" instead of a short-range one. This "knowledge making" comes from using text. Students read literature in their particular field, listen to conversation about that literature, and learn the language of the field and why problems or questions are present. The collaboration in this type of project is in meeting regularly, in gathering and making sense of information and ideas, in co-authoring presentations, and in holding workshops. Due to the nature of this format, both extravert and introvert learners have the time to study and learn in their own ways.

Another way to organize a collaborative classroom is to pose problems at the end of one class in preparation for the next. Then when the groups come together, the extraverts are ready to discuss the topic while the introverts have had their time to process alone first. If doing peer review, papers can be given out at the end of one class for discussion at the next, which causes the same result as the previous activity.

Diana George (1984) offers excellent advice for peer review in the composition class. She suggests using recapitulation to begin peer review of an essay. By this she means having the student talk about the paper before it is read to the group. The student reviews the paper, mentions the trouble spots, and leaves room for suggestions. It gives the group a place to start and allows the introvert thinker to process while the paper is being read.

George also suggests possibly taping the group discussion. She offers this as a way to revise pieces while also reminding the group how they have contributed to the revision of the paper. It also offers the introvert time to consider the discussion alone after class.

It is a good idea to meet with the groups outside of class when possible. This is one way to get a better understanding of the particular group dynamics and to determine if your personal goals are being reached. Are the students collaborating? Have they been able to work through conflict or power struggles? Are they reaching the goal of completing the project? Are you able to facilitate without dominating? Are you really developing a collaborative class or is it, as Reither and Vipond (1989) warn against, "an overlay on courses still otherwise governed by traditional preoccupations" (p. 855)? Students are usually painfully honest once they trust that you really believe in the collaborative concept. These group meetings are often illuminating experiences for both you and the students.

DEVELOPING COLLABORATIVE MINDED STUDENTS

Because many students are suspicious of collaborative learning because they have not experienced it or have only participated in very few collaborative activities, it is important to learn to broaden students' awareness of type and the need to rethink ideas. Students usually have to be taught the goals involved in collaborative learning. Trzyna and Batschelet (1990) offer several goals for consideration:

1. Mediating conflict between competition and collaboration;
2. Learning how to help others to learn and converse;
3. Helping others master content areas and disciplinary assumptions;
4. Working together to produce a common report, proposal or project. (p. 25)

Students often have to be taught how to respect each other and how to use the skills involved with mediating conflict that comes from a lack of interpersonal communication skills.

Group members can learn to help each other by finding out about each other. Karis (1989) suggests that team members have a time to discover each other's talents, skills, and backgrounds because conflict often occurs in groups where there is a lack of identification between the students. Karis advises that conflict can be positive, however, if it brings with it a better understanding of each other.

The third goal of collaboration, to help others master the content areas and disciplines, must also consider personality type. Problems that occur in this area may be nonparticipation, domineering behavior, or a dichotomy between the desire to cooperate and the desire to compete. The combination of these problems may result in a lack of learning (Trzyna & Batschelet, 1990). Considering not only the content to be learned but the manner in which students learn best is an important element for a successful group.

Finally, the group must consider the successful completion of the project. Karis (1989) noted that groups that fail usually have no shared meaning for the project. When conflict arises to the degree that the project is stalled, Karis urges the group members to find a shared understanding within the group. What is it that they all can agree on? Second, the students should be urged from the onset of grouping that changing one's viewpoint is not a sign of weakness or error. She described it as "revising our image of the world" (p. 120).

SUMMARY

Although people tend to have a dominant personality type, "there can never occur a pure type in the sense that a person is entirely possessed of the one mechanism with a complete atrophy of the other" (Jung, 1921, p. 187). It is important to offer this avenue for growth. As students try to develop their unpreferred styles, their writing may be awkward. Encourage students so they will continue to develop. Supporting and challenging students becomes a distinct challenge for the instructor. Students need a pat on the back as well as a gentle nudge. Challenge writers to achieve balance. Once they gain confidence in their own style, challenge them to develop their unpreferred style and recognize the unrealistic expectation that they will become balanced writers in one course (Jensen & DiTiberio, 1989).

Fontana (1986) urges the consideration of personality type in conjunction with the other variables of life that influence action. Cattell and others maintain that personality and personal motivation account for much of a student's achievement. It cannot be denied, however, that numerous investigations have demonstrated increased academic achievement among students taught according to their individual learning styles (Dunn & Dunn, 1992).

Awareness of personality type theory enables instructors to develop classroom activities that correspond with learning styles and preferences. It also helps teachers understand the relationships between how they teach and how their students learn (Sides, 1990). When considering collaboration in light of personality type, it is important to recognize the primary objective of collaboration that Karis (1989) asserts is to "use language to induce cooperation in each other" (p. 114).

Type is only an explanation for what happens in the classroom; it is never an excuse for not participating. However, a powerful teaching insight can be gleaned from its study. Personality types vary and should be valued; likewise, writing processes vary, and writers do not and should not be forced to structure their writing experiences in exactly the same manner. If collaborative activities are structured and planned, then the classroom can be a place of optimal learning for every student.

REFERENCES

Britton, J., Burgess, T., Martin, N., et al. (1975). *The development of writing ability* (11-18). London: Macmillan.

Bruffee, K. (1972). The way out: A critical survey of innovation in college teaching. *College English, 33,* 457-470.

Bruffee, K. (1973). Collaborative learning: Some practical models. *College English, 34,* 634-643.

Bruffee, K. (1984). Collaborative learning and the conversation of mankind. *College English, 46,* 635-652.

Clark, C.L., & Connelly, C. (1993). *Collaboration: Mutual empowerment/silencing? or both?* (ERIC Document 360639).

Clark, I. (1993). Portfolio evaluation, collaboration, and writing centers. *College Composition and Communication, 44,* 515-524.

Dunn, R., & Dunn, K. (1992). *Teaching secondary students through their individual learning styles.* Boston: Allyn and Bacon.

Ede, L., & Lunsford, A. (1990). *Singular texts/plural authors: Perspectives on collaborative writing.* Carbondale: Southern Illinois University Press.

Fontana, D. (1986). *Teaching and personality.* New York: Basil Blackwell.

George, D. (1984). Working with peer groups in the composition classroom. *College Composition and Communication, 35,* 320-326.

Gomez, M.L. (1991). Learning to teach writing through collaborative inquiry. *Journal of Staff Development, 12,* 40-43.

Jensen, G., & DiTiberio, J. (1989). *Personality and the teaching of composition.* Norwood, NJ: Ablex.

Jung, C.G. (1921). Psychological types. In The *collected works of C.G. Jung.* Princeton, NJ: Princeton University Press.

Karis, B. (1989). Conflict in collaboration: A Burkean perspective. *Rhetoric Review, 8,* 113-126.

Kroeger, O., & Thuesen, J. (1988). *Type talk.* New York: Delacorte Press.

Lawrence, G. (1984). *People types and tiger stripes: A practical guide for learning style.* Gainesville, FL: Center for Applications of Psychological Type.

Reither, J., & Vipond, D. (1989). Writing as collaboration. *College English, 51,* 855-867.

Schroeder, C. (1993). New students—new learning styles. *Change, 25,* 21-26.

Sides, C. (1990). Psychological types and teaching writing. *Writing on the Edge, 1,* 23-40.

Storr, A. (1983). *The essential Jung.* Princeton, NJ: Princeton University Press.

Strasma, K., & Gavin, F. (1992, Spring/Summer). Collaboration within writing classes: An ethnographic point of view. *The Writing Instructor,* pp. 111-127.

Trzyna, T., & Batschelet, M. (1990). The ethical complexity of collaboration. *Writing on the Edge,* 23-33.

Chapter 6

Personality and Reading Response Journals

Vicki Tolar Collins
Oregon State University

In *The Composing Processes of Twelfth Graders*, Janet Emig (1971) suggests that a profitable line of research in composition would be to ascertain whether a relationship exists between the composing processes of a given group of students and their scores on a number of standardized personality tests. George Jensen and John DiTiberio (1989) responded to Emig's suggestion in their book *Personality and the Teaching of Composition*, which interprets early data and develops theory on the ways personality type, as measured by the Myers-Briggs Type Indicator (MBTI), affects or is manifested by the composing processes of individual students. Furthering research on personality and composing processes, this chapter responds to Emig's (1971) suggestion that composition scholars investigate whether "there is a correlation between general personality traits and preference in the modes of writing" (p. 96).

While teaching composition at a large state university strong in technical fields, I became interested in the choices of mode students make when they are offered options in ways to respond to a literary text. For example, many technically inclined students who are oriented toward logic and factual data prefer to respond to works of literature by summarizing or analyzing the text, using what Emig (1971) would call "extensive mode," whereas other students who are oriented toward emotion respond by relating the work to their own lives and experiences, using Emig's "reflexive mode."

Although most studies of students' composing choices have been situated in structured research situations, I have chosen to study student choices of mode in the context of a composition course in which students write about literature. Basing the study on the writing processes of students keeping a reading response journal, I was able to examine a large number of student responses over the length of an entire course in composition. Using student scores on the MBTI along with journal responses, I attempted to answer the following research questions:

1. Do students of the same personality type tend to approach literature through the same mode of journal entry? If so, which types prefer which modes?
2. Are the criteria students use to identify their "best" journal entry consistent within type?
3. Does personality type play a role in frequency of use of personal voice as reflected in use of first-person pronouns in journal entries?

The choice of the reading response journal as the genre for this study requires further comment. When we study the writing processes of student writers, we are generally studying writers under stress, for as Edward White (1985) pointed out, "the demand to write is almost always an external demand" (p. 104). This is particularly true in the world of academic discourse in which students must contend with the stresses not only of the particular assignment, rhetorical situation, and method (and threat) of evaluation but also with conventions of discourse peculiar to a certain discipline.

When a doctor administers a physical stress test to a patient, she begins with a baseline reading of how the patient's body performs when not under stress. Analogously, I want to suggest that in order to understand how students accommodate themselves to various academic stresses on their writing processes, we need to know how they write when they are not under stress. I do not believe this task has been accomplished by researchers in composition.

If we define the basic task of academic discourse as responding in writing to a new data set, then I would argue that the ungraded reading response journal provides a low-stress academic writing situation in which we can see students responding to texts (new data sets) in their most preferred way.

The objectives of this study are important because we have had no baseline reading of what choices students make in academic writing when they are not under the stresses of a structured rhetorical situation, grades, and so on. If we learn how students prefer to respond to texts, we can identify additional skills they need in writing situations that do not draw on their strengths or preferences. Furthermore, if teachers can use a well-respected and easily administered testing instrument such as the Myers-Briggs Type Indicator (which some colleges and universities administer to all freshmen as a part of advising) for understanding student writers, teachers may be better able to make some sense out of the apparently chaotic sea of individuals that surges past them year after year. We may also learn how to design fairer assignments, why student voices differ, and why students do not always value what we value in their own writing.

Some of the underlying assumptions of this study need to be addressed. Any system, such as Isabel Myers's (1987) Jungian-based theory of personality type, that seeks to find patterns in student preferences and orientations can be accused of stereotyping and limiting students, of putting them in a box. Jensen and DiTiberio (1989) respond to this charge by stating:

> Although the MBTI makes use of key words and letters (as abbreviations for those words) to describe people, these symbols do not signify static traits, but instead indicate a person's preference for a particular cognitive process. A person's preference for one of a pair of opposite cognitive processes is similar to a preference for either using one's right or left hand. When people sign their name with their preferred hand, they usually do so quickly, effortlessly, almost unconsciously. However, if asked to sign their name with their unpreferred hand, they usually experience more difficulty. As we prefer one hand over the other, Jung's model suggests that we have psychological preferences on a number of bipolar dimensions. . . . Because we use the preferred cognitive process more frequently, it matures more rapidly. The unpreferred process, which may be used each day but less habitually, develops more slowly. We may feel, even as adults, childishly awkward when using it. (p. 5)

Just as we classify writers as basic or skilled, male or female, technical or creative, student or experienced, expert or novice, good or poor, so we may profitably look at the writing processes of students who vary according to personality type and cognitive functions of personality. According to George Frisbie (1990), "The core of the Jung/MBTI approach is the functions, which are reflections of cognitive processes. Behaviors characteristic of these functions represent cognitive styles" (p. 17). The four core function combinations are sensing and thinking (ST), sensing and feeling (SF), intuition and feeling (NF), and intuition and thinking (NT).

As final contextualization of the research, I claim the following beliefs about writing on which I based this study:

1. With Murray (1987) and others, I believe that students write to learn.
2. With Berthoff (1981) and Elbow (1973), I believe that students write to figure out what they mean.
3. With Berthoff (1981), I believe that students write to question and learn by questioning.
4. With Pearsall and Cunningham (1988), I believe that students write to show mastery.
5. With Iser (1974), I believe that readers construct texts. To extend Iser, I believe that they construct texts in ways that are consistent with personality preference.
6. With Bartholomae (1985), I believe that students must "invent the university," that is, understand the demands and conventions of the particular academic discourse into which they have entered. To extend Bartholomae, students must also learn to recognize how their own preferred ways of responding to new data in writing may or may not work in various rhetorical situations.

METHOD

Participants

One class of 22 students enrolled in English Composition at a large land-grant university were the subjects of this study. Sixteen were freshmen, and six were sophomores or juniors. All were Caucasian or non-Hispanic. None would be considered a basic writer, and none qualified for an honors section. Based on testing by the university testing center, all 16 Myers-Briggs types were represented among the students except ENTJ, which is the type of the instructor.

Materials and Design

As a regular course requirement, students kept a journal responding to works in a literature anthology. Students were required to submit journal entries on two works per class meeting, turning entries in at the beginning of the class meeting during which the works would be discussed. Students were given a sheet of 10 suggested types of journal entries from which to choose (see Appendix A) and were asked to code each entry indicating which type or types of entry they had written.

Drawing on knowledge of type preferences, I designed the 10 journal entry options to include a wide choice of approaches or modes that I thought would appeal in task and wording to different personality types. For example, some entries are more impersonal and analytical, whereas others call for a writer to relate the work to his or her own experience. Table 6.1 indicates which core function groups were predicted to prefer each entry mode. Student writers had free choice of which approach to use and were told that a journal entry could draw on more than one approach.

Journal entries were not graded but were given a check, check plus, or check minus to indicate completeness of the assignment. Check minus did not denote a "wrong" response but rather that the journal entry was not sufficiently developed or did not reflect adequate engagement with the assigned text. Although the journal was required for the course, students were told that no overall letter grade would be assigned for the journal.

Late in the term, students were asked to choose their "best journal entry," revise it, and write an analysis of their revision process. (This was graded and counted as a regular essay assignment.) Further data on the journal writing process were gathered through a written survey at the end of the course.

Table 6.1. Predicted and Actual Journal Mode Choices.

Journal mode[a]	Predicted to appeal to	Preferred by
1. Summarize	ST	ST, NT
2. Analyze character	SF, NF	ST,SF
3. Connect to other readings	NT	none
4. How text reflects the human condition	SF, NF	SF, NF
5. Connect text to your own life	SF, NF	SF, NF
6. Interpret	NT	NT, ST, SF
7. Analyze conflict	NT	none
8. Ask questions	SF, NF	SF, NF
9. How text challenges your views	ST, NT	none
10. Own entry	NT	NT, SF

Note. This table indicates which cognitive function group was predicted to choose each journal mode and which group(s) chose each mode.
[a]For complete journal assignment, see Appendix A.

RESULTS AND DISCUSSION

Although Jensen and DiTiberio (1989) suggest that each personality preference affects an individual's writing process, my data indicate that in selection of mode, extraversion-introversion preference and judging-perceiving preference are less statistically relevant than the central core functions of sensing-intuiting preference and thinking-feeling preference. Thus in this study core functions are used rather than full personality type. Myers and McCaulley (1985) explained: "The essence of Jung's comprehensive theory that relates to psychological types is the belief that everyone uses four basic mental functions or processes which are [sensing, intuition, thinking, and feeling]. . . . The four processes postulated by Jung . . . represent an individual's orientation to consciousness" (p. 12). Frisbie (1990) suggests that core functions also offer a valid indicator of cognitive styles. Results of this study are presented for the four core functions groups: sensing feeling (SF), sensing thinking (ST), intuitive feeling (NF), and intuitive thinking (NT).

When journal entries were examined by core functions, the answers to the research questions were significant:

1. Students of the same core functions did tend to choose the same mode of journal entry.
2. Criteria students used to select their "best" journal entry were consistent with core functions.
3. Use of first-person pronouns did vary consistently with core functions.

Journal Entry Choices, Predicted and Actual

Table 6.1 indicates which core functions were predicted to choose each entry mode and which core functions did prefer each mode. Table 6.2 indicates the percentage of total entries chosen by each group.

Use of First-Person Pronouns

At the end of the term, students were asked to count the total number of times they had used a first-person pronoun in journal entries. The following chart compares the average use of first-person pronouns for students of each core function group, in order of decreasing frequency:

CORE FUNCTION	AVERAGE USE OF FIRST-PERSON PRONOUNS
Sensing-Feeling	65
Intuitive-Feeling	49
Intuitive-Thinking	34
Sensing-Thinking	22

Table 6.2. Journal Mode Choices by Cognitive Functions.

Journal mode[a]	ST	SF	NF	NT
1. Summarize	27%	11%	16%	23%
2. Analyze character	12%	12%	9%	4%
3. Connect to other readings	1%	2%	3%	2%
4. How text reflects the human condition	7%	11%	13%	9%
5. Connect text to your own life	6%	12%	13%	5%
6. Interpret	14%	14%	10%	23%
7. Analyze conflict	5%	3%	4%	4%
8. Ask questions	13%	15%	22%	6%
9. How text challenges your views	1%	3%	2%	0%
10. Own entry	14%	17%	8%	24%

Note. This table indicates, by cognitive function group, what percentage of journal entries were of each mode.
[a]For complete journal assignment, see Appendix A.

Because all students produced approximately the same quantity of writing, the greater frequency of first-person pronouns does not reflect some groups simply having written longer entries than others.

With these summaries of data in mind, I examine the journal writing of each core function group in more detail.

Sensing Thinking (ST) Writers

Type theory holds that individuals who prefer sensing and thinking are practical and matter-of-fact, orderly, precise, and careful about rules and procedures. STs tend to be good at observing and ordering, filing and recalling, and sequencing and categorizing (Frisbie, 1990).

In writing journal entries, ST writers most frequently chose to summarize the poem or short story, summarizing about twice as often as they used their next two preferred entries—#6, "Interpret the meaning of this work," and #10, "Write whatever else you want to say about the work." STs were the least likely of any group to speculate on how a work comments on the human condition and the second least likely group to ask questions about a text. They also used #5, "What connection does this work have to you?," half as often as writers preferring SF. Of the ST writers who did occasionally relate works to their own experience, all were extraverts.

The ST preference for summary reflects a primary need to clearly understand the facts and order of a work: What is the story or poem actually about? What happens when? But their second preference, for interpretation, indicates a willingness to move beyond summary and look for meaning in a work (although sometimes their interpretations look like summaries). The ST's search for meaning is not likely to lead to speculation on large issues such as how a literary work reflects what it means to be human or personal issues that connect the work to the writer. The fact that STs frequently chose to write about literature in their "Own entry" indicates a desire for freedom of thought and expression that would not be predictable from typical type theory's description of this type, which emphasizes their preference for predictability and order. It is interesting to note that STJs valued writing on their own as strongly as STPs.

One interesting finding about ST writers in this study resulted from analyzing their criteria for choosing their "best" journal entry to revise for a grade. Two ESTJs, Brady and John, said they chose entries that showed their mastery of analytical skills. Brady wrote, "I felt like I had a good understanding of what `Up-Hill' was about and how the speaker uses metaphors." John chose his entry because it demonstrates "one of the things I learned this quarter about poems . . . that the author of the poem and the speaker of the poem do not have to be the same."

However, not all STs made their choices based on mastery. Jon's (ESTP) preference for sensing is evident in his criteria: "`Blue Girls' instantly attracted my senses because of John Ransom's relaxing attitude. With all the pressures and burdens of college, `Blue Girls' was a welcome, relaxing change and made me daydream of a careless world of girls dancing in a beautiful park." Chris (ESTP) sounded more like writers who prefer feeling in his criteria, writing, "Of all the poems, I liked this one the most." Jim (ISTP), Mark (ISTJ), and Joe (ISTJ) also bypassed mastery as a criterion and instead chose entries because they were about poems to which the students could personally relate. Jim (ISTP) said he chose an entry as his best because the poem reminded him of his father, but Jim's journal entry did not mention his father. Joe (ISTJ) wrote that he could see himself in the role of the young recruit in "The Man He Killed," but he did not mention himself in the entry. Mark, another ISTJ, wrote that he chose his entry because "I liked the poem because the subject dealt with animals. Since my career is to become a veterinarian, this subject interested me." His entry, however, does not mention his personal interest in animals but speaks impersonally on the implications of the poem for animal rights and the importance of respect for animals. Mark chose the poem because he saw a connection to himself, but in the journal entry he focused on a public issue rather than on his own experience.

In spite of the fact that the majority of ST writers valued entries on poems to which they personally related, they referred to themselves in the journals (i.e., used first-person pronouns) less often than any other group and one third as often as SF writers. This discrepancy may account for misjudgment by English teachers about ST students. English teachers at the college level (90% of whom are intuitives, according to Jensen & DiTiberio, 1989) may regard ST students as coldly logical and unable or unwilling to "relate" to literature. It appears, however, that ST students do relate to literature in a personal way and do value works that correspond to their own experiences. Nevertheless, they may appear distanced from the text because they often do not write in a personal, first-person voice.

Sensing Feeling (SF) Writers

Type theory suggests that students who prefer sensing and feeling combine a preference for gathering data through their senses and dealing with concrete, practical matters with a disposition to make decisions based on personal values and their own feelings. They have a desire to be personally invested in what they are doing (Frisbie, 1990).

When writing journal entries the SFs preferred entry #10, which students called their "own entry" and which allowed them to write "whatever else you want to say about the work." Their next most preferred entry was #8, "What in this work did you not understand? Ask questions and explore. You do not have to be 'right,'" followed closely by #6, "Interpret the meaning of this work." SF writers also used, slightly less frequently, choice #5, "What connection does this work have to you, to your life, to your ideas, or to people you know?"

These choices suggest that SF writers value having freedom to approach literature in their own way. They also want to express their individual reactions to a text. They are not afraid to ask questions about a work they do not understand. (It is discussed later that certain other types almost never asked questions.) Furthermore, SF students, whether introverts or extraverts, are interested in trying to find the meaning of what they read and relate that meaning to their own lives. It should be noted that SF writers showed less strength of preference in journal mode than the other three groups, as the SFs chose seven journal modes with nearly equal frequency (variance < 5%).

The personal orientation of SF writers is also reflected in the frequency with which they used first-person pronouns in their journal entries. Writers who prefer sensing and feeling referred to themselves using first-person pronouns more than any other type, almost three times as often as writers who prefer sensing and thinking.

When SFs were asked to choose their "best" journal entry for revision and explain why that particular entry was chosen, they, more than any other type, based the choice on their personal pleasure and satisfaction, either with the poem itself or with the journal entry. Julie (ESFJ) wrote, "I chose to write on this journal entry because I really enjoyed writing it. I related the poem to my own personal experience." Jenny (ISFP) explained her choice: "It's one of my best because I said why I liked the poem as well as interpreting it, and I think that it is well written. I like my interpretation, and I liked how I applied it to today." Kyle (ESFP) chose his entry to revise because it gave him an opportunity to write about his father and because he was homesick. Kyle explained, "The journal entry says a lot about the relationship I have with my father." SF writers see their "best" writing as that which they enjoy and that in which they can discuss connections between the literary work and their own lives.

Intuitive Feeling (NF) Writers

Type theory sees individuals who prefer intuition and feeling as insightful, creative, mystical, and interested in ideas oriented with people. They tend to be good at imagining, forming hypotheses, and making combinations (Frisbie, 1990).

NF journal writers most frequently chose to write entries in which they asked questions about the work. Their next preferred journal approach was #1, summary, followed closely by #4, "Speculate on how this work comments on the human condition," and #5, "What connection does this work have to you?" The willingness to ask questions and explore the unknown in a work of literature not only indicates a tolerance for ambiguity but also a willingness to let the reader (i.e., the teacher) know that the writer has not mastered the text. Because the sample included only one NFJ as opposed to four NFPs, I cannot be certain of the possible judging-perceiving influence on this willingness to question. The one INFJ chose to ask questions less often than the NFPs in the sample. The frequency of summary by NFs was surprising and does seems counter to type. Writing about the human condition and relating the work to self indicates that NF writers value the personal and the human connection in their writing as they do in their lives.

These preferences for the personal and the connected also appear in the criteria NF writers used for selecting their best journal entry. Jennifer (ENFP) chose her entry because "the poem has a meaning that I applied to my feelings about male chauvinism." Similarly Kane (INFJ) wrote, "I especially like this entry because I am applying lessons in literature to my own life." Linda (ENFP) stated, "The poem `Dreams' appealed to me because I believe the story behind the words," indicating the NF preference for focusing on values. Lori (ENFP) chose her entry on Adrienne Rich's poem "Rape" because she could relate to the poem, "not because I have been raped but because I am a woman. I like to relate poems to my life." Lori's criteria reflect her preference for relating literature to self as well as her feeling of connection to all women. Only Cathy (INFP), who frequently expressed her insecurity about reading poetry, chose an entry based on mastery: "I chose this entry because I understood the poem."

NF journal writers averaged 49 uses of first-person pronouns in their journal entries, second highest frequency of any type, indicating that their preference for relating literature to themselves is expressed in a personal voice.

Thus NF journal writers can be described as speculative, willing to reveal what they do not know, and interested in connecting literature to themselves and to humankind. But their choices also indicate a need to be sure they understand the work. This last quality may signal a maturity and balance in NF writers that would not be expected based on Jensen and DiTiberio's (1989) description of them as likely to focus too heavily on generalities.

Intuitive Thinking (NT) Writers

Individuals preferring intuition and thinking are described in type theory as speculative, logical, interested in theory and understanding, and good at synthesizing and interpreting. Competency is important to them, as is thinking things through. They are skillful at discovery, problem solving, and comparing and contrasting (Frisbie, 1990).

It should be noted prior to the discussion of journal preference in NT writers that the sample population included no NTJs, so the influence of perceiving on these data cannot be assessed.

NT writers most frequently wrote using #10, "Write whatever else you want to say about the work." Their next two preferences were only slightly less frequent: #1, summary, and #6, "Interpret the meaning of the work." These entries (# 10, #1, and #6) accounted for nearly 75% of NT entries. No other group focused so heavily on three preferred modes. NT writers were the group least likely to ask questions and reveal what they did not understand. Whether introvert or extravert, NTs rarely chose to discuss connections between literature and their own experience. They also were the second lowest group in use of first person pronouns.

These data indicate that NT writers highly value the freedom to write in their own way. The seeming contradiction between frequently using both summary (surface understanding) and interpretation (deeper understanding) may be clarified by Curt (ENTP), who explained his system for writing journal entries: "If I understand the work, I interpret it. If I do not understand it, I write a summary." In typical NT fashion he has designed a logical system that works for him and to which he is loyal. Either way, the NT writer is careful to indicate understanding, which he values. This need to seem competent may be reflected in the NT's infrequent use of the question entry.

Although the logical and usually impersonal NTs may not write about literature in a personal voice or connect the works to personal experience in journal entries, their criteria for selecting their best entry to revise belie this apparent distance. Sean (ENTP) wrote that he chose his entry about the poem "Double-Play" because "Wallace shows a different way of looking at a part of baseball. Being a baseball player myself, the double play was just a part of the game. Wallace's description made me realize the grace involved in baseball, as well as other sports." Clearly, Sean's choice was related to the poem's expanding his own way of seeing sports. Todd (INTP) chose his entry on the same poem because "I understood the poem, was able to reflect that comprehension in my journal, and relate it to my own experience as a baseball player." Todd's rationale reflects not only his need to demonstrate competence but also his personal connection to the poem. Both Bill (INTP) and Curt (ENTP) chose entries they saw as "representative" of all their entries. Bill wrote that he values interpretation because it "causes one to think for oneself" (note his impersonal voice here, which is typical of Intuitive-Thinking types). Curt mentioned not only his clear interpretation of the poem but also the fact that the teacher had liked his first version.

Therefore, although NT writers may not use a personal voice or express emotional connections to the literary works, teachers should not assume that they are unable or unwilling to connect to literature in a personal way. They seem to value the personal connection not because of the recognition of similitude, as with SFs, but because of the new insight the work of literature may offer them about their own experience.

Least Preferred Modes

A word should be said about the least preferred journal entries. Interestingly, all four core function groups avoided the same journal approaches. The most avoided topics were:

#3. In what ways does this work remind you of other works you have read? Draw connections.

#7. Discuss the conflicts or tensions that appear in this work or section.

#9. How do the ideas in this work challenge, stretch, or violate your usual ways of thinking?

Number 3, drawing connections to other works, would theoretically be appealing to NT writers who enjoy synthesis and connections, but even they may lack the confidence in their literary knowledge to approach a work from this direction. Numbers 7 and 9 demand a willingness to deal with conflict and ethical ambiguity. It is possible (and in fact Perry would affirm) that most freshmen are not mature enough in cognitive functions to choose to deal with this sort of tension.

Value of the Journal Assignment

The end of term survey asked students to identify the value of the journal assignment based on their own experience. Thirty-three percent saw its value in the practice of writing; for example, they liked having the opportunity to try new writing techniques. Sixty-six percent said that writing journals was valuable because it improved their appreciation and understanding of literature. Thus the assignment was valued for encouraging both learning to write and writing to learn. Neither personality type nor core functions were reflected in which students gave which response.

Use of the Journal Assignment Sheet

In the survey, students were asked whether they usually decided what type of journal entry to write before they began writing or wrote first and then decided what type of journal entry they had written. Responses to this question correlated with the judging-perceiving preference rather than the central core functions of personality. All students but one who prefer judging stated that they typically began by looking at the assignment sheet and deciding what type of entry to write. Nearly all students who prefer perceiving stated that they wrote first and then looked at the list to see what type of entry they had written.

This provides an interesting, if unanticipated, insight into how writers may use assignment sheets. My first reaction to these responses was to question whether they negated the usefulness of my study. As an ENTJ myself, I had always assumed that students would use the assignment sheet to decide ahead of time which approach to take to an assignment. After all, an assignment sheet is designed to direct and shape the journal response. If only judging types are making a conscious choice of what approach to use ahead of time, I considered the possibility that perhaps the choice of modes is orderly and predictable for judging types but random and unpredictable for perceiving types.

Upon examination of the data, I concluded that even though perceiving writers wrote first and coded their entries later, their coding still indicates their preferred modes of writing about literature. Although the coding is postscriptural, perceiving writers selected approaches consistent with those of judging writers in their core function group. The fact that choices made by perceiving writers *without* benefit of the assignment sheet are consistent with choices made by same-function judging writers *with* benefit of the assignment sheet is further evidence that these responses grow from some orderly internal cognitive structure.

Jensen and DiTiberio (1989) suggest that, in general, perceiving writers tend to select broad topics and only limit topics as deadlines approach. When they revise, perceiving writers often need to cut unneeded material and refocus the paper. The consistency with which perceiving types in my study ignored the assignment choices until they had said what they wanted to say about a text may help us understand the general phenomenon of perceiving writers' unfocused first drafts: They need to respond to the text or topic in their own way before they can conform to a teacher's assignment. Jensen and DiTiberio suggest that perceiving writers "may lose sight of their original goals while writing." It is possible that at times they do not even set goals when they begin to write. Goal setting tends to be a judging activity.

These data also suggest that teachers with a judging preference may have unrealistic expectations of how students use an assignment sheet. In evaluating student texts, teachers may highly value student fulfillment of details of a writing assignment, which is an easier task for judging writers, who start with the teacher's assignment, than for perceiving writers, who start with their own response to the topic or text.

FURTHER IMPLICATIONS FOR TEACHING

The results of this study affirm the reading response journal as more than a way of checking up on who has read the assignment: The journal can become a tool for planning what strategies and skills to present to a certain class, small group, or individual. As Emig (1971) suspected, writers do make choices of mode, at least in journal responses, that are consistent with their core functions of personality type. But in the academy, students cannot always choose their mode of response. This means that students learning academic discourse may at times be working against their own personality preferences and preferred modes of writing.

Understanding students' preferred choices of mode and responses to texts in low-stress writing situations can help teachers identify additional skills individuals or groups will need when assignments or writing tasks are more structured or more demanding. For example, SF and NF students who prefer to write in the first person and who like to relate texts to their own lives may need practice recognizing rhetorical situations, such as some technical and academic writing tasks, in which more "objective" and formal voice is appropriate, and they may need instruction on how make the shift. Conversely, we can teach ST students, who prefer summary to other approaches, the difference between summary and interpretation and help them practice their interpretive skills. They also need to learn to recognize rhetorical situations in which they may write most effectively using their often-avoided personal voice.

The journal also may be the place where students can learn to "grow their own meaning" (Elbow, 1973) before they have to adjust to the codes of the academy. Students' "growing their own meaning" can, in fact, lead to improved learning and improved attitudes toward reading and writing about literature, as indicated by the 66% of students for whom the main value of the journal was an increased appreciation and understanding of literature. I began using the reading journal in an attempt to reduce the hostility toward literature exhibited by many technically oriented students. I hoped that if I invited all students to approach literature through their own personality strengths there would be less resistance to reading and responding in class. This is, in fact, what happened. In introductory literature courses, I have found that technically oriented students who write frequent journal entries engage the literature with energy and interest, easily holding their own with their liberal arts classmates, in both engagement with the literary works and depth of insight. An outside observer would be hard pressed to distinguish the engineers from the English majors. It is not an overstatement to say that my literature classes have been transformed.

Awareness of personality type and student writing choices can also transform writing assignments, as teachers become better able to frame assignments that are appealing and fair to students of various types or core functions. For example, in the course that was the subject of this study, one poetry assignment invited students to choose either (a) to write an essay in which they analyzed an Emily Dickinson poem, or (b) to write a poem and in a separate essay analyze their own use of voice, tone, imagery, and diction. Students who prefer a more objective assignment might choose #1, whereas students who want to express their own connection to poetry study might choose #2. Sixteen of 22 students wrote their own poems and analyzed them, reflecting, in my opinion, the positive effect of journal writing on students' attitudes toward and comfort with poetry.

Results of this study can also remind teachers that student criteria for assigning value to their writing may be quite different from the criteria of the teacher or the academy. For example, students may choose their "best" entry because they value seeing themselves in the work, expressing emotions, or demonstrating mastery, whereas the teacher may assume that students would choose an entry marked by excellence in clarity, organization, and use of detailed support. It is significant that students in the study were more likely to judge an entry as "best" based on personal connection to the literary work than on any objective quality in the writing of the entry. The implications of this difference bear further investigation.

Finally, as teachers become aware of how type preference affects students' writing processes, we will also understand how our own type preferences affect our expectations of and prejudices toward student writing, our evaluation of student texts, and our own writing processes.

IMPLICATIONS FOR COMPOSITION RESEARCH

Knowledge of students' baseline writing preferences according to personality type provides a foundation upon which other researchers can attempt to replicate and extend basic information about personality and writing process, identify other academic writing tasks that are low stress and appropriate for similar study, and conduct research to learn whether a relationship exists between composing processes of students performing specific academic writing tasks and their personality type as measured by the Myers-Briggs Type Indicator. Researchers might also look for differences by personality type in various stages of the writing process. The implications for revision, which will be considered in a separate article, are intriguing and worthy of further exploration.

As Donald Stewart (1988) points out, researchers have personalities, too. Their preferences may manifest themselves not only in how they envision the composing process but also in how they interpret findings in their studies. For example, David Bartholomae (1985) in "Inventing the University," Nancy Sommers (1980) in "Revision Strategies of Student Writers and Experienced Adult Writers," and Linda Flower and John Hayes (1980) in "The Cognition of Discovery: Defining a Rhetorical Problem," all demonstrate a preference for complex, open-ended student texts, which are much more natural for perceiving writers than for those who prefer judging. Researchers, like teachers, may tend to value most highly writing that conforms to *their own* personality preferences.

As teachers and researchers, let us remember that our students "invent the university" (Bartholomae, 1985) and the discourse they need to function there not only as a result of the nurture (or lack of nurture) they have received in the education system; they also invent the university and its discourse using their own preferences in judgment, data gathering, and cognitive style, that is, their own individual personalities. They come to us with their *own* ways of knowing, selecting, evaluating, reporting, concluding, and arguing.

Just as Berthoff (1981) advises teachers to begin where the students are, my research indicates that we should also begin with who our students are. And recalling the related roots of the words *journal* (*journel*, daily) and journey (*journée*, a day's travel), we can use their journals and our knowledge of personality preferences to help them on their journeys as writers and readers.

REFERENCES

Bartholomae, D. (1985). Inventing the university. In M. Rose (Ed.), *When a writer can't write* (pp. 273-285). New York: Guilford Press.

Berthoff, A. E. (1981). *The making of meaning: Metaphors, models and maxims for writing teachers.* Upper Montclair, NJ: Boynton/Cook.

Elbow, P. (1973). *Writing without teachers.* New York: Oxford University Press.

Emig, J. (1971). *The composing processes of twelfth graders.* Urbana, IL: National Council of Teachers of English.

Flower, L., & Hayes, J. (1980). The cognition of discovery: Defining a rhetorical problem. *College Composition and Communication, 31,* 21-32.

Frisbie, G. T. (1990). Cognitive styles: An alternative to Keirsey's temperaments. *Journal of Psychological Type, 16,* 2-18.

Iser, W. (1974). *The implied reader* (W. Iser & D. H. Wilson, Trans.). Baltimore: Johns Hopkins University Press.

Jensen, G. H., & DiTiberio, J. K. (1989). *Personality and the teaching of composition.* Norwood, NJ: Ablex.

Murray, D. (1987). *Write to learn* (2nd ed.). New York: Holt, Rinehart and Winston.

Myers, I. B. (1987) *Introduction to type* (4th ed.). Palo Alto, CA: Consulting Psychologists Press.

Myers, I. B., & McCaulley, M. H. (1985). *Manual: A guide to the development and use of the Myers-Briggs Type Indicator.* Palo Alto, CA: Consulting Psychologists Press.

Pearsall, T., & Cunningham, D. (1988). *Fundamentals of good writing.* New York: Macmillan.

Sommers, N. (1980). Revision strategies of student writers and experienced adult writers. *College Composition and Communication, 31,* 378-388.

Stewart, D. (1988). Collaborative learning and composition: Boon or bane? *Rhetoric Review, 7,* 58-83.

White, E. (1985). *Teaching and assessing writing.* San Francisco: Jossey-Bass.

APPENDIX A
GUIDELINES FOR READING JOURNAL
EH 103-VICKI COLLINS

Instead of daily reading quizzes, you will write a reading journal entry for each work or section of a work assigned in the course. Journal entries will count in your grade. Your goal should be for each entry to reflect your thoughtful reading of the assigned work or section.

Some Guidelines:

1. Title each reading journal entry with the title, author, and page numbers of the work.
2. Minimum acceptable length for an entry is about 1/2 page handwritten. More is fine.
3. Reading journal entries may be written more than one to a page.
4. For full credit, the journal entry must be turned in at the beginning of class on the due date, before the work is discussed in class. Place your entries on the teacher's desk before class.
5. After entries are returned, they should be kept in a three ring folder or binder. The entire journal must be turned in to the instructor at the end of the course.
6. Some suggestions on how to approach the reading journal entries follow. You may use any, all, or none of these.
7. To the right of the title of each entry, indicate the number of the suggestion you have used to write that entry.

   Remember to code each entry. For example, if in an entry you discuss conflicts and tell what you did not understand, put 7,8 next to the title of the entry.

   Keep this sheet in your journal folder or binder for reference. Refer to it when you are writing a journal entry.

   Obviously there is no "right" way to respond to any of these topics. But the more you think about the reading and reflect your thinking in the journal entry, the more your reading and writing will improve. I encourage you to try your ideas out. The purpose of this assignment is for you to improve your understanding of the readings by writing.

   One goal of this course is to encourage and reward risk-taking in your thinking and writing. The reading journal is a particularly good place to try some things that are difficult or challenging.

   The journal entries will be read and recorded daily. Normally I will not comment on them. If you would like a comment, response, or answer to a question, write "Please Respond" on the entry. The journal does count in your grade.

Approaches to Journal Entries

1. Summarize the work (plot or major ideas).
2. Focus on one or more characters. What makes him/her tick?
3. In what ways does this work remind you of other works you have read? Draw connections.
4. Speculate on how this work comments on the human condition

(i.e. what it is like to be a human being).

5. What connection does this work have to you? To your life? To your ideas? or to people you know?
6. Interpret the meaning of this work.
7. Discuss the conflicts or tensions that appear in this work or section.
8. What in this work did you not understand? Ask questions and explore. You do not have to be "right."
9. How do the ideas in this work challenge, stretch, or violate your usual ways of thinking?
10. Own entry. Whatever else you want to say about the work.

Chapter 7

Personality Type and Revising by Student Writers

Jane Bowman Smith
Winthrop University

Many of my freshman writers, regardless of type, have seemed to operate within the boundaries of what these students and I call the "efficiency model." They want to finish the product in the most efficient way possible, which results in a rushed or truncated process with editing the only form of revision. They view writing as an assignment, an exercise; it is something to get done and hand in. Even after I pose questions intended to help them resee and develop their content, many obstinately (in my opinion) focus on sentence-level editing, making only those changes that I have specifically noted. Freshmen interested in writing as a *means* of making meaning, who are able and willing to write recursively, are members of a small minority.

Research has suggested at least three reasons for students' resistance to revision. Both Nancy Sommers's (1980) "Revision Strategies of Student Writers and Experienced Adult Writers" and Sondra Perl's (1980a) "A Look at Basic Writers in the Process of Composing" argue that students have not been taught more "global" strategies. Andrea Lunsford's

(1992) "Data, Methods, and Analysis," a study of teacher evaluation in high school, suggests another reason for the students' approach to revising; secondary teachers tend to write distanced, value-free responses that ignore content and focus on arrangement and sentence-level correctness. Students in a sense are being trained by their teachers' evaluation styles to focus on diction and grammatical errors. A third possible reason is the students' dependence on speech as a means of accomplishing the writing task. Sommers's (1980) study argues that "the students understand the revision process as a rewording activity. They do so because they perceive words as the unit of written discourse. That is, they concentrate on particular words apart from their role in the text" (p. 381). Thus, she continues, the sound of what they are "saying" in the paper is important; they focus on the word and its immediate connection to speech rather than the more abstract thinking demonstrated in the paper as a whole— something farther away from the immediacy of verbal communication.

Yet this research does not fully explain why, even after a semester of work on revision, combined with discussions of writing as a meaning-making activity that furthers thought, many students still seem to define writing primarily as a means to inform and to use a linear process in which revision and editing are seen as a single "step" that consists largely of work that improves correctness. Jungian typology theory, however, suggests reasons for this behavior. This particular view of writing as a means primarily to inform the reader and of a composing process that is best accomplished in a series of carefully performed steps is usually held by sensing types. Jungian theory also argues that intuiting students will define writing differently, and that their composing process will reflect this difference. I have not always seen my intuiting freshmen acting in accordance to their type, however. They, too, describe the "steps" of the composing process and worry about surface correctness.

Because neither composition research nor Jungian personality theory fully explains what I have seen in my classrooms, I decided to examine students' commentaries about both their writing and their composing processes in order to compare the responses of sensing and intuiting students, with particular attention to their revising processes. I hypothesized that a careful analysis of their responses would show that my students' revision strategies in fact *were* influenced by their types, and that sensing students would be more concerned with imparting information and would have a sequential revision process, working to improve the text in a series of steps and paying careful attention to surface details. Intuiting types, however, despite their use of a sequential process and a concern for errors, would probably be more concerned with making meaning and would compose more recursively, gradually clarifying and developing their ideas and leaving details until the last minute.

Because I suspected that freshmen were not as able to use their own preferences to their fullest potential, I decided to compare the freshmen's responses to more experienced writers in my advanced composition classes. The actual results of my study only somewhat confirmed my hypothesis. Although the freshmen did reveal their preferences in the way they revised—sensing students tended to examine the "parts" of their essays, whereas intuiting students tended to be more concerned with the idea and the essay as a whole—both groups of freshmen described their revision as a sequential process, often with little understanding of what they were doing. Both sensing and intuiting writers within their "groups" differed widely in their abilities to use their preferred process effectively; some of the most inexperienced (or least confident and practiced) writers displayed only a limited ability, whereas many of the more experienced writers still seemed to be "perfecting" the process natural to their type. (It was also extremely difficult to separate the sensing and intuiting influences from the students' other preferences—particularly feeling or thinking and judging or perceiving.)

This study suggests that although students' preferences for either sensing or intuiting certainly influences their revising, one cannot state simply that students will always display the traits usually connected with their preferences. In this study, sensing students were more likely to suggest their type in the way that they revised than were intuiting students. Both groups of freshman writers usually revealed their ignorance about writing by relying heavily on what their teachers had told them. This study also raises questions about the relationship of the individual student's definition of writing and the purpose(s) he or she believes it serves to the student's composing and revising processes.

METHOD

Over a period of two years, I have assigned a writing journal in my introductory and advanced composition classes and have also had students write self-assessments of their completed papers before they hand them in. In their journals, students write regularly about their use(s) of writing, their composing processes as they complete assignments, and the assignments themselves. In an attempt to make the assignment useful to both sensing and intuiting type students, I asked them specific questions but encouraged them to see, if they chose, the questions as simply a "starting point." Their responses to my questions allowed me to study the ways in which sensing and intuiting types discuss their revising processes, whether their processes are "true to their type," and also whether significant experience with writing changes the students' descriptions of their processes.

My procedure for categorizing their responses involved a complex series of readings and note takings in order to categorize "key words" and descriptions that related to type. There were two very important difficulties: Given the self-reflective nature of these assignments and their open-endedness, all four groups of students moved away from the specific questions to discuss what interested them personally. This made it hard to compare responses. I also have to assume that some of these responses were written so as to please the teacher, whether consciously or unconsciously. (Ironically, however, the students may have misread my type; they usually wrote as if they believed an emphasis on surface details would please me!)

This is also a small study; there are 20 sensing and 19 intuiting types who are freshman writers, and 16 sensing and 19 intuiting types who are "more experienced" writers—74 writers in all. The freshmen were enrolled in my regular entry-level composition classes. The more experienced writers were generally junior and senior English majors or writing minors who enrolled in my upper-level advanced composition classes—one class aimed at future English teachers and another a nonfiction writing workshop. All the students agreed to be typed, and we discussed personality theory in class. Table 7.1 details the students' types.

One thing I had not anticipated was the preponderance of judging types in my study; I believe that this had an effect on many of the students' responses, particularly their desire for early closure and "efficiency," which certainly affects the amount of revising a writer is willing to do.

Although I believe that using my own students is problematic, in this case the advantages outweighed the disadvantages. I knew, for example, what students were being taught about the composing process

Table 7.1. Students' Types.

Inexperienced Sensing		Inexperienced Intuiting	
ISFJ = 4	ESFJ = 8	INFJ = 3	ENFJ = 7
ISTJ = 5	ESTJ = 2	INTJ = 1	ENTJ = 1
ISTP = 1	INFP = 2	ENFP = 4	
	INTP = 1		
19 judging, 1 perceiving		12 judging, 7 perceiving	
Experienced Sensing		Experienced Intuiting	
ISFJ = 5	ESFJ = 5	INFJ = 6	ENFJ = 6
ISTJ = 3	ESTJ = 3	INTJ = 1	ENTJ = 1
		INFP = 2	ENFP = 2
		ENTP = 1	
16 judging, 0 perceiving		14 judging, 5 perceiving	

and the value of writing; furthermore, I doubted that students outside my classes would be honest either in answering surveys or in writing sustained journal entries about their composing processes and reflecting on what they had learned.

RESULTS AND DISCUSSION

Inexperienced Sensing Writers

One thing that concerned me was how little these 20 students knew about writing as a process. They knew almost nothing about how to revise—or how to prewrite, for that matter. Their journal entries reveal writing to be an almost unexamined skill that they take for granted on the one hand and fear on the other, because their own language turns on them, coming back from the teacher with red ink marking the errors in their spelling, grammar, and punctuation. When asked, they stated that they enjoy writing more when they are "interested in the subject," but they did not explain whether they enjoy this kind of writing because they enjoy communicating or whether their interest makes the process of writing easier. They do not seem to understand that the teacher will *read* their work: To them, reading is really *grading*, a different sort of thing altogether.

In general, these 20 students reveal their sensing preference in their attention to the *details* of their papers. Their commentaries suggest they believe that word choice and sentence-level editing are very important; they regularly stress their focus on individual words, their reliance on the dictionary and thesaurus, and their attention to the "sound" of their texts. Although they generally do not use the term *voice*, they seem to be making a connection between their writing at the sentence level and their speech; they want the essay to "sound right." When it does not, they change a word. Yet they do not have complete confidence in their ability to control their words. Erika [ESFJ], for example, feels her best quality is her ability to choose the "precise words to display her point of view," yet her biggest problem is being "too verbose." Jason [ISTP] wishes that writing were more like math; he dreads putting his ideas into words: "Why can't there be one right answer?" he asks. Janelle [ESFJ], who admits to writing anxiety, is afraid to write because she uses "incorrect words and sentence structure."

These students also regularly mention their ability to gather data or "facts": They stress the "informational" aspect of language and of writing. In *Personality and the Teaching of Composition*, George Jensen and John DiTiberio (1989) described one of the most significant differences between sensing and intuiting types: "Sensing types gather perceptions by looking first at the tangible particulars of their environment. Usually their abstractions emerge later, after nurturing their data or after writing a draft or two" (p. 47).

Natalie [ISFJ] is a good example of many of these students who are actually comfortable with research, perhaps because she is dealing with facts: "I feel that the area in which I am the best writer is research writing. It is easy for me to organize facts and translate them into a paper. In high school, I could write a research paper in no time." Natalie, however, is not describing an argumentative research paper: She is comfortable writing a "research report," which demands only that she find and organize data from the library. Her own analysis and interpretation of her data is not mentioned in this journal entry, and she had difficulty generalizing from her facts.

What Jensen and DiTiberio (1989) notice about the sensing type students' need to "nurture their data" (p. 47) is borne out by these students as well. Although the inexperienced sensing writers have largely mastered the "data gathering" aspect of invention, they have difficulty interpreting the data. In order to explain this part of the process, they often use phrases such as "relate all the material" or "tie it together." Janelle [ESFJ] explains her realization that she has to interpret her data without really describing what she means:

> It took one long night of me revising and rewriting to (hopefully) have done a good job. While I was revising, I thought that I was going to have to take out a large portion of my paper, but I finally realized that I just had to tie it all together and that is what I did.

Several students made similar comments: They are tempted to remove sections of their paper that are giving them trouble rather than to work out the conceptual connections among their ideas.

Applying a theory from their research to their own experience or another text is also difficult for this group of students. In a conference with me, for example, Kimberly [ISTJ] lamented that she would need to change the topic of her research project because she had been unable to find specific information. When I questioned this, remembering that she had earlier told me that she had found many articles on her general subject, she responded:

> Yes, I know I said that, and it's true that I found lots of articles on gender and on stereotyping. The problem is that none of them says what I wanted to say about my topic. They weren't talking about gender stereotyping in that particular film.

When I told her that she could certainly use the information about gender stereotyping and apply it to the film herself, she was concerned; she had "never [done] this in high school," she said, "and I can't really imagine how to do that on my own."

Kimberly stayed with her subject, however, and eventually wrote a much more positive self-assessment:

> I'm glad I didn't change topics after all, even though this was a very frustrating paper at times. I really feel triumphant now, because I actually did it! I saw what the books were talking about when I re-examined the film.

Kimberly's achievement is important; she has learned an essential analytical skill. She also has a sense of pride in her accomplishment.

Cathy [ISFJ] wrote about this same struggle with her own interpretation and analysis in a self-assessment of a paper: "I struggled with analyzing/developing my ideas further. I numbered my surveys and added them in when necessary. I took out some quotes that seemed to be just extra words." Her description suggests that she, too, is more comfortable when dealing with data than when developing her ideas. Words such as *numbered, added,* and *tried to add more* suggest that she would prefer to treat language like math. Her sense that some of her quotations were just "extra words" might stem from her difficulty with analysis; she might be better at gathering facts than at demonstrating the relationships among the facts and her idea. Yet it is also possible that she is becoming aware of her sensing tendency to "pour on the facts" without determining which are the most important. Cathy's awareness of this difficulty suggests she may be working with her less-preferred function and thus moving toward a more balanced composing process.

These students' ability to deal with data also tends to break down when they are writing longer papers; their commentary reveals their problems in dealing with large amounts of information. They had difficulty determining what was irrelevant, in relating examples to their point, and in creating hierarchies of information.

Their difficulty in making meaning is revealed in their comments about thesis statements in particular as well as other "meaning creating" aspects of the text, such as introductions and conclusions. Leslie [ISFJ] gives a good example of this:

> I don't know how to capture the reader's attention. Should I ask a question or give background information? I don't know what the best way is. My next problem is the conclusion. How do I end my paper? I never know how to "wrap it up." I don't know whether to state my opinion, ask a question, or list the main topics in each of my paragraphs. When I can't think of an ending, I restate the thesis.

Rather than experiment with several possibilities, Leslie seems to want the one "best way" to deal with her problem. Although she mentions "capturing the reader's attention," an interest in audience that is probably a result of her feeling preference, she seems to be thinking more of capturing the *teacher's* attention because that is what she has been told to do. She wants to rely on a strategy or technique to "control" the difficulty of writing, but she relies on strategies that she has been taught rather than "playing" with the language to create her own strategies for solving her problem. In part, her difficulty may stem from what can be inferred of her definition of writing and its purpose. Writing is something "to do," something that is "said" to the reader. She seems to want to package her idea within a prescribed form rather than develop her thought through writing.

These sensing students also have difficulty developing their ideas. Natalie's [ISFJ] self-assessment is typical: "I have a problem of just concentrating on one main point. By doing this, I often write about the same point over and over, just repeating it in different terms." Her attempt to develop her ideas, to use writing to deepen her thought, results in simple repetition of "the same point." When she writes narratives, however, and describes the real world, she does not have this difficulty.

Jeremy's [ISTJ] discussion of the connection between writing and thought is particularly telling:

> I find that once I get started writing on a subject, then my ideas begin to flow and I have no trouble writing about them. The drawback here is that while writing, I usually come up with new ideas, and they come out on paper in an unorganized manner. I also have a tendency to change the way I want to explain my idea during the writing stage. I tend to get frustrated then because I have already spent time thinking on this idea and now that has become wasted time.

The student efficiency model operates here: For Jeremy, exploratory thinking is wasted time because it forces him to adapt or change his paper. This suggests his resistance to the making of meaning. For Jeremy, writing a paper seems to be merely an assignment—not something to invest oneself in.

From what they write in their commentaries, revision is often easier for this group of students than prewriting or invention; especially when they need to structure an argument or draw conclusions from facts, they report that they dread the invention and drafting stage. Their reasons for finding revision easier may be related to the way in which they approach revising. Thomas Thompson (1994), in an essay entitled "Personality Preferences, Tutoring Styles, and Implications for Tutor Training," described sensing students as using "a linear writing process in which they complete each step before moving on to the next one" (p. 138). He sees this as the "traditional" writing process of prewrite, draft, and revise, and adds that "many sensing types, with their penchant for following rules, follow the 'rules' for the composing process that their teachers taught them" (personal communication, October 10, 1995).

This reliance on a linear process comes out in the students' references to the "steps" of composing in general, and specifically in their revision. "In writing," says Brad [ESTJ], "I have learned to do four things: first I do my prewriting, then I write my rough draft, then I do my revising, and finally I make a final copy." Brad emphasizes that he has learned this. Yet his description of his actual revising process might appear odd to some instructors:

> While revising, I look for agreement errors, spelling errors, punctuation marks, etc. Once I have found all my errors, then I am ready to write my final copy. In writing my final copy, I make my essay as perfect to my knowledge as is possible.

His careful list of the specific errors he looks for is a clear indication of his sensing preference, as is his apparent desire to *do* what he has been taught. Yet his approach is in fact the opposite of what his college teachers would suggest. He edits first and *then* evaluates the content of the essay to determine whether it fits his concept. Putting sentence-level editing first may be a carryover from high school learning, but it also confirms Jensen and DiTiberio's (1989) claim that sensing types have predictable problems with revising. They tend to make few changes in the content of the paper, instead simply proofreading. In fact, when Brad revised the draft of a research paper to which I had responded, he paid careful attention to my comments on sentence-level problems but left larger issues—such as my questions about his content and argument— alone. Although Brad has learned that revision is important, it still seems to have been imposed from the outside.

Other students in this group begin with larger issues first, but they still describe the process of revision as being one of steps or phases, as does Heather [ESTJ]:

> When I revise my paper, I first try to make sure that my thesis is clear. I will read over it (the paper) and see if I can pick out what my thesis is. After I feel that my point is stated properly, I look over the arguments in the paper. If I feel that my claims are not supported well, I try to expand on them. All this, the overall effect of the paper, is one of the most important aspects of the paper. The last thing I worry about when I am revising is my grammar.

Heather seems to have moved away from the more typical sensing preference for examining details to an awareness of the importance of the more global aspects of her paper—the thesis and "point" she is making and the arguments she musters. Yet she is still atomizing her paper, examining it in smaller parts that are more manageable. It may be, too, that her use of the phrase "one of the most important" is significant within the class context. Most instructors—who are probably intuiting types—would question what could be as important as "the overall effect of the paper," suggesting a potential conflict in the way the intuiting professor and the sensing student look at writing.

The examination of these students' journal entries and self-assessments suggests several important facts about inexperienced writers who are sensing types. Their sensing preference leads them to favor the more practical uses of writing and to listen carefully to their teachers in order to follow their advice. The students in this group follow a *strictly* linear process; they believe that they should be able to receive the assignment, think a bit, write the introduction and especially the thesis, and then use the thesis as a "control" for the rest of the essay. None of these 20 students described a recursive writing process. When they see problems with this approach, as does Kimberly, for example, it is not due to any perceived limitations in composing in this way but rather in not having adequate strategies to choose from in each "phase" of the process that troubles them.

It seems likely, from what they have written, that their use of steps is personally very effective; it enables them to complete their assignments in an efficient and competent way. Possibly, their training in high school has reinforced their sense that this is the natural order of things. When they revise, they also make use of a series of steps but the potential of this particular revision process is often not fully realized. Perhaps their teacher's discussion of revision in high school—where it is often seen as punishment—discourages them from developing its fullest potential. Of the four groups of students, this group most often describes revision as fixing errors, and the students in the group usually know exactly what errors to look for in their own work. These students have the most difficulty using language to develop and deepen their thinking; they are also the least likely to play with language. It seems possible that this relates to their practical definition of writing as *primarily* a means to share information.

Sensing Writers in Advanced Classes

The 16 more experienced sensing students in the advanced composition classes *do* have an understanding of writing as a process; they write knowledgeably about both prewriting and revising strategies. Of these 16 students, however, only four define themselves as "creative writers"; many of the others are planning to teach at the secondary level. Perhaps in part because these students are all either English majors or writing minors, they never mention a fear of being graded, nor do they assume that the teacher's reading of the paper is the same as grading it. When they imagine their audience, they see a person whose purpose for reading is to receive information, and they often create heuristics that enable them to probe and improve the clarity of their writing. Oddly, only one student specifically mentioned that she enjoys writing more when she is engaged in her subject matter, but class discussion confirmed that these students, like the sensing freshman writers, enjoy writing most when they are interested in their subjects.

Like the freshmen, this group of experienced writers reveals their sensing preference in their attention to the details of their texts—the actual words, their use of punctuation, and their sentences. When discussing their revision process, 12 of the 16 specifically discuss these details. However, they show greater maturity in their definition of revision: Only five of these students essentially edit their papers without revising them, and each of the five admits to "knowing better." These students have also learned to draw conclusions from their data; only three discuss their struggles to interpret data or to "make a point."

Finally, like the freshmen sensing writers, these students state that revision, for them, is best accomplished through a series of steps. In this group, 12 of the 16 discuss their systematic and practical stages of revision. Unlike the freshmen, however, whose discussions often seem to be rote, their "steps" are purposive, clearly aimed at revising each aspect of the paper despite their proportionally greater attention to the surface features of the text. They can explain why they use a series of steps: Their process seems to be more in line with Donald Murray's (1993) suggestions in *Write to Learn*, a means of revising as sweeping purposively through a text, focusing on one aspect at a time. The students examine their writing carefully; revision is no longer handled as if with a checklist. The four students who revise more recursively—who state they rewrite and edit intensively while drafting—tend to express frustration with this process, making it easy to speculate that they might be using a procedure that is unnatural to them.

Like the freshmen, this group of experienced writers reveal their sensing preference in their concern for the details of their texts. Lynn [ISTJ], for example, carefully described her revision of sentences:

> On the first draft, I changed mostly the sentence structure and some content. On the second draft, I went back and reviewed my action verbs to describe my work experience. I was looking, in a way, for more effective phrasing of my sentences.

Later in the same commentary, Lynn discussed in detail what she had learned from the class's text, Erika Lindemann's (1987) *A Rhetoric for Writing Teachers:*

> I think Lindemann points out two techniques that would improve my revising. The first is to use Christensen (p. 180) to evaluate paragraph relationships. The second is the "Paramedic method" (p. 182). The two ideas that would be most helpful to me are circling the prepositions to help keep me from being too wordy and circling the "to be" forms.

Lynn's emphasis on sentences is more mature than the error hunting that concerned the freshmen; they are concerned with correctness, she with improving her style. Yet like the freshmen, she views her text as a concrete product.

Several of these students, as does Lynn, describe a close connection between the actual phrasing of their sentences and the content of the essay. Stephanie [ISFJ] described her individual sentences *as* the content of her essay:

> After I work on the overall organization, the next thing I check for is content. I look to see if my statements make sense and are easy to understand. At this point, I also try to make sure I don't repeat the same phrase over and over again. I change any sentences, words, or phrases that make my point difficult to understand, or take away from what I'm trying to say.

Stephanie connects content to her actual sentences, focusing on clarity and stylistic revision. She seems to define her role as writer as a "clear communicator"; as she projects herself into the role of her audience, her goal is readability and ease of understanding.

Most of the more experienced sensing writers define revision as teachers of composition would wish; they "re-see" all aspects of their texts. Only 2 of the 16 view content revision—the development of meaning—as proof of erroneous thinking, as did Jeremy. Sarah's [ESFJ] comments on revision, like Jeremy's, suggest a deeply negative attitude toward change:

> Basically I hate rewriting a paper. I don't mind revising it and "fixing" the mistakes or even making sentences more concise—but changing the work too much makes me feel like I failed.

Revision, when seen as "editing," is acceptable; "rewriting" is not. This resistance is maintained *despite* discussion in class of the benefits of revision. Jeremy [ISTJ], a freshman, sees revision and the change of his idea as a waste of time; Sarah connects revision with "failure." Each shows that the lingering myth of "getting it right the first time" still influences students. (Both Sarah and Jeremy are also judging types, which certainly affects their desire for closure.)

Like the sensing freshmen writers, this group of students primarily manages the process of revision by approaching it as a series of steps: 12

of the 16 describe an orderly process of working through the paper and focusing on a different "task" each time. What I found most intriguing is a fairly common desire among even these experienced writers to work on their sentences *before* they revise their content or structure. The adage, "Why correct sentences you may need to delete?," does not, apparently, make much sense to these sensing types, as Tad [ISTJ] explains:

> Any paper will be incomprehensible if it lacks proper spelling or sentence structure. Thus, these are two of the first things I check when revising for this very reason. After I check spelling and sentence structure, I check documentation. . . . These things are all mechanical errors, and not a part of the thinking process of the paper. *Then* I begin checking the thesis and the overall structure of the paper to make sure it flows and can be understood.

Tad's first sentence could refer to either himself or the reader, but it seems likely to me that he, himself, finds his errors to be too distracting as he works on what is for him the harder part of revising—working on the "thinking" part of his paper. He presents these ideas about editing and revision as if they are his own, not just something the teacher has said in class. His revision strategy—to start with the mechanical errors—may also be the sensing type's natural movement from the small to the large. He concludes his entry with the statement that "revising can be done easily, providing one follows a schedule of sorts. Randomly reading through the paper, or spot checking, almost guarantees an error or two."

This group of sensing students sometimes examines the paper part by part, as Marshall [ESTJ] explains:

> I think technically, revising and editing are NOT easy, the way some people in the class have said, but easier than objectively critiquing a paper that is literally a part of you. The idea that the whole is greater than the sum of its parts [sic]. I mean that it is easier to look at the individual parts objectively than to look at the whole. When one looks at a paper, we need to be scientists, *skeptical*, looking at the parts analytically. By doing so, the whole should be well formed.

Marshall's comment about "critiquing a paper that is literally a part of you" suggests that it is hard for him to be objective and stand back from the "whole." He is better able to examine the parts of the essay and believes that if each part has been carefully revised, the essay as a whole will be coherent and complete. Marshall also reveals his thinking preference in words such as *objectively* and *skeptical*.

Some of the students in this group, however, although still using a series of steps, begin their revising with more global issues. Brandi [ESFJ] wrote, somewhat wryly:

> When I do begin revising, I read for clarity first. Does the reader understand my point? Does my thesis clearly state what the paper is going to be about? Does the organization of the draft follow the thesis? Usually, I answer "no" to all these questions. When I am satisfied that the draft is understandable, I read it for grammatical mistakes.

Brandi has learned to dialogue with her text and has internalized questions that enable her to project her reader's response to what she has written. Her questions suggest her practical definition of writing; she is concerned with its "clarity." As a sensing type, Brandi naturally relies on a series of steps to revise, but she has apparently absorbed her teachers' suggestions to deal with larger textual concerns first and to edit last.

Only two of these writers describe a writing process that could be seen as recursive. Yet both describe struggling with this kind of composing, as Amanda [ISTJ] reveals in her self-assessment:

> Both the cover letter and resume were very hard for me. As I worked on the cover letter, I had to make constant revisions. The first paragraph alone I had to rewrite at least five times because I kept trying to cram all of the information in that paragraph. I initially followed that with a description of my work experience, then I had to revise that by adding a paragraph describing my activities as a student teacher because they were pertinent. I then had to revise the paragraph that I had planned to use second to flow from the now-preceding paragraph!

As discussed later, Amanda's description is less clear than the intuiting students' descriptions of their recursiveness; her frustration—partly a result of an overload of facts—also is obvious in this commentary. It is tempting to speculate that the "messiness" of this process bothers her.

What are the apparent effects of writing experience for junior and senior sensing types? This study suggests that the strengths of sensing types—their attention to the details of their texts, for example—are maintained, and the students have come to understand their emphasis on them. As Lynn in particular demonstrates, this attention to detail can lead to a sophisticated understanding of sentences and a willingness to perfect one's style. Writing practice also seems to help them learn how to generalize and to draw conclusions from the wealth of data they collect.

This group of students has internalized strategies for revision and are generally able to describe what they do effectively. Even the students who resist revision have learned or created their own techniques to help them manage the process. Many have also developed their own heuristics, with questions that they use regularly to analyze the development of their ideas, their structure, and their audience's probable response. These students' competent discussion of composing and particularly revision as a series of steps suggests that some researchers may place too much emphasis on the importance of "recursiveness" in writing, at least for some students. There is no real evidence that these students revise less effectively as a result of using a sequential or linear process, whether they begin their revising by checking for errors or by considering their thesis as a reflection of their essay's ideas.

Inexperienced Intuiting Writers

Unlike the sensing freshmen writers, the intuiting freshmen *do* discuss the writing process; they seem more knowledgeable about prewriting techniques, however, than about strategies for revision. I am not sure why the two groups of freshmen differ in their awareness of writing as a process; I can only speculate that this is a natural result of both their different definitions of writing itself and their understanding of its uses. Unlike the sensing students, who define writing most often as imparting information, these intuiting students define writing as something that expresses and allows them to develop their ideas. Of these 19 students, only 6 express a fear of being graded, and all blame their past teachers' focus on errors for this fear. I had expected that the intuiting freshmen would be much less concerned with the surface features of their texts than were the sensing freshmen, and in one way they are; when they discuss their revising strategies, 15 comment more extensively on how they improve the content and organization of their papers than on how they edit. Only 3 equate revision with editing. Only 4 of these 19 students, however, neglect to mention editing at all. Apparently, their high school education has alerted them to be careful of the surface features of their texts—even though this would not be a natural reflection of their preference.

Although both groups of the sensing students express confidence in their command of diction and particularly facts, the intuiting students see their ability to focus on their ideas and to make meaning as their strength. This confirms Thompson's (1994) description of the tendency of intuiting types to:

> [focus] attention on patterns and possibilities suggested by the data rather rather than on the data themselves. People who habitually favor perception (i.e., intuitive types) attend to the whole picture rather than to its parts and are likely to become good at grasping abstract or symbolic relationships; they may even consider an emphasis on sense experience to be unnecessary or annoying. (p. 138)

Kelvin [ENFJ], for example, simply stated: "I love to write because I love expressing my views." JoAnne [ENFP] likes "to write about books or events [she finds] have a deep meaning." Nikki [INFJ] believes her strengths include "good thoughts and ideas that are true and genuine."

The intuiting students, however, sometimes see their ability to generate a multitude of many potential ideas as causing them problems. Len [ENFJ] stated:

> Though I usually think of many exciting and interesting topics, I think of several concepts at once; therefore, I cannot think of what to write. Also, because I try to squeeze in all of my thoughts, my papers sometimes appear choppy.

Len gets confused because he has too many options, and he is aware that trying to deal with *all* of them is a mistake. Yet his comment about trying to "squeeze in" everything suggests he does not want to let them go. Just like the sensing students who are aware that their greatest strength—a sensitivity to words—could become a problem, Len sees potential difficulties in his ability to engender ideas.

Jensen and DiTiberio (1989) also note the intuiting student's desire to handle assignments in unique or creative ways, which may result in ultimately ignoring the assignment altogether. Of these 19 students, 10 (when simply given a journal assignment that asked them to describe their composing process) use a creative or unique approach. One would expect students—especially when they knew the entry would not be graded—to make fewer demands on themselves by writing more straightforwardly. Two of the students wrote highly narrative entries; Coco [INFJ] essentially loses sight of the topic altogether in order to describe her physical reactions to writing:

> My first problems derive [sic] in my paper when the teacher stands up and says, "Okay, you are going to turn in a 400-word paper to me at the end of class." Right away my heart begins to pump like the air from a machine going into a flat tire. Also, my eyes begin to fill with water, causing my vision to blur. The nerves in my nervous system give a whole new meaning to the term "nervous wreck." The paper I'm supposed to write is a monster chasing me down a dark hall in my mind.

Coco's imagination leads her in several different directions; first, she visualizes the class and the teacher, then she creates a simile to describe her physical reaction. Unfortunately, although it is fresh and interesting, it is not one that fits the class setting! Two more descriptive sentences follow, and then, finally, she ends with a metaphor—possibly a return to the schoolroom idea. However, Coco lacks control over her creativity. These several strategies draw attention to themselves and do not further the point she is making. The other eight students also individualize the assignment. Two experimented with point of view, and several created effective single metaphors to begin their entries.

It is perhaps not surprising that when these students were asked "what do you find difficult about writing?," most said "grammar" or "mechanics," the least imaginative part of writing. Intuiting types, particularly if also feeling, seem to be bothered by a teacher's emphasis on surface details—the kind of attention that sensing types may also dislike yet seem to take for granted. Harvey [INFP] described the effect of a teacher's "error orientation" in an entry describing his writing history:

> I had never thought of myself as a writer until about a year ago. Before that time, anything I wrote was (in my opinion) *on an elementary school level.* I believe the reason was that my teachers never encouraged me, they simply corrected my grammatical errors and graded me (this usually earned me a D). The change came when I wrote my first essay for my Senior English class. For the first time in my life, the teacher returned the paper with words of encouragement about my ideas in more abundance than the grammatical corrections. My writing still isn't the best in the world, but after that paper, I wanted to improve.

Although Harvey's feeling preference is clear in his response to praise, it is also apparent that his previous teachers' attending to what he perceived as superficial details and ignoring his ideas resulted in his being "turned off." Once a teacher responded to his ideas, as opposed to his grammatical errors, his attitude toward writing also changed.

Only 2 of these 19 students cited the difficulties that resulted from generating too many ideas. I was surprised that only one student (who in fact was probably the brightest student in this group) mentioned that she sometimes had difficulty dealing effectively with her evidence. Jensen and DiTiberio (1989) comment that the writing of intuitives can appear to be more mature because it deals so heavily in abstractions, but add that "attending to direct findings, facts, and evidence, which comes so naturally to sensing types, is quite difficult for developing intuitives" (p. 91). The intuiting students' ignorance of this potential problem in their writing was in striking contrast to the sensing freshmen's awareness that they had trouble interpreting their data—the parallel problem for sensing types. This lack of awareness by the intuiting students supports Jensen and DiTiberio's (1989) claim that teachers tend to value the writing of intuitives because of its abstractions; teachers perhaps comment on the sensing students' difficulty with thesis statements, but pass over the intuiting students' lack of evidence.

What surprises me most, however, is these students' descriptions of their revising. They sound a great deal like the inexperienced sensing students; they use a sequential process, and they often describe what they do in "steps." Only three of these students seem to write recursively, using the process of writing and crafting their words to create meaning. These three draft and revise simultaneously on their computers as they move from rough notes to a draft; it is difficult to tell from what they say, however, whether they are actually using writing and language to develop their ideas or are simply getting their work done "efficiently." The other 16 describe their revising in much the same way as do the sensing students, although most begin with larger concerns such as thesis and organization and leave editing for last. Jensen and DiTiberio (1989) comment that the revising of intuiting types "may be more effective if they resolve the unnecessary complexities of their ideas, check their facts, and, as a last step, clean up the mechanics of spelling, punctuation, and the like" (p. 174). They imply that intuiting students may neglect these details but this is not a problem for the students I studied. It appears likely that their secondary education has made them very aware of errors in their texts.

In this group of students, 16 describe a sequential revising process. Dana [ENTJ], for example, sounds like the freshmen sensing students quoted earlier in both her resistance to revision and her reliance on a sequence of steps:

> Revising a paper that you have written is a difficult task because it is like you are admitting you made mistakes; no one likes to do that. I feel that there are four essential components to revising your own paper. When I revise my paper, I want to make sure that I have answered the question completely in my thesis and essay, that the structure of my essay matches that of my thesis, that I have presented arguments for both sides, and that I have edited carefully.

Dana's view of writing is that of "teacher ownership." She wants the paper to be a demonstration of what she has learned in the class; she may also be "carrying over" the view of revision as punishment that she learned in high school. Dana also seems to believe that good writing is writing that is perfect the first time. Yet her response focuses less on surface details, which is often the major concern of the sensing students, and more on the content and ideas of her paper. Rather than list specific errors she looks for, as do many of the sensing types, she merely makes sure that she has "edited carefully." Word choice and sentences are not even mentioned.

Many of the intuiting students seem to have been influenced by what they were taught in high school; they describe their composing and revising processes as a series of steps, yet they are not as focused on correctness as are the sensing students. Crystal [INFJ] is an example of those who seem to be in a transitional period, moving from an old linear strategy to one that allows her to make meaning:

> I have learned the way to compose my papers are to first gather my ideas to see what emphasis I want my papers to have on my reader. [sic] After gathering my ideas, I would make an outline, because it allows me to see how my essay will be structured. From my outline, I can begin the rough

draft of my paper. Once I finish my rough draft, I look over the essay to see if my ideas flow smoothly, and to see if anything needs editing. I check the grammar and citations of my sources to make sure they are accurate. Then I revise to see if the point of my paper is supported and made relevant.

Crystal reports on what she has learned from her teachers, yet when she looks over her prewriting, she thinks about its meaning with reference to the reader. Her use of the word *emphasis* implies that she has generalized from the facts, and that facts do not speak for themselves. Crystal's description of her revising is confusing, however. It is difficult to know whether she examines her ideas and errors simultaneously or whether she actually rereads and works through her text in four separate stages.

Some of these inexperienced students, however, have moved beyond what they learned in high school and are more alert to their own meaning, which implies a different definition of their writing. The students' self-assessments also suggest that they profit from an examination of their revising process. Hugh [INTP] reads and rereads the paper to determine whether the thesis, which he sees as a controlling idea, fits what he actually wrote. He stated:

> I usually examine the thesis and conclusion of my papers. I have seen that in some of my past papers my thesis statement ends up not being specifically related to the actual paper I wrote. I begin reading my thesis only after I have reread my paper and feel familiar with the content, and then I make sure the thesis "fits." If it does not, then I change it to fit the paper. Some may consider this backwards, but I feel like my thesis is flexible. I also check the rest of the introduction and my conclusion. I make sure they will leave an impact with the reader. I want them to make the reader think.

This excerpt is in striking contrast to some of the sensing freshmen's responses. Although they sometimes see a change in their thinking as "a waste of time," Hugh is able to take advantage of this potential growth and see his thesis as "flexible." Hugh, however, is not as concerned with imparting information but rather with his own developing thoughts and with his need to "make [his] reader think."

Although the intuiting students usually use the term *steps* when discussing the revising process, in some cases the term seems to be used for convenience. Laura [INTJ], for example, apparently describes her process in steps because that allows her to analyze it more easily:

> There are several things that I consider when revising a paper. Usually, in the actual process, these steps overlap and blend together somewhat. However, when they are separated, they proceed in the following order of importance.

The fact that these steps "overlap" suggests that her process may actually be recursive. Her phrase, "when they are separated," implies that she is consciously separating them in order to observe them more analytically for the purposes of description. As Laura describes her revising, she focuses almost exclusively on the "idea" and the content of her essay. Editing is presented almost as an afterthought:

> The next thing to do is make sure it is good for others to read. This can be very difficult and usually it is better to set the paper aside for awhile so that I can look at it more objectively. The rest of the revision process only entails polishing the paper and adding the finishing touches.

Unlike the sensing freshmen, Laura does not specify the errors she typically makes; she is much more concerned with the larger issues of writing than she is with details.

Several of the best writers in this group are very aware of their audience. Chris [INFP] realizes that his commitment to revision has changed as he has gained an appreciation for his power over the reader:

> Revising a paper can be a long or short process. One year ago when I said "I just finished revising my rough draft" it meant I hit spell check and then printed the paper out. Now when someone asks me how I revise a paper, a new and ever changing definition enters my mind. All my work comes back to the idea, "will the reader want to read my essay?" Like the conclusion for example. I ask myself, Is it effective? Do I like it? Will the reader remember this essay and what it is about? Finally, does it make me sit back and just think?

Chris's ability to probe his text—the sense that he is making meaning through language that can and should engage the reader—is very advanced for the freshmen I studied. Like Hugh, Chris is determined to make his reader think as a result of reading his essay. His use of the phrase "the changing definition" of revision also suggests his awareness that he will continue to learn about writing as he matures. I found it interesting, however, that a significant difference between the freshmen and the more experienced intuiting writers is their ability to apply the theory they have learned. The freshmen, even when they have understood the concept of the audience and have created heuristics to help them imagine the reader's response, are less able to actually achieve this in the essay itself. The experienced writers not only grasp the theory but are able to apply it.

James Newman (1990), in his *Cognitive Perspectives on Jungian Typology*, discusses Isabel Briggs Myers's hypothesis that intuitives are naturally better with language than are sensing types because words, as symbols, have to be translated into meaning by intuition. His research supports Myers's view "and suggests that the ability to comprehend complex linguistic forms is one of the principal capacities of the intuitive function" (p. 6). The responses and self-assessments of the students I studied suggest that intuitives are just as able to *generate* linguistic forms as to comprehend them. Even the least able of these writers deal more, in their commentaries, with their ideas than did the sensing types; the best writers, even as freshmen, have a sophisticated understanding of the connection between the development of their thoughts and the act of writing and hope to make the reader think in response to their texts.

Their creativity and desire for uniqueness, a reflection of their intuiting preference, is not always within their control; they present other challenges to their teachers in their tendency to write abstractly, sometimes getting overwhelmed by their ideas, and in their apparent ignorance of the importance of evidence. At least in this study, the freshmen acted differently from what one would expect of intuiting types in two ways: They are very aware of errors in their texts, and they most often describe a sequential composing and revising process. Both are much more predictable for sensing types. From the way they discuss these issues in their commentaries, however, it seems most likely that being alert to errors is a result of their schooling and particularly the way in which they have been graded. It is not easy to determine, with the freshmen, whether the sequential composing and revising is a result of their education or their own preferences.

Intuiting Writers in Advanced Classes

Of the four groups, this group of students' descriptions of their composing process most closely resembles the writing of Sommer's (1980) experienced writers. They have "[adopted] a holistic perspective and the perception that revision is a recursive process" (p. 386). I think it is significant that of these 19 students, 11 define themselves as creative writers; the others are planning to teach secondary school or to write professionally. The fact that so many of these students identify themselves as creative writers affects their definition of writing and assuredly the way(s) in which they write. Although the sensing students have learned to clarify their communication in order to impart information effectively, these students (like the intuiting freshmen) tend to use the act of writing to deepen and develop their thought and to affect their readers.

I was surprised that this group of students is not so obviously "creative," so intentionally unique in their approaches to their assignments, as are the inexperienced intuiting students. A more careful examination of their writing, however, reveals the difference; the advanced students do consistently use figurative language, as does Sam [ENTJ]: "Editing is nothing more than a buffing of the existing wax—a polishing." The difference is that the language is used effectively and does not stand out—or away—from its context. Their discussion also suggests that they have begun to see analytical writing as creative, just as is "creative writing."

Of the four groups of students, the experienced intuiting students are generally most able to project themselves into the mind of the reader and also to imagine the reader as someone other than the teacher. Jackie [INFJ], for example, wrote in a journal entry:

> For the last paper—resume and cover letter—I put myself in the mind of the employer who would be reading the material. I also pretended that I really was going to send this resume out and thus wanted to make sure it would be a reflection of who I really am.

Jackie's sense here that the writing should reflect "who she is" suggests the connection these intuiting students often seem to feel between their writing and their own identity, as well as her ability to imagine who her reader "is."

Like the inexperienced intuiting students, these more experienced writers express their intuiting preference in their ability to engender ideas. Kim [ENFP] described an idea's coming suddenly into her mind as "an impact—the POW! of creativity." Despite Kim's very physical image, this group's commentaries often reveal the abstract quality of intuitive writing. Jeff's [ENFP] description of a specific revision is almost completely lacking in concrete details:

> I decided to focus my revising more on the content of the paper—I knew I needed to do a better job of making myself look good [on the application letter]. I think that the smartest way to have approached revising this paper is to look at the paper through an employer's eyes and to grade the paper myself as an employer would grade it.

His commentary is very general; he does not suggest how, specifically, he could "make himself look good," although obviously he would need to do that with specific facts about himself. And although he is aware that an employer will "grade" his resume, he again ignores (or at least does not specifically mention) the relevant details that the employer would look for.

When asked what they found difficult about writing, many—not surprisingly—said "grammar," but Tracey [INTJ] suggested another difficulty for intuiting students: "I am not a spontaneous writer. Writing is a very slow process for me. I have to take time to think about what I want to write. I hate in-class writing of any kind because I don't usually have time to get things together." Although Tracey's process may well be a reflection of her introversion—a need to think things through before writing them down—it also suggests that she has become almost dependent on the challenge of using writing to develop her thought.

Despite these students' general acceptance of the importance of revision, and their willingness to revise with great patience, three students did comment on their resistance to doing it. In each case, the student's resistance to revision seems to be connected to a "myth" about creativity. Michelle [INFP], for example, seems to cling to a romantic definition of inspiration:

> I really usually do not spend a lot of time revising. Something in *A Rhetoric for Writing Teachers* really stood out to me, the part about how sometimes students feel that there is a "mysterious genius" in them and they don't want to admit that their genius has failed them. Well, that's the kind of writer I am. I do think I could improve my rewriting techniques if I would just place greater emphasis on saying what I mean, and THEN worry about how to say something.

Yet Michelle does see that revision would help her final product, and even her reason—the "mysterious genius"—relates to her intuiting preference for creativity and uniqueness. Unlike the sensing students, she is not resistant to revision because she is "efficient" or "organized."

Of the 19 students, 8 describe their revision process as a series of steps. Like the inexperienced intuiting students, however, their "steps" are not always clearly separated and specific. The 11 students who describe their composing and revising processes recursively, however, most closely fit the "model" that has recently been seen as the most mature writing process, as does that of Seanna [INFJ]:

> Revision is a continuous process for me. It begins right after I write my first sentence and doesn't end until I'm satisfied with the completed paper. Halfway through the paper, I may have found a new idea to develop that's particularly interesting or makes a good point. At the same time, I may not develop an idea I originally intended because I spent time with other ideas.

Seanna has moved beyond the "student efficiency model" and no longer seems to be controlled by either the teacher's assignments or ownership of her text; her journal entry also reveals the patience and confidence that many of these students have developed as they have learned to perfect their writing.

The intuiting students in this group seem to have an advantage over the sensing types I studied in their ability to see their text as a whole. Even the experienced and very talented sensing writers tend to deal primarily with the parts of their papers when revising. Tracey [INTJ] is the best example:

> When I finally decide that I am ready to put pen to paper, I am constantly going back and rereading what I have already written. This I guess is the way I keep a sense of where I have been. My need for reinforcement is constant. I have an internal sense of the way the paper ought to flow and

> I have to keep checking on it. When I do return to the paper, I do a lot of
> the same as far as drafting. I will read it several times and just think about
> it. I can't just reread the first sentence and start making changes. My
> revisions come in much the same manner that the first draft does.
> Sometimes I spend a lot of time just rereading and thinking. I don't
> measure what I have accomplished by what I have actually written down.

Tracey's use of phrases such as "an internal sense of the way the paper
ought to flow" and her resistance to making immediate changes as she
reads suggest her ability to concentrate on the meaning of her entire text
rather than on its component parts.

The experienced intuiting students do not seem to have made the
same "leap ahead" in writing ability as do the experienced sensing
students, perhaps because so many of the freshmen who are intuiting have
a fairly sophisticated knowledge of writing. Like the freshmen, the
experienced intuiting students value creativity and uniqueness, but they
are able to control and use it rather than be used by it. Their
experimentation with both language and form is purposive.

The more experienced intuiting students often still write in an
overly abstract form, particularly when self-assessing. They tend to write a
general overview rather than listing the details they need to address. Yet
their actual revising processes deal with both the global and surface
features of their texts. Not all these students write recursively; many revise
by using a series of steps. This may be a result of their judging preference,
a desire to be organized and systematic and to reach closure. Their ability
to explain why they do this suggests that this is not a simple "following of
the teacher's directions."

Real growth, however, occurs in the experienced intuiting
students' ability to imagine the reader and to project the reader's needs.
When the freshmen make statements such as "I want to make the reader
think," the more experienced students picture the reader responding to the
text and make changes accordingly. Some of these students also display a
greater ability both to read the text in a sophisticated way to see whether
the mental picture matches what is on the page and to use rereading as a
spur to develop meaning.

CONCLUSION

Almost 20 years ago, in "Understanding Composing," Sondra Perl (1980b)
argued that composing is a recursive process:

> In recent years, many researchers including myself have questioned the
> traditional notion that writing is a linear process with a strict plan-write-
> revise sequence. In its stead, we have advocated the idea that writing is a

> recursive process, that throughout the process of writing, writers return to substrands of the overall process, or subroutines (short successions of steps that yield results on which the writer draws in taking the next set of steps). (p. 364)

Perl's redefinition of composing, together with the work of other researchers, affected not only the way in which teachers have viewed composing but also the way in which we have viewed revision. Their work also established a general trend in research and shaped the way composition—at least at the college and university level—was taught. I remember the impact this particular essay had on me as I struggled with my dissertation; my own dissatisfaction with the sequential model of composing had been validated. Composing was a recursive process. My pleasure arose from the fact that Perl could indeed have been describing the way in which I compose and, in particular, revise.

In rereading this essay recently, I realized that over the past years I have often evaluated my students' ability to revise on the basis of their ability to revise *recursively*. Those who used a sequential process, who revised in a series of steps, seemed to be, simply, wrong despite my study of personality theory. Perl's (1980b) essay also provided a definition of writing, one that resonated for me:

> It is also important to note that what is there implicitly, without words, is not equivalent to what finally emerges. In the process of writing, we begin with what is inchoate and end with something that is tangible. In order to do so, we both discover and construct what we mean. . . . In writing, meaning cannot be discovered the way we discover an object on an archeological dig. In writing, meaning is crafted and constructed. It involves us in a process of coming-into-being. (p. 367)

Perl's definition of writing as a meaning-making activity is surely one we wish to share with our students; it is at the heart of the humanist tradition. And my study suggests that many of my students, when they gain experience, can agree. It is much more likely, however, that these students will prefer intuiting than sensing. The sensing students in my study—admittedly still developing writers—did not share this notion of writing's purpose any more than they revised recursively. Perl seems to ignore the practical and utilitarian uses of writing in her description, and this is where sensing students tend to begin.

The sensing students I studied—and there were some very accomplished writers among them—view their role as writers, the text they produce, and their reader quite differently than do the intuiting students. Most of these sensing students see themselves as gathering and making sense of information when they write. They focus on the text as an artifact in the real world; their focus on the word itself, on the sentence, and even on their errors suggests their sense of crafting something usable and practical, as if they were artisans of language. When they imagine the audience reading, they see the reader's purpose as learning information from their text, and so their revision is motivated by a need for clarity. Their sequential process, a careful working through the text step by step, seems to be a natural result. Thus their revision has two goals: First, to impart information clearly to the reader and, second, to "craft" the text or to polish it as an artifact.

The intuiting students in this study are not as easy to categorize. The freshmen generally connect writing with expressing their ideas, whereas many of the more experienced writers seem to share Perl's definition of the meaning-making aspect of writing. For them, writing is closely connected with their creativity, and their ideas have impact both on themselves and on their audience. They seem to imagine the act of reading as prelude to thought; the reader will not simply gain information but will engage actively with their texts, both in the act of reading and beyond. As a result, their revision seems to be more global, more concerned with the text as a whole rather than with its parts. Yet I do not want to oversimplify here: Not all the intuiting students shared these views; some viewed writing more literally and revised more practically, and I am not sure how to explain the apparent lack of connection between their views, their strategies, and their type.

What are the implications of this study for our teaching? Simply, awareness of our own preferences—which can so easily become prejudices—and understanding that our students are likely to be different. Jensen and DiTiberio (1989) argue:

> As a general rule, instructors should first encourage students to develop their strengths, to apply their preferred processes to writing before attempting to produce well-rounded prose. Those students who were never encouraged to write in a way that suited their cognitive style may need support and encouragement even to develop their natural strengths. (p. 106)

This seems to me to be excellent advice. My study suggests that teachers need to be flexible as they help their students to revise. Because most instructors at the college level are intuiting, our intuiting students can clearly benefit from our experience. What we have learned about revising will help them: Concentrating on the main idea of the text, seeing the text as a whole, imagining the reader reading and making meaning of our language, and harnessing our desire for creativity and uniqueness so that it serves our purposes. When we help our sensing students, however, we must step outside the process that seems so natural and intuitively "right."

We need to help them focus more effectively on the text as an artifact and to shift their emphasis from their errors to polishing their sentences. We need to respect their sense that writing is ultimately practical, a means of sharing information. We need to help them flesh out the steps they go through as they revise, encouraging them to deal not only with the superficial aspects of their texts but also the larger aspects, such as the thesis, that tend to trouble them. Finally, we must make sure they have adequate strategies to rely on in each phase of their very different revising process.

REFERENCES

Jensen, G. H., & DiTiberio, J. K. (1989). *Personality and the teaching of composition.* Norwood, NJ: Ablex.

Lindemann, E. (1987). *A rhetoric for writing teachers* (2nd ed.). New York: Oxford University Press.

Lunsford, A. (1992, March). *Data, methods, and analysis.* Paper presented at the Conference on College Composition and Communication, Cincinnati, OH.

Murray, D. M. (1993). *Write to learn* (4th ed.). Fort Worth, TX: Harcourt Brace.

Newman, J. (1990). *A cognitive perspective on Jungian typology.* Gainesville, FL: CAPT.

Perl, S. (1980a). A look at basic writers in the process of composing. In L. N. Kasden & D. R. Hoeber (Eds.), *Basic writing: Essays for teachers, researchers, administrators* (pp. 13-32). Urbana, IL: National Council of Teachers of English.

Perl, S. (1980b). Understanding composing. *College Composition and Communication, 31,* 363-377.

Sommers, N. (1980). Revision strategies of student writers and experienced adult writers. *College Composition and Communication, 31,* 378-388.

Thompson, T. (1994). Personality preferences, tutoring styles, and implications for tutor training. *Writing Center Journal, 14,* 136-149.

Chapter 8

Personality Type in the Foreign or Second Language Classroom: Theoretical and Empirical Perspectives

Rebecca L. Oxford
University of Alabama

Literacy involves the ability to read, understand, and draw conclusions from written texts and to communicate effectively in writing, whereas oracy involves the ability to understand spoken language and to communicate effectively in speech. In this chapter, I am concerned with both literacy and oracy in two language environments: foreign language and second language. A *foreign language* is ordinarily defined as a language learned in a setting where it is *not* the primary means of daily communication. An illustration is Spanish as learned by a Russian person in Moscow or Vienna. A *second language* is typically defined as a language learned in an environment where it is the main vehicle of communication for most people. An example is English as learned by a Chinese person in Milwaukee or London.

In both the foreign and the second language learning situation, personality type is likely to be a powerful predictor of how—and how well—a person develops literacy and oracy. Personality type is measured by the Myers-Briggs Type Indicator or MBTI (Myers & McCaulley, 1985) and its longer version, the Type Differentiation Indicator (Saunders, 1989) or TDI, as well as the Keirsey Temperament Sorter or KTS (Keirsey & Bates, 1984). These instruments are by no means identical.

The MBTI (Form G) is a 126-item, self-report questionnaire designed to reveal basic personality preferences on four scales: extraversion/introversion, sensing/intuition, thinking/feeling, and judging/perceiving, all of which are explained in detail later in this chapter. The MBTI has internal consistency reliabilities averaging .87 and test-retest reliabilities of .70-.85 (Myers & McCaulley, 1985). Concurrent validity is established in correlations with other instruments of personality, vocational preference, learning style, and management style (.40-.77), and construct validity is supported by many studies of vocational preferences and creativity.

The TDI is a longer and more intricate 290-item form of the MBTI (Form J). It provides data on 27 subscales for each of the four MBTI dimensions: extraversion/introversion (e.g., gregarious-intimate, expressive-contained), sensing/intuition (e.g., realistic-imaginative, pragmatic-intellectual), thinking/feeling (e.g., questioning-accommodating, reasonable-compassionate), and judging/perceiving (e.g., planful-open, systematic-casual). The TDI also includes seven additional scales indicating a sense of overall comfort and confidence versus discomfort and anxiety. Reliability of 23 of the 27 TDI subscales is greater than .50, an acceptable result given the brevity of the subscales (Saunders, 1989).

The KTS is a 70-item questionnaire that also measures personality type. The KTS is a derivative of the MBTI, but it does not have a large bank of psychometric information. Keirsey and Bates (1984) do not include any reliability and validity data on the KTS in their book, which includes the instrument. Wallace and Oxford (1992) reduced the KTS to a shorter form and discovered an internal-consistency reliability in the .60s. They also learned that the KTS has validity regarding the link between student grades and teacher-student personality type conflicts (see information later in this chapter). Despite their differences, these three instruments are all useful for assessing personality type in the language classroom.

This chapter explores personality type in the foreign or second language classroom. As shown in this chapter, interesting and potentially important linkages exist between personality type on the one hand, and language performance and learning strategy use on the other. Cross-cultural type differences abound. Gender differences in personality type are also prevalent (see Keirsey & Bates, 1984; Oxford, 1993, 1995) but are not discussed in this chapter because of length constraints. Conflicts between contrasting personality types are evident in the language classroom, especially between teachers and students or between two different cultural groups, as shown in this chapter. These conflicts might be even more significant in language classrooms than in other kinds of classrooms because such conflicts seriously affect the amount and type of communication in which the language learner is willing to engage. The chapter closes with recommendations for the language classroom. The entire chapter helps us comprehend more clearly how people learn to communicate meaning. The variables discussed here open up new avenues of understanding for teachers and researchers alike.

FOUR DIMENSIONS OF PERSONALITY TYPE

The MBTI, TDI, and KTS assess four dimensions of personality type: extraversion/introversion, sensing/intuition, thinking/feeling, and judging/perceiving. These dimensions are extremely important to language learning (and to learning in general). However, these four dimensions are not the final word on who people are and how they behave. For example, these four aspects do not reveal personality pathologies such as manic depression, schizophrenia, autism, and borderline personality. Moreover, they do not explain or predict "negative" personality traits in a person such as the tendencies toward excessive prevaricating, equivocating, exaggerating, complaining, belittling, or ego inflating. Pathologies and negative personality tendencies are beyond the realm of the four dimensions. Also excluded from the four basic dimensions of personality type (but partially included in one subscale of the TDI) is the area of sensory preference: visual, auditory, tactile, and kinesthetic. This dimension is important for understanding how people learn, either in the classroom or outside of the classroom. In addition, the four dimensions of personality type do not thoroughly cover certain important cognitive and affective variables such as intelligence, motivation, anxiety, ego boundaries, and so on, although these often correlate with personality type (Ehrman & Oxford, 1995).

Although the four dimensions do not cover every aspect of personality or cognition, I have found in my own research that they explain many of the behaviors and interactions that occur in the language classroom. I have also found that temperament types are useful as well. Three of the personality type dimensions—intuition/sensing, thinking/feeling, and judging/perceiving—are combined in various ways to produce four temperament types: intuition/thinking, intuition/feeling, sensing/perceiving, and sensing/judging. These are explained in full by Keirsey and Bates (1984).

The personality type dimensions are extraordinarily helpful and have frequently been used to explain "learning style" (Lawrence, 1984; Oxford, Ehrman, & Lavine, 1991). In this chapter I describe each of the four dimensions of personality type and make theoretical and empirical applications to language learning processes. For each of the four type dimensions, I first give definitions and theoretical background, followed by personalized examples from foreign or second language situations. Then I demystify each dimension still further through an explanation of cross-cultural research. This is followed by verbatim case studies of actual personality type conflicts as described by the people involved.

EXTRAVERSION/INTROVERSION

Definitions and Theoretical Background

The first dimension of personality type is *extraversion/introversion,* which influences the grouping of students in the classroom and the types of activities preferred by the learner. According to Jungian theory, this dimension concerns the source of energy of each individual. Myers and McCaulley (1985) have sharpened our understanding of extraverts and introverts, and Oxford, Ehrman, and Lavine (1991) have linked this information to the language classroom. In the general U.S. population, approximately three-fourths of the people are viewed as extraverted and the rest as introverted (Keirsey & Bates, 1984).

   Extraverted learners of foreign or second languages gain their energy and focus from events and people in the outside world. They have many friends, and they like group work. They do not want to stay in the same group for too long, however. Extraverted students prefer conversation, role-plays, and other highly interactive activities. Sometimes extraverts move from one thing to another very rapidly because they are interested in so many events and issues. Therefore, they find it hard to concentrate deeply for a long period of time.

   Introverted learners of foreign or second languages, on the other hand, are stimulated most by their own inner world of ideas and feelings. Their interests are deep, and they have fewer friendships than extraverted students (but often strong ones). They prefer to work alone or else in a pair with someone they know well; they dislike lots of group work in the language classroom. Introverts find it easy to concentrate on one thing for a long time and dislike moving rapidly from one group or issue to another. With introverted students, it is often useful to employ the "think-pair-share" sequence, in which the student starts by working alone and gradually eases into group work.

Cross-cultural Research

The primarily North American adult learners in a foreign language study by Ehrman and Oxford (1995) were mostly introverted. As noted earlier, the general U.S. population is chiefly extraverted. The individuals in the Ehrman and Oxford study were chosen to participate in foreign language instruction because they were linguistically and academically talented and heading for international government careers. Students who were assessed as expressive (an extraverted trait) on the TDI were found to use social strategies for language learning. However, extraversion/introversion appeared to have almost no correlation with end-of-training language proficiency in this study.

In an earlier study of the same kind of foreign language learners (Ehrman & Oxford, 1989), these researchers discovered that extraverts significantly preferred visual and affective strategies, reflecting a preference for the outer world and for being in touch with feelings. In that study, introverted language learners more often used strategies for searching for and communicating meaning, which related to the introverts' interest in the inner world of ideas. In a follow-up foreign language case study by Ehrman and Oxford (1990), extraverts used social learning strategies consistently and easily, whereas introverts rejected such strategies or used them in rare instances. Cognitive strategies were occasionally applied by extraverts but with far less comfort than social strategies. For introverts, metacognitive strategies such as planning and evaluation were clearly preferred, with a general rejection of affective and social strategies. These findings fit well with Jungian theory about the preferred sources of energy of extraverts and introverts.

African-American high school students tended to be extraverted in a general, nonlanguage-learning study (Nuby, 1995). According to voluminous research cited by Nuby, African Americans have been shown to like group sharing, nondirective teacher functioning, novelty, freedom, and personal distinctiveness (clothes, jewelry, names) within the group setting. Nonverbal behaviors such as strutting, touching, making or avoiding eye contact, and rolling the eyes are all highly extraverted ways by which African Americans convey messages in groups and to the teacher. In the same investigation by Nuby (1995), Native American high school students also showed themselves to be extraverted. As Nuby explained, Native Americans were highly extraverted and cooperative within their own cultural group, but this ethnic comraderie coexisted with a suspicion of "outsiders."

Arabic-speaking students of ESL or EFL are typically very gregarious, overtly verbal, and interested in a whole-class, extravert-pleasing mode of instruction (Harshbarger, Ross, Tafoya, & Via, 1986; Willing, 1988). Likewise, Hispanic students of ESL or EFL are in general highly extraverted. They want a close relationship with the teacher, respond to social goals, do not care about impersonal rewards, and like physical touching in class and out. Hispanic students cooperate overtly in class by working in groups, talking together, and helping each other concretely. In one study, Oxford and Burry-Stock (1995) found that Puerto Ricans often used a variety of social strategies for learning EFL on the island of Puerto Rico. These are all indicators of a strong extraverted tendency among Hispanics. Language teachers, according to Harshbarger et al. (1986), sometimes totally misinterpret Hispanic students' extraverted interest in the teacher as a bid for favoritism and their peer-helpfulness as a sign of cheating.

The cooperation shown by African Americans, Native Americans, Arabic speakers, and Hispanics is related to their overall leaning toward extraversion. However, cooperation can also be related to the group solidarity of certain kinds of introverts. According to Harshbarger et al. (1986), Japanese and Korean students of ESL or EFL are often quiet, shy, and reticent in language classrooms. They dislike public touching and overt displays of opinions or emotions, indicating a reserve that is the hallmark of introverts. These ethnic groups, Japanese and Korean, contain many introverts but have a traditional cultural focus on group membership, cooperation, solidarity, and face-saving (Harshbarger et al., 1986; Hofstede, 1986).

On their home terrain, Chinese students in general show strong cooperative tendencies and group concerns, although many of them would also be classified as introverts. In the Chinese system, all children are expected to maintain the same level of achievement because "the cooperative nature of the culture requires that everybody help everyone else" (Hudson-Ross & Dong, 1990, p. 123). For Chinese students, overt cooperation does not occur in the classroom, but it may occur outside of school. "Because caution, conservatism, and compliance are valued in Asian cultures, traditional Asians may appear to be indecisive, timid, overcomforming, and unassertive" (Cheung, 1985, cited in Nuby, 1985, p. 45). This might be why many Asian students are reluctant to participate in speaking activities or other tasks that demand a display of extraversion.

The kind of cooperation shown in Chinese ESL or EFL classes is different from that of Hispanic ESL or EFL classes (Nelson, 1995). Chinese students cooperate subtly by maintaining relationships, group harmony, and cohesion; they seldom work in small groups and are expected to listen, take notes, and leave. Hispanics, on the other hand, rapidly form small groups and very obviously help each other.

No cultural groups preferred group work in Reid's (1987) large, cross-cultural study of college students of ESL and college students who spoke English natively. This finding was especially surprising for Hispanic students, who show themselves as highly group-oriented and extraverted in most studies. Native English speakers rated group work lower than all other cultural groups; perhaps this relates to the competitive, individualistic nature of their educational experience. A very different picture arose for Rossi-Le (1995), who replicated and expanded Reid's work with a sample of adult immigrants that included native Spanish speakers and a wide variety of Asians (Chinese, Vietnamese, Laotians, and others), all learning ESL in the United States. In Rossi-Le's study, all ethnic groups indicated a preference for group learning, thus possibly reflecting a difference in age, maturity, or experience and a possible absorption of the North American extraverted tendency.

Extraversion/Introversion Conflicts

Two extraversion/introversion clashes are shown below. Both of these conflicts involve an introverted student and an extraverted teacher. As noted earlier, Keirsey and Bates (1984) stated that a large majority of the U.S. population is extraverted. Therefore, it stands to reason that this culture's teachers, who choose a profession in which they work with large numbers of people, would reflect an extraverted tendency and that clashes would occur with introverted students.

Young, an introverted Korean student of ESL, encountered a conflict with a very extraverted teacher from California. Young is a typical representative of Korean culture in terms of introversion. Although Introversion versus extraversion seems to be the primary problem, there might have been several other conflicts as well. Judging (wanting quick closure) versus perceiving (wanting to wait before reaching a conclusion) is one such conflict. Also, Young's Feeling (emotional) orientation made her even more sensitive to the anxiety of conflict, whereas the teacher's thinking (objective, distanced from emotion) focus made him indifferent to such concerns. Finally, there might have been a conflict between Young's sensing (concrete-sequential) learning and the teacher's apparent intuition (full of nonsequential creativity). More about these dimensions is given later in this chapter. Here are Young's comments:

> I am an Introvert, Sensing, Feeling, and Judging learner. I am also strongly visual. The reason I have a strong visual learning preference is mainly due to my previous learning experiences in Korea, I believe, where most teachers emphasize learning through reading and tend to pour a great deal of information on the chalkboard. . . . I once had a style conflict with one of my professors at a California university, when I took an elementary communication class. The professor was a strong Extraverted, haptic [hands-on] person who always wanted his students to demonstrate certain kinds of motions and actions in class. The professor himself liked to act, dance, mime, and move around in the classroom. He rarely wrote down his lecture points on the chalkboard. I have no doubt that many of the activities that the professor developed were excellent for the course.

Personally, however, I had difficulties adapting to such activities because I am an Introvert and I am not a haptic learner. I often skipped the required group activities. Frankly, I did not enjoy the course at all. In the classroom I had often been anxious because I didn't want to be called to be a demonstrator in front of the whole class. Outside the classroom, I had always been nervous about being with a group of Extraverted American students; I was the only foreign and Introverted student in the group.

Introverted, feeling Myra was terrified by an extraverted, thinking teacher of Spanish as a foreign language. This teacher embarrassed her in class and wanted her to perform in public among strangers. Here is Myra's story:

The teacher was very stern, forceful, and expected us all to catch on instantly. Many of us had never had Spanish in high school. She came into class on the second day and started having us say the name for the month of August. I sat way in the back behind a much larger person thinking I would not have to say anything. She walked right back to me and asked me to say agosto. I could not trill the "g" as she expected. She made me say it over and over again, feeling my throat; then she made me feel her throat as she said it. I was so embarrassed. As we left, a nice looking young man in the elevator said, "I really felt sorry for that girl." I said, "That girl was me." I was petrified every time I had to go into that room again. I had to take three more quarters of Spanish, and I would take anyone but her, even if I had to skip quarters and risk forgetting everything I had previously studied.

SENSING/INTUITION

Definitions and Theoretical Background

The second aspect of personality type consists of *sensing versus intuition*. This dimension refers to how people take in and use information. The sensing versus intuition aspect is part of Myers' and McCaulley's contribution (1985), and Gregorc (1979) has done extensive research with four related categories (concrete sequential, abstract sequential, concrete random, and abstract random), which cannot be discussed in detail here due to space constraints. Applications to foreign and second language learning have come chiefly from Oxford, Ehrman, and Lavine (1991). Keirsey and Bates (1984) cite research showing that three-quarters of the U.S. population are sensing and the rest are intuitive.

Sensing students of a foreign or second language use strategies that focus on concrete facts in a step-by-step, organized fashion. Abstract principles and underlying language systems are not very important to sensing learners, who prefer to do the task at hand and then move sequentially to the next activity. These learners are frequently slow and steady, progressing at their own rate but able to achieve learning goals if those goals are made very clear. Randomness and lack of consistency in lesson plans are difficult for such students to handle in the language classroom. A sensing student prefers language learning materials and evaluation techniques that can be applied in a concrete, sequential, linear manner that involves the physical senses. If the language teacher or another student diverges from the planned topic of discussion by telling an amusing anecdote, the sensing learner is frequently distressed by the lack of continuity. Compared with intuitive students, sensing students are likely to follow the teacher's guidelines to the letter, be focused on the present, demand full information, and avoid compensation strategies that demand creativity in the absence of complete knowledge.

Intuitive students of a second or foreign language think in abstract, large-scale, nonsequential ways. They are able to distill the main principles of how the new language works and thus conceive of the underlying language system. They are often bored by concrete, step-by-step learning and would rather take daring intellectual leaps. The intuitive learner tries to build a mental model of language information. He or she deals best with the "big picture" in nonlinear, random-access mode. Interesting discussions that veer off the assigned topic for the day are perfectly acceptable to an intuitive student. An intuitive student, when asked for a list of three possibilities, is likely to come up with 15 because of a general orientation toward creativity and futurism. The intuitive student is comfortable without having all the information and feels free to use guessing, predicting, and other compensation strategies in the absence of full knowledge.

Cross-cultural Research

In a highly sophisticated group of North American adults learning a variety of foreign languages in an intensive instructional environment, Ehrman and Oxford (1989) found that intuitive students outperformed other students in the use of language learning strategies. These researchers discovered very striking correlations between intuition, on the one hand, and the use of strategies for searching for and communicating meaning, affective control, employing authentic language, and formal model building on the other hand. In combination with extraversion, intuition also related positively to the use of visualization and memory strategies. In combination with judging (briefly mentioned earlier), intuition related positively to the use of general study strategies.

Equally apparent was the fact that sensing had no significant relationship with the use of any learning strategy categories in the Ehrman and Oxford (1989) foreign language study. This means that sensing students in this study did not typically use strategies that were associated with effective language learning. Those sensing students who performed well typically mastered strategies that were more often used by intuitives. The general language performance of sensing students, as assessed by foreign language proficiency ratings, was far worse than that of intuitives.

In a follow-up case study of the same highly selective group of North American foreign language learners, Ehrman and Oxford (1990) saw a slightly different picture, particularly of sensing learners' strategies. These researchers discovered that sensing students reported a strong liking for memory strategies and were the only type group to do so. Sensing students also reported some use of cognitive and metacognitive strategies but (along with the judgers) rejected compensation strategies such as guessing. Intuitives, on the other hand, made extensive use of compensation strategies; they and the perceivers were the only ones to report frequent use of compensation strategies. Intuitives used some affective strategies.

In sum, Intuitives did much better than sensing types in terms of overall foreign language performance and learning strategy use in an intensive language instructional setting (Ehrman & Oxford, 1989, 1990). Sensing types showed great practical interest in facts and details and made choices that followed a clearly definable series of steps in a serial-processing mode. Many such learners disliked guessing strategies that involved ambiguity; the concrete, hands-on orientation of these learners was linked to a desire for unambiguous structure. Intuitives in the same studies searched for general patterns and principles. They preferred a random-access, parallel-processing mode of learning as though they owned the entire "language territory" from the start and did not have to inch their way along. They liked guessing strategies and were not upset by ambiguity.

In Ehrman and Oxford's (1995) study with the same kinds of foreign language learners, most tended to be intuitive. They showed characteristics such as abstract, imaginative, theoretical, intellectual, and original on the TDI. This is not the general tendency of the U.S. population, which is probably more sensing (Keirsey & Bates, 1984), as noted earlier. In the Ehrman and Oxford (1995) study, the most important scale on the MBTI regarding correlations with language proficiency ratings was sensing/intuition, in favor of the intuitive students. Again, intuitives compared with sensing students were far better foreign language learners. The TDI aspect that correlated best with language proficiency was "intellectual," an Intuitive characteristic, and this aspect was the most strongly related to language aptitude of any of the personality variables. Intuitives also outshined sensing learners on the use of cognitive strategies. Four of five sensing/intuition subscales on the TDI correlated with overall teacher ratings as a "good student," with intuition as the significant factor.

Sensing students who were termed "realistic" on the TDI tended to use social learning strategies, although there was little other significant correlation between sensing and learning strategy use. In a related study using analysis of variance (Ehrman, 1994), sensing types consistently showed lower language proficiency than intuitives.

Some cultures (such as many Far Eastern and Arabic-speaking countries) encourage development of a sensing personality type, which is reflected in foreign or second language learning. The sensing type of language learner often uses a restricted set of very structure-related language learning strategies such as memorization, planning, analysis, sequenced repetition, detailed outlines and lists, structured review, and a search for perfection. (See Oxford & Burry-Stock, 1995, regarding Taiwanese, mainland Chinese, Japanese, and Egyptian EFL students whose learning strategy use reflects the sensing personality type.) Arabic-speaking learners of EFL or ESL are particularly prone to verbatim memorization of long passages, which are often copied to enhance students' writing. Some language program administrators call this "plagiarism," but it is not considered such in Arabic countries. Many Korean students of ESL or EFL like following rules (Harshbarger et al., 1986), and this is usually a sign of a sensing personality type (Keirsey & Bates, 1984). More flexible strategies, though not always higher-order thinking strategies, and a more facilitative, nonauthoritarian view of teachers are often found among the pluralistic North Americans.

In Nuby's (1995) nonlanguage-learning study of high schoolers, Native Americans and African Americans were generally sensing, favoring linear, factual, hands-on learning with concrete results. However, when contrasting the two groups, Native Americans were somewhat more intuitive than African Americans in this study, although both groups were sensing.

Sensing/Intuition Conflicts

Here we see two sensing/intuition conflicts. In both cases, the teachers are sensing and the students intuitive. This stands to reason because Keirsey and Bates (1984) assert that the large majority of teachers (and of the U.S. population in general) are sensing.

Alicia's intuitive, feeling type made her typical of other Latin American students. Though she was born into a Spanish-speaking family, she grew up with English and later studied Spanish as a foreign language. She experienced severe difficulties with a sensing, thinking teacher of Spanish from the southeastern part of the United States. The feeling type has been briefly described before as making decisions emotionally, whereas the thinking type makes decisions through logical analysis. The main problem here is not feeling/thinking, however; it is the intuitive versus sensing contrast, in which Alicia is highly creative and the teacher is excessively dogmatic, overcorrecting, and rule-bound. Alicia explains:

> My style wars began in a graduate course [in Spanish literature]. The teacher and I are not compatible at all. My style of language learning is causing great friction with his teaching mode. I'm unhappy, I dread the class, and I'm under a great deal of stress in and out of the class. I am always prepared for the day's work, [but] I like to have fun while I'm learning. My teacher is close-minded. Everything has to be done his way. He is dogmatic and will not change his views or methods of teaching for anyone. . . . I'm a global learner; he likes to have everything detailed at length with no explanation given. I'm having to use rote memorization in order to study, and that is no joy; nothing has meaning, everything is just a blur. He is slow, and I'm impulsive, but not to the point that I do not take my studies seriously. He uses over-correction methods which really dampen the atmosphere of learning in the class . . . I do hope that I will make it to the end of the course without an ulcer or have a nervous breakdown before the exam. This has really been a nightmare and a very forceful style war in my learning career.

Intuitive David experienced a course in Spanish as a foreign language taught by a sensing teacher who disallowed David's intuitive creativity and communicative urges. To cover all the chapters, the Spanish teacher reverted to the worn-out comfort of the sensing, sequential, noncommunicative grammar-translation method. David explains what happened:

> In the course of the semester my feelings ranged from hopeful enthusiasm to disappointed frustration. The beginning of the semester started out well. The teacher was very energetic, friendly, and enthusiastic; she claimed she would only speak the target language, promised numerous chances for students to practice dialogues in "real life" situations, and the text and corresponding video seemed interesting, attractive, and flexible. But rapidly I came to recognize that her primary obligation [and her own desire] were to "cover" the required amount of material in the required amount of time. The students simply had to keep up or drop out. My hopes for a communicative class never materialized.

> Pages and pages of material, including dialogues, vocabulary lists, and new grammatical structures, were required for memorization each day, and nearly all of this was without being practiced or heard, and out of any context. The dialogues that were practiced in class usually consisted of about ten minutes of reading from the text with a partner. The video was generally fast-forwarded to the demonstration of new sounds, again out of context, which the students simultaneously read as they appeared and then practiced no more. The teacher's enthusiasm rapidly turned to ironic badgering as the students dropped further and further behind any sort of

"natural" or spontaneous ability to produce the language. It was a race to keep a handle on the basics of grammar and vocabulary so they could be identified on an exam. The teacher nearly always used English, or rather a mixture of the most elementary target language and English. . . . The essence of what was taught was grammar-translation, the most outdated, uninspiring, and unsuccessful method of foreign language teaching today.

THINKING/FEELING

Definitions and Theoretical Background

The *thinking versus feeling* dimension is the third aspect personality type, according to the Jungian-based work of Myers and McCaulley (1985). This aspect relates to how and why a person makes decisions, either via subjectivity (kindness, concern for emotions) or via objectivity (justice, concern for correctness). According to Keirsey and Bates (1984), roughly half of the U.S. population is thinking and the other half is feeling.

A *thinking* student of a foreign or second language is not readily concerned with social and emotional subtleties, except possibly as data for analytically understanding a particular problem or issue. This type of student makes decisions based on objective logic and analysis. The thinking person operates from an objective set of logical premises that lead inexorably to a conclusion. This individual believes that justice is more important than kindness. In the language classroom, the thinking person insists on analysis of language data. The thinking type is often highly critical of him- or herself, as well as of others, because of the high standards this person sets and the analytical evaluation this person applies.

Related to thinking is analytic processing. An *analytic* ("left-brain dominant") language student likes small details better than the overall picture. The analytic student has no trouble picking out significant details from a welter of background items and prefers language learning strategies that involve dissecting and logically analyzing the given material, searching for contrasts, and finding cause-effect relationships. Analytic learners do not like to guess without adequate time to reflect, nor do they like to use compensation strategies like paraphrasing when they do not know a particular word. They would rather look up the information and have it exactly right. Such strategies often slow down overly analytic students and keep them from obtaining sufficient conversational practice.

A *feeling* student of a second or foreign language is sensitive to social and emotional factors. His or her decision making is likely to be influenced by the feelings of others, the emotional climate, and personal and interpersonal values. The feeling person operates with a subjective constellation of values, emotions, and feelings. This person believes that kindness is more important than justice. In a language learning environment, the feeling person is more concerned about empathy with other learners, with the teacher, and with native speakers of the new language than about language analysis.

Associated with feeling is global processing. The language student with a *global* (sometimes called "right-brain dominant") style seeks the big picture right away. Global language learners usually choose holistic strategies such as guessing, predicting, searching for the main idea, and engaging in extensive communication. They dislike grammatical minutiae, avoid analysis, and enjoy compensation strategies like guessing, paraphrasing, or using synonyms. On the other hand, their lack of concern with accuracy sometimes causes global students to "fossilize" their errors early.

The contrast between thinking and feeling functioning appears to be at least somewhat related to *field independence versus field dependence*—the degree of ability to separate insignificant background details from truly significant details. Research on this theme started more than two decades ago (see a summary by Witkin & Goodenough, 1981) and has steadily developed with applications to foreign and second language learning (see Abraham, 1985; Hansen & Stansfield, 1981; Oxford, Ehrman, & Lavine, 1991). Abraham (1985) examined the field independence and field dependence of language students in relation to grammar teaching methods: analytic (rule-oriented, deductive) versus global (non-rule oriented, inductive). Abraham discovered that, as expected, field dependent students performed best in language classrooms where analysis was not emphasized, whereas field independent students excelled in classrooms where analysis was the dominant approach. Based on the work of Day (1984), Chapelle (1995), Chapelle and Roberts (1986), and Hansen and Stansfield (1981), we can point to some clear evidence that field independent (thinking) people do better on tests of grammatical accuracy. It would be expected that field dependent (feeling) students would outperform thinking students in communicative tasks, but more research is needed.

Cross-cultural Research

In a series of studies of highly sophisticated North American learners in an intensive foreign language instructional environment (Ehrman & Oxford, 1989, 1990), Thinking students showed characteristics that seemed to resemble reflectivity, analyzing not just the language but their own language performance as well. Some of these learners were highly self-critical, and their language performance was harmed by overreliance on negative and overly reflective thinking. Feeling people, who were more socially attuned than their thinking colleagues, often performed better on the predominantly communicative tasks in their program.

Ehrman and Oxford (1989) discovered that feeling students of foreign languages used more social strategies than thinking students. In addition, feeling students used significantly more general study strategies. Feeling students were overall better foreign language learners than were thinking students. In the follow-up case study (Ehrman & Oxford, 1990), the researchers found a dramatic contrast between the foreign language learning strategies of thinkers and feelers. Thinkers, perhaps because of their enjoyment of analysis, exhibited the strongest preference for cognitive strategies of any personality type, but feelers rejected most cognitive strategies, especially analysis. Thinkers commonly reported using metacognitive strategies, which were totally unreported by feelers. Thinkers rejected the social strategies so important to feelers or used them only with conscious effort.

In a later study with the same general group of foreign language learners, Ehrman and Oxford (1995) found that the majority were quite Thinking-oriented; on the other hand, they did show a few definite feeling tendencies, such as acceptance and tenderness on the TDI. In this study, Ehrman and Oxford found on the TDI that "questioning" (a thinking trait) correlated significantly with speaking proficiency. Students who reported themselves on the TDI as "defiant" (a thinking characteristic) were slightly ahead of their compliant classmates in both speaking and reading proficiencies. However, overall thinking/feeling had no significant relationship with proficiency, although certain subscales did.

Many Hispanic students, according to Harshbarger et al. (1986), are more global (therefore, feeling) than analytic (therefore, thinking). Indicators of this feeling orientation are that Hispanic students of ESL or EFL typically base judgments on the closeness of personal relationships rather than on logic, and they often express feelings openly (Oxford, Hollaway, & Murillo, 1992). Sometimes (though not indicated by Harshbarger et al.) Hispanic ESL or EFL students appear more impulsive than reflective. Also, Oxford and Burry-Stock (1995) discovered that Puerto Rican learners of EFL frequently use affective strategies and reflection to handle anxiety, thus underscoring a Hispanic tendency toward the feeling orientation.

By comparison, Japanese students of ESL or EFL generally desire that the teacher respect their privacy, are not forthcoming about their personal feelings, and tend to make judgments based on analysis and objectivity. Japanese students might be classified as more thinking than feeling (Oxford, Hollaway, & Murillo, 1992). (Like the Japanese, Korean ESL or EFL students want to avoid embarrassment and maintain privacy.)

In her nonlanguage-learning study, Nuby (1995) found that both African-American and Native American high school groups were thinking rather than feeling learners. It was interesting that both groups showed the same thinking personality type, just as they both exhibited extraversion and sensing.

Thinking/Feeling Conflicts

The following illustrations show thinking/feeling conflicts. In both, there is a conflict between a thinking teacher and a feeling student.

Joy, a global, feeling-oriented, intuitive North American student, ran into emotional and academic problems with an analytic, thinking-focused, sensing teacher of Chinese as a foreign language in the United States. She describes the situation:

> It seems that my predominant style is global with some bit of analytic showing forth at times. . . . I aim for perfection in written Chinese yet I do not aim for perfection in spoken Chinese, in terms of pronouncing the tones exact. (Chinese has four tones that we don't have—each word has a different meaning, according to tone.) My focus in verbal Chinese is communication, and I've learned that I can successfully communicate without giving a perfect "performance." This attitude toward the spoken language met with some conflict when I was being tutored by a Chinese teacher this past year. She was aiming for perfection in pronouncing the tones, and had me repeat words many times because my production of the word was not exactly correct. This led to a great deal of frustration on my part to the point of almost breaking into tears, reflecting my sensitive and feeling orientation, as I could not hear and reproduce the distinctive sounds she was demanding.

Allen, a feeling person, likewise felt a conflict with two thinking, accuracy-oriented, grammar-based foreign language teachers (the Russian teacher and the second Latin teacher) but experienced great comfort with a feeling teacher (the first Latin teacher). Notice the great affective waves apparent in his explanation:

> I took Russian in my sophomore year. In the first two weeks we covered the alphabet, and then we hit the grammar. I immediately got lost. I wanted to go back to the grammar. I got out of Russian by dropping the course.
>
> Then I took Latin. I had a very patient instructor who taught step-by-step and helped me extensively. I wanted personal attention, and he gave it in abundance. He was a Jesuit priest from Mexico who had taught for 30 years. He could be very strict, so some students thought he was an asshole, but I didn't. . . . He guided me very well, told lots of stories of the old country, and was very nostalgic. He showed tremendous patience, following the pace of every student. He made sure I understood everything. I got a B in the course and was happy, not anxious at all.

The next semester I got a new teacher of Latin. This second Latin teacher was very analytical, expecting you to know grammatical patterns, declensions, conjugations, and so on. I got a C and two Ds from that professor and felt very anxious and frustrated.

JUDGING/PERCEIVING

Definitions and Theoretical Background

Judging versus perceiving is the fourth personality type dimension highlighted by Myers and McCaulley (1985) and applied to the language classroom by Oxford, Ehrman, and Lavine (1991). Keirsey and Bates (1984) assert that approximately half of the U.S. population is judging and the other half is perceiving.

This dimension concerns the individual's degree of tolerance of ambiguity, which refers to acceptance of confusing situations for long periods of time. As noted by Ely (1995), language learning is fraught with uncertainty about meanings, referents, and pronunciation, so a degree of ambiguity tolerance is helpful to language learners.

Judging students of foreign or second languages are hardworking, organized, and planful; have a low tolerance for ambiguity; and possess a strong need for clarity. They want lesson directions and grammar rules to be clearly spelled out. Judging students are likely to plan language study sessions carefully and do lessons on time or early. To avoid ambiguity, they will sometimes jump to hasty conclusions. Such students avoid spontaneous conversations and games in the language classroom. They prefer to prepare their vocabulary lists and review the relevant grammar rules before any given social interaction using the language. Judging students, because of their fear of the frequent ambiguities of language learning, often suffer reduced risk-taking ability. Such students occasionally "freeze up," allowing their inhibitions to take over completely (Ely, 1995). Students who avoid risks are stalled by actual or anticipated criticism from others or by self-criticism that they themselves supply.

Students of foreign or second languages who are able to tolerate moderate to high levels of confusion, known as the *perceivers,* are likely to persist longer in language learning than students who are overly frightened by ambiguity. Perceivers do not worry about not comprehending everything because they readily accept a degree of confusion. They are noted for taking in lots of stimuli and postponing decisions or judgments. Compared with judgers, perceivers view language learning far less seriously, treating it like a game to be enjoyed rather than a set of tasks to be completed and judged. Perceiving can be a benefit in some situations, particularly those that require flexibility and the development of fluency, but a detriment in highly structured and traditional classrooms.

Judging/perceiving relates to some degree to the impulsive/reflective cognitive processing dimension. Most of the research on this dimension, called "conceptual tempo," was done in the 1970s. *Impulsive* (fast-inaccurate) students show quick and uncritical acceptance of initially accepted hypotheses. Overly impulsive students can be error-prone, both in the productive skills of writing and speaking and the receptive skills of listening and reading. *Reflective* (slow-accurate) students prefer systematic, analytic investigation of hypotheses and are usually accurate in their performance in all skills. Other possibilities are fast-accurate (always preferred but not typically achieved) and slow-inaccurate (the worst case). Note that judgers, who need rapid closure, can be either impulsive or fast-accurate. Perceivers, who prefer slow progress toward conclusions, can be either reflective or slow-inaccurate. Thus, the rapidity or slowness reflected in judging/perceiving does not determine the degree of accuracy.

Cross-cultural Research

Ely (1989) discovered that the degree of ambiguity tolerance significantly predicted U.S. students' choice of many (although not all) foreign language learning strategies. Similarly, Ehrman and Oxford (1989) found strong connections between judging/perceiving and learning strategy use in their study of carefully selected North American foreign language learners. In that study, judgers, who were in the great majority, showed a significant preference for general study strategies, which involve getting tasks done and completing assignments. Perceivers showed a significant preference over judgers in use of strategies for searching for and communicating meaning. This might have resulted from a moderate statistical correlation between intuition and perception (Myers & McCaulley, 1985). An important part of searching for and communicating meaning is staying open to further information in order to guess at meaning from context, even when there are unfamiliar elements. Perceiving students often used better (more communicatively oriented) foreign language learning strategies and were generally better language learners than judging students, who required rapid closure (Ehrman & Oxford, 1989).

Ehrman and Oxford (1990), in their follow-up case study research on foreign language learners, found that Judgers had a clear preference for metacognitive strategies such as planning and evaluation, which perceivers typically rejected. Judgers liked social strategies for instrumental rather than affiliative reasons (i.e., to get the job done). Judgers, who are uncomfortable with ambiguity, strongly rejected compensation strategies such as guessing, but perceivers enjoyed such strategies. Perceivers freely used cognitive strategies not mentioned by judgers, and they were the only group to indicate a spontaneous preference for affective strategies, which judgers rarely used. Judgers and perceivers were opposites in use of compensation, metacognitive, and social strategies.

In a later foreign language study, Ehrman and Oxford (1995) found that judging/perceiving as an overall dimension had no strong correlation with language proficiency. This might have occurred because perceiver flexibility (found to be helpful in an earlier study by Ehrman & Oxford, 1989) is balanced within the perceivers themselves in the 1995 study by judging persistence and self-disciplined hard work. In the 1995 study, students who were rated as planful, systematic, and methodical (all judging traits) on the TDI were also found to be frequent users of metacognitive strategies for planning and evaluating. Therefore, the use of metacognitive strategies for foreign language learning seems to be linked with an orderly, judging personality.

Many ESL and EFL students come from cultures in which ambiguity is not tolerated well and judging is encouraged. Harshbarger et al. (1986) noted that Korean students of ESL or EFL insist that the teacher be the authority and are disturbed if this does not happen. Japanese students of ESL or EFL, though reflective themselves, often want rapid and constant correction from the teacher and do not feel comfortable with multiple correct answers. Many Asian students in various subject areas, according to Sue and Kirk (1972), are less autonomous, more dependent on authority figures, and more obedient and conforming to deadlines than students from other cultural backgrounds.

Arabic-speaking learners of ESL or EFL often see things in black/white, right/wrong terms and sometimes refuse to compromise; to these students, written texts take on an "always correct" aura, and the teacher who accepts more than one answer as right seems weak or ignorant (Oxford, Hollaway, & Murillo, 1992). Note that this can occur among more conservative groups in many different cultures.

In comparison, Hispanic ESL or EFL students are not described by Harshbarger et al. (1986) in such very judging, closure-focused terms. They appear more flexible about deadlines, dates, and clarity. In fact, the *mañana* concept (putting things off until tomorrow) fits well with a more perceiving persona. A concern for social harmony might lead Hispanic students to a greater desire for flexibility, which is characteristic of the perceiving person.

Judging/perceiving was the only dimension in which Native American and African-American high school students truly differed, and this difference was between perceiving for the Native Americans and mixed type for the African Americans, according to Nuby's (1995) general, nonlanguage-learning study. In her study, Native Americans demonstrated a need for flexibility, variety, novelty, and change and a powerful desire for unstructured classrooms. African Americans in this investigation exhibited a mixed preference for judging and perceiving. Their need for closure, stasis, and structure was approximately equalled by their opposite need for flexibility, change, and spontaneity.

Compared to North American students, Japanese learners show greater reflection in any subject area (Condon, 1984). This is demonstrated by Japanese ESL and EFL students' concern for precision and for not taking quick risks in conversation (Oxford, Hollaway, & Murillo, 1992; Oxford & Lavine, 1992). Quite typical is the "Japanese student who wants time to arrive at the correct answer and is uncomfortable when making guesses" (Nelson, 1995, p. 16).

In nonlanguage-learning studies, Native American learners sometimes appear overly perceiving—or even passive or uninterested. A reluctance to try something too soon and the fear of being "shamed" (equivalent to the fear of "losing face" in other cultures) may account for the seemingly unresponsive classroom attitude of Native American students (Longstreet, 1978).

Judging/Perceiving Conflicts

Two conflicts between judging and perceiving are shown below. One is a cross-cultural clash between a group of mostly perceiving Japanese and a group of mostly judging North Americans, and the other is a disharmony between a judging student and a perceiving teacher.

The first judging/perceiving clash was reported by Mary, an EFL teacher who was one of the judgers needing rapid closure (and less reflection time) in a cross-cultural situation in Japan:

> Discussion of cultural conflicts [in personality types] reminded me of a faculty meeting I attended some years back when I participated in an English summer school for Japanese students. The purpose of the meeting was to collect ideas for the culminating event of the summer. The American teachers, accustomed to brainstorming, immediately began throwing out ideas, waiting for some to be rejected and some to be explored. The Japanese, whose words are as weighty as deeds, did not respond to the ideas or propose any of their own. A deep silence settled over the room. Soon the Americans began jiggling keys in their pockets and moving uncomfortably in their chairs. The Japanese allowed the silence to continue while the stress of the room built, until finally one teacher proposed a well-thought-out activity that everyone could approve. The meeting ended with satisfied Japanese and strung-out Americans.

The second judging/perceiving clash shows Cassandra, a graduate student in French as a foreign language, who was in conflict with her perceiving professor. She explains:

> My first graduate class was taught by a professor who was obviously totally opposite from me. His directions for the papers he assigned were ambiguous and auditory. Each time I would write a paper, he would grade the paper differently. He would give no specific reason why! I felt frustrated. . . . The next semester I was teamed with an analytic, closure-oriented [Judging] professor who handed out a seven-page syllabus. He left no stone unturned. I was at home.

I have now described and illustrated the four personality type dimensions and presented type conflicts in the words of the people involved. Next comes a description of a study of ESL teacher-student personality type conflicts. These conflicts had a direct effect on students' grades.

A STUDY OF PERSONALITY TYPE CONFLICTS AND THEIR INFLUENCE ON TEACHERS' EVALUATIONS OF ESL STUDENTS

In a study of teacher-student personality type differences in a multicultural university ESL program, Wallace and Oxford (1992) found that students and teachers experienced conflicts 82% of the time, that is, in 326 out of 396 possible comparisons of personality type dimensions. The instrument used was the Keirsey Temperament Sorter (Keirsey & Bates, 1984), which covers the four personality type dimensions described earlier.

In this study, the ESL students were significantly more extraverted (47%) than their North American teachers (27%), and the teachers were dramatically more thinking (55%) than their students (19%). The teachers did not appear to be clearly representative of the U.S. population, which is far more extraverted and slightly more balanced in thinking/feeling than this teaching cadre. The greater extraversion and feeling orientation of the students suggested greater personal and interpersonal sensitivity, as contrasted with more impersonal objectivity on the part of the teachers in this sample. However, the teacher-student differences on the sensing/intuition and judging/perceiving dimensions were not as striking. Wallace and Oxford felt that cultural influences were a major contributor to the personality type differences.

Wallace and Oxford discovered that, in the *writing* area, personality type differences between students and teachers consistently and negatively affected student' ESL grades, whereas type congruence positively influenced students' ESL grades. In *reading* and *grammar*, type differences negatively affected ESL grades for significant numbers of students. However, type conflicts did not affect students' ESL grades in *speaking* in the Wallace and Oxford study.

Thus, clashes in personality types can have a dangerously detrimental effect on student grades, particularly when teachers do not understand these conflicts. Instructors who are more familiar with and accepting of type disharmony are no doubt less likely to downgrade the students whose type differs from their own. Now I offer some practical suggestions for handling personality type in the language classroom. These recommendations are helpful for all other kinds of classrooms as well.

PRACTICAL SUGGESTIONS FOR DEALING WITH PERSONALITY TYPE IN THE LANGUAGE CLASSROOM

Here are some recommendations for dealing with different personality types in the foreign or second language classroom:

1. *Assess the personality type of both the teacher and the students.* Assessment instruments such as the Myers-Briggs Type Indicator (Myers & McCaulley, 1985), the Type Differentiation Indicator (Saunders, 1989), and the Keirsey Temperament Sorter (Keirsey & Bates, 1984) are useful in determining each individual's personality type. These instruments are sensitive to the kinds of type differences that are affected by culture. Sharing general information about the results demonstrates the teacher's interest not only in what students learn but also in how students act and how they process information. It can also establish a good foundation from which to teach new language learning strategies.

A whole-class discussion of the personality type assessment results is crucial so students see that the foreign or second language class is indeed a mixture of types. This kind of discussion is particularly important in a second language class, where people usually represent many cultures and where personality types might therefore be extremely heterogeneous. Such a discussion is also helpful in foreign language classes, where the cultural diversity of the learners may be less than in a second language classroom but where there are likely to be varied personality types nonetheless.

I have personally found in Russian, German, Spanish, ESL, and EFL classes (as well as in nonlanguage classes) that students are intensely interested in discovering their own personality types and the types of their peers and teachers. When type discussions are constructive, students' initial interest in self-awareness is rewarded and deepened.

2. *Alter teaching strategies in order to offer a wide range of activities that fit the needs of students of all types.* Ellis (1989) points out that language teaching strategies should be matched when possible to the students' personality types or learning styles. "Matching is best achieved

by the teacher catering for individual needs during the moment-by-moment process of teaching (i.e., by emphasizing group dynamics and offering a range of activity types)" rather than by assigning students and teachers together based on personality type or learning style (p. 260). Without help, students can occasionally adapt on their own—but this causes students to suffer "some cost to their own ease of mind and the type of proficiency they develop" (p. 260).

Though language teachers cannot be expected to change their personality types, they can alter their teaching strategies to provide a variety of activities to meet the needs of different students' personality types. Again, this is particularly essential in a second language setting because a myriad of greatly different personality types (often related to different home cultures) will be the rule, not the exception. In foreign language classes, where students tend to come from similar cultural backgrounds, personality type differences are probably less dramatic but nevertheless exist.

To cope with the students' differences in personality type, teachers of second or foreign languages can consciously decide to offer a range of multisensory, abstract and concrete learning activities that meet the needs of many students (Oxford, Ehrman, & Lavine, 1991). Teachers can provide some activities that tap the subjective warmth of the Feeling type and other tasks that encourage the objectivity and precision of the Thinking type. Teachers can offer some activities that allow students to work alone (for the Introvert) and some activities that foster extended interaction (for the extravert). Intuitives and perceivers will thrive with tasks that stimulate invention, multiple possibilities, and openness, and sensing students will prefer activities that involve concrete, sequential, single-right-answer work. All of these options are possible in the classroom of the teacher who is aware of personality type differences, but they do not frequently occur in classrooms of teachers who do not understand type differences and needs.

3. *Provide variety in grouping of students.* The extravert is more than eager to express some ideas orally in the presence of several or many class members. The introvert may need some encouragement to share ideas aloud and may want the safety of jotting down a few notes first and perhaps sharing with one other person before being invited or expected to participate in a group discussion. Cooperative learning structures are highly applicable to the language classroom and can accommodate both introverted and extraverted students. Noting in the lesson plan where there is provision for large-group, small-group, pair, and individual response is a good idea.

Teachers can put students in groups according to their personality types from time to time. By this I mean identifying a single personality type dimension, such as sensing/intuition or extraversion/introversion, that appears to make a difference in a particular classroom population. Based on this single dimension (rather than all four of the dimensions, which taken together can become a bit complex for group-management planning), try type-alike groups for greatest efficiency. Also use type-varied groups for generating greater flexibility of ideas and behaviors. Working with people whose types are different from their own helps students to understand themselves and their colleagues—as long as any conflicts are discussed tactfully and insightfully. Teachers should avoid grouping Introverts with each other all the time. It is often helpful to include perceiving students and judging students in the same group; the former will make learning more lively and more fun, and the latter will ensure that the task is done on time and in good order.

Grouping brings up a host of cultural issues related to the nature of the individual versus the group. In a second language classroom, with many cultures present, grouping might need to be done more carefully and with greater sensitivity than in a foreign language classroom, in which students often come from a single home culture.

4. *Prepare a learning environment that welcomes and accommodates a variety of personality types.* The language learning environment can establish the class climate as either exclusive, limiting which personality types are accepted, or inclusive, welcoming many varied personality types. Second and foreign language instructors can enhance their success and that of their students by displaying a keen interest in personality types.

Through the use of cultural and linguistic displays in the foreign or second language classroom, the teacher can do much to eliminate or lessen conflicts in personality type. An eclectic room that sends messages like "There are many different ways to experience the language" is a room that encourages learners with varied personality types to feel at home, regardless of their background culture. Bulletin boards containing photographs of former classes at work can do much to establish a warm, accepting class climate. Snapshots of students working together in small groups or involved in a lively discussion let extraverts know there will be time for interaction, while some photos of students doing individual research reassure Introverts about the balance of individual and group activities. Bulletin boards or display cases can send positive messages to students. Those that feature highly creative art projects or models constructed by students can stimulate intuitive learners. Step-by-step, orderly posters of grammar and vocabulary (done by sensing students) can provide a means of expression for those students. Environmental alterations like these, particularly those that have a multicultural rather than a monocultural emphasis, can help learners of all personality types feel they belong in the classroom.

5. *Change the way personality type conflicts are viewed.* Foreign and second language teachers can help students see type differences as opportunities for growth, rather than paralysis. They can make communication about type contrasts an ongoing process that is a part of the total language class experience. In this way students can continue to learn from the experiences of others as well as increase their own self-awareness of personality type.

CONCLUDING COMMENT

The importance of personality types in the foreign or second language classroom is immense, as demonstrated in this chapter. Research results show that personality types affect students' choice of learning strategies and their ultimate language proficiency (both in literacy and oracy, as defined at the beginning of this chapter). Evidence is also presented in this chapter about key cultural differences in every dimension of personality type.

Language teachers who do not comprehend the significance of teacher-student clashes in personality type appear to evaluate their students somewhat unfairly and probably do not provide adequate instructional diversity. Teachers who are well informed about personality type are likely to be more willing to adjust their instructional strategies to accommodate learners' diverse needs and to grade equitably, without projecting their own type preferences onto their students.

Second and foreign language teachers around the world should heed this chapter's recommendations concerning attention to personality type. Doing so would make the language classroom a warmer, more inclusive place where learners experience greater success. When learners experience greater progress, teachers feel more successful as well.

REFERENCES

Abraham, R. (1985). Field dependence/independence in the teaching of grammar. *TESOL Quarterly, 19*(4), 680-702.

Chapelle, C. (1995). Field-dependence/field independence in the L2 classroom. In J. Reid (Ed.), *Learning styles in the ESL/EFL classroom* (pp. 158-168). Boston: Heinle & Heinle.

Chapelle, C., & Roberts, C. (1986). Ambiguity tolerance and field independence as predictors of proficiency in English as a second language. *Language Learning, 36,* 27-45.

Cheung, F. (1985). *Therapy with Asian families.* Washington, DC: Center for Minority Group Mental Health Programs, National Institute of Mental Health.

Condon, J. (1984). *With respect to the Japanese.* Yarmouth, ME: Intercultural Press.

Day, R. (1984). Student participation in the ESL classroom or some imperfections of practice. *Language Learning, 34,* 69-98.

Ehrman, M. (1994). The Type Differention Indicator and adult language learning success. *Journal of Psychological Type, 30,* 10-29.

Ehrman, M., & Oxford, R. (1989). Effects of sex differences, career choice, and psychological type on adult language learning strategies. *Modern Language Journal 73,* 1-13.

Ehrman, M., & Oxford, R. (1990). Adult language learning styles and strategies in an intensive training setting. *Modern Language Journal, 74,* 311-327.

Ehrman, M., & Oxford, R. (1995). Cognition plus: Correlates of language proficiency. *Modern Language Journal, 79*(1), 67-89.

Ellis, R. (1989). Classroom learning styles and their effect on second language acquisition: A study of two learners. *System, 17,* 249-262.

Ely, C.M. (1989). Tolerance of ambiguity and use of second language learning strategies. *Language Learning, 36,* 1-25.

Ely, C.M. (1995). Tolerance of ambiguity and the teaching of ESL. In J. Reid (Ed.), *Learning styles in the ESL/EFL classroom* (pp. 87-95). Boston: Heinle & Heinle.

Gregorc, A. (1979). *Style Delineator.* Maynard, MA: Gabriel Systems.

Hansen, J., & Stansfield, C. (1981). The relationship of field dependent-independent cognitive styles to foreign language achievement. *Language Learning, 31*(2), 349-367.

Harshbarger, B., Ross, T., Tafoya, S., & Via, J. (1986, April). *Dealing with multiple learning styles in the ESL classroom.* Symposium presented at the annual meeting of Teachers of English to Speakers of Other Languages, San Francisco, CA.

Hofstede, G. (1986). Cultural differences in teaching and learning. *International Journal of Intercultural Relations, 10,* 301-320.

Hudson-Ross, S., & Dong, Y.R. (1990). Literacy learning as a reflection of language and culture: Chinese elementary school education. *The Reading Teacher, 44,* 110-123.

Keirsey, D., & Bates, M. (1984). *Please understand me.* Del Mar, CA: Prometheus.

Lawrence, G. (1984). A synthesis of learning style research involving the MBTI. *Journal of Psychological Type, 8,* 2-15.

Longstreet, E. (1978). *Aspects of ethnicity.* New York: Teachers College Press.

Myers, I., & McCaulley, M. (1985). *Manual: A guide to the development and use of the Myers-Briggs Type Indicator.* Palo Alto, CA: Consulting Psychologists Press.

Nelson, G. (1995). Cultural differences in learning styles. In J. Reid (Ed.), *Learning styles in the ESL/EFL classroom* (pp. 3-18). Boston, MA: Heinle & Heinle.

Nuby, J.F. (1995). *Learning styles: A comparative analysis of the learning styles of Native American and African-American students.* Unpublished doctoral dissertation, University of Alabama, Tuscaloosa, AL.

Oxford, R.L. (1993). Instructional implications of gender differences in language learning styles and strategies. *Applied Language Learning, 3,* 1-35.

Oxford, R.L. (1995). Gender differences in language learning styles: What do they mean? In J. Reid (Ed.), *Learning styles in the ESL/EFL classroom* (pp. 34-46). Boston: Heinle & Heinle.

Oxford, R.L., & Burry-Stock, J.A. (1995). Assessing the use of language learning strategies worldwide with the ESL/EFL version of the Strategy Inventory for Language Learning (SILL). *System, 23*(2), 153-175.

Oxford, R., Ehrman, M., & Lavine, R. (1991). Style wars: Teacher-student style conflicts in the language classroom. In S. S. Magnan (Ed.), *Challenges in the 1990s for college foreign language programs* (pp. 1-25). Boston: Heinle & Heinle.

Oxford, R.L., Hollaway, M.E., & Murillo, D. (1992). Language learning styles: Research and practical considerations for teaching in the multicultural tertiary ESL/EFL classroom. *System, 20*(4), 439-456.

Oxford, R., & Lavine, R. (1992). Teacher-student style wars in the language classroom: Research insights and suggestions. *ADFL Bulletin, 23,* 38-45.

Reid, J. (1987). The learning style preferences of ESL students. *TESOL Quarterly, 21*(1), 87-111.

Rossi-Le, L. (1995). Learning style and strategies in adult immigrant ESL students. In J. Reid (Ed.), *Learning styles in the ESL/EFL classroom* (pp. 118-125). Boston: Heinle & Heinle.

Saunders, D. (1989). *Type Differentiation Indicator manual.* Palo Alto, CA: Consulting Psychologists Press.

Sue, D.W., & Kirk, B.A. (1972). Psychological characteristics of Chinese-American students. *Journal of Counseling Psychology, 19,* 471-478.

Wallace, B., & Oxford, R. (1992). Disparity in learning styles and teaching styles in the ESL classroom: Does this mean war? *AMTESOL Journal, 1,* 45-68.

Willing, K. (1988). *Learning styles in adult migrant education.* Adelaide: National Curriculum Resource Centre.

Witkin, H., & Goodenough, D. (1981). Cognitive styles: Essence and origins—field dependence and independence. *Psychological Issues,* Monograph 51.

PART TWO

Personality and Professional Literacy

Chapter 9

The Psycholinguistics of Revising*

Alice S. Horning
Oakland University

Despite lots of interest and concern about teaching the writing process in recent years, remarkably little of substance is known about revising as an aspect of the process. Much of what has been written about revising seems self-evident. Perhaps researchers feel they already know everything they need to know from the work done in the early 1980s (Gebhardt, 1983; Sommers, 1980). Perhaps revising is so often conflated with editing that writing texts and other works that deal with the writing process present it as kind of a last step just before writing is offered to readers. Perhaps revising is not as important as prewriting, drafting, appropriate use of sources where relevant, and other issues, or perhaps it is so integrated with these processes as to be impossible to analyze separately. Revising is not well understood and deserves a lot more attention. Insights about revising that lead to useful strategies in teaching are available through research showing the relationship of revising behavior to personality preferences.

---

*I thank the following for their assistance with this project: Wallis Andersen, Carole Crum, Naomi Quenk, and Catherine Rush.

Revising is a key part of the writing process. As writing pedagogy and assessment move toward the use of student portfolios, revised work will be an essential part of student abilities examined for evidence of writing skill (White, 1994). More attention and a different kind of attention to revising is thus warranted. The studies reported here will demonstrate that revising behavior is shaped by the personality preferences of the writer, whether student or expert; in addition, the findings suggest that by contrast to students, expert writers revise more effectively. Experts can shift to nonpreferred strategies, making use of their inferior functions in revision more easily than can students, and do so when there are emotional issues at stake.

The studies to be presented examine how both students and mature, capable writers engage in the revision process. To examine the influence of personality type, both student subjects and the expert writers have completed the Myers-Briggs Type Indicator. The studies examine individual cases of revising by students working on typical undergraduate research papers and cases of revising by experts working on varied types of documents. Because of the close analysis of text changes involved, a multiple-case case study format has been used for this research. The students' documents are fairly uniform in that they are all formal research reports prepared for a first-year college research writing course. The expert writers' documents include a letter of recommendation, a performance appraisal, and a memo. One expert is a Ph.D. candidate and revised a section of her dissertation for the study. The variation in the types of documents worked on by experts is another reason why a case study analysis is valuable. The contrast between the students and the experts sheds light on ways to help student writers move into the expert category.

REVIEW OF THE LITERATURE

The theory being tested here derives from general views of revising in the theory and pedagogy of writing. For example, a standard handbook on writing, newly revised, divides revising into macro and micro revision (Mulderig, 1995). Macro revision focuses on the "larger elements that make an essay successful . . . focus . . . organization . . . evidence" (p. 200), whereas micro revision addresses sentences, diction, and other changes sometimes associated with editing. The author offers suggestions for using peer and instructor critiques in writing, and then goes on to discuss paragraph development, paragraph coherence, sentence-level changes, and revisions to diction (p. 226-293). Similarly, Frank Smith's (1994) psycholinguistic analysis of writing makes a distinction between editing ("cleaning up the text," p. 127) and review, which he defines as "writers reading a text for their own purposes" (p. 127). Beyond these basic distinctions, discussions of writing and revising give generic advice but do not look at the process itself and how it is shaped by writers' personality preferences. Previous research offers some insights on how people with different personality preferences typically approach revising, and these insights support the hypotheses under study here.

The first hypothesis states that personality type shapes the revising processes of both student and expert writers. In this area, the seminal work is that of George Jensen and John DiTiberio (1989) on personality and teaching composition. In their discussion, Jensen and DiTiberio present findings from both beginning and expert writers, and the findings allow them to synthesize the different types' approaches to writing and revising. Although there is more to the influence of type on writing than how each individual dimension influences writers' work on revision tasks, the following observations make a good starting point for analysis of revision strategies. Jensen and DiTiberio describe, in the "Handouts on Personality and Writing" included in their book, each dimension's typical revising strategies as follows:

Extraverts: Discussing drafts with others helps them both to realize the need for revision and to understand what needs to be revised. Some (especially if J) may not revise unless they receive spoken feedback. Their first drafts tend to need editing out of unrelated material. Those ideas that remain can be written about in greater depth.

Introverts: They spend more time than extraverts between drafts considering revisions. They may, as a result, revise more extensively. Throughout the writing process, they tend to write alone, asking for advice only from close friends or during private sessions with teachers. When revising, they may need to relate their ideas to experience.

Sensing: Even during a first draft, they closely attend to mechanics (grammar, spelling, handwriting, etc.). Similarly, they often tend to view revising as merely "correcting" or proofreading. They should be encouraged, when revising, to explain the implications of the data presented in the first draft by adding or rewriting topic sentences, thesis statements, summaries and so forth.

Intuitive: Their revisions may be more effective if they resolve the unnecessary complexities of their ideas, check their facts, and as a *last* step, clean up the mechanics of spelling, punctuation and the like.

Thinking: They value feedback that is given with a clear rationale (such as, "It is important for you to provide more details so that your reader will better understand your ideas"). In revising, they may need to enliven their writing with some personal examples and qualify blunt statements.

Feeling: If overly criticized, they may wish to ignore revising or writing in general; when revising, they may need to clarify the content and improve their organization.

Judging: When revising, they need to reevaluate decisions that may have been made hastily or arbitrarily, more thoroughly analyze their ideas, expand their writing to clarify or qualify, and improve transitions.

Perceiving: Their first drafts tend to be long and thorough but also too inclusive. When revising, they may need to cut down the length of the paper or to refocus its direction. (pp. 171-177)

These preferences play themselves out in different ways with different individual writers, as do all aspects of personality type. The strategies typical for each dimension are generally confirmed in the data from both student and expert writers to be discussed later.

It is already clear that expert writers deal with text in ways influenced by their type. I have demonstrated previously that expert writers respond to texts in ways that are influenced by their personality type (Horning, 1993). These responses focus on two text features: cohesion, which makes a text a unified whole rather than a disconnected series of sentences, and redundancy, which provides psycholinguistic insurance that the message sent will be received accurately. In particular, my previous research suggests that intuitives have a strong preference for cohesion "because it supports the relationships among ideas in a text, and also . . . redundancy, because, at least at the discourse level, the use of such redundancy is precisely to reveal the larger patterns of the ideas in the text" (p. 158).

My findings show that thinking and feeling types both seek structure in a text, and although the specific kind of structure differs at each end of the dimension, the overall preference is for textual structure to be signalled clearly by markers of cohesion or redundancy. Similarly, viewing types in terms of temperament, following the ideas of Keirsey and Bates (1984), both intuitive-thinking temperaments and intuitive-feeling temperaments show special sensitivity to language and respond in ways consistent with their type results when temperament is considered (Horning, 1993).

The second hypothesis under study here states that expert writers revise more effectively due to their ability to make use of nonpreferred strategies from their inferior functions; expert writers make this use of nonpreferred strategies when they are writing about emotional issues. Expert writers have been studied some in the literature in composition, chiefly in terms of workplace writing situations (e.g., Couture & Rymer, 1993). With the exception of Jay Woodruff's (1993) interviews, four out of five of which are with creative writers, not much attention has been paid recently to the revising processes of expert writers.

Expert writers can turn to nonpreferred strategies from their inferior functions when their preferences do not work well for them in revising. The inferior function is the least developed function in the structure of personality according to Jung. In Quenk's (1993) discussion, the inferior is thought to erupt under conditions of fatigue, illness, and stress, as well as under the influence of any mind-altering drug. Quenk points out that not every episode of these conditions will necessarily cause an eruption of the inferior. She also notes that from Isabel Briggs Myers's (1980) point of view, the inferior could provide a new and useful perspective. This potential usefulness of the inferior is demonstrated by the cases to be discussed here. These expert writers were clearly writing in conditions they perceived as stressful when they made positive use of strategies consistent with their inferior functions.

The literature, then, shows that writers approach revision in ways that are consistent with their type preferences. Both student writers and expert writers show this clearly in the documents to be examined later. In addition, however, the study of expert writers engaged in revising shows that they produce better writing due to their ability to use nonpreferred strategies. The purpose of these studies is to demonstrate the role of type in revising and writers' various abilities to use both preferred and nonpreferred strategies when revising documents.

Because revision will become more important in portfolio-based evaluation of writing both within courses and across courses in program assessment, a fuller understanding of revising strategies is essential. Specifically, two hypotheses are to be examined in studies of student and expert writers. The first hypothesis states that revising behavior is consistent with personality preferences, following the work of Jensen and DiTiberio. The second hypothesis states that, by contrast to student writers, expert writers revise more effectively because they can shift to nonpreferred strategies more easily and effectively and do so especially when there are emotional issues at stake.

STUDY 1: STUDENT WRITERS REVISING

The literature in rhetoric and composition studies has for years focused on ways to encourage students to develop their writing process, suggesting strategies for prewriting and revising in addition to focusing on the final product. In general, the discipline has stressed the need to have students learn how to engage in the parts of writing, with less stress on the final outcome. Some of the current interest in portfolios of student work comprises another attempt to move students to focus on process and "show their work" through the stages of drafting and revision, rather than just the final paper. Students, however, still worry about the grade they get, usually based largely on the final outcome. In studying students' revising processes, it is difficult to see the impact of personality type, because their focus is so often on correctness and satisfying teachers' requirements. The student writers' data provide, as a result, only limited evidence. To examine both hypotheses, the research papers of four student writers have been analyzed.

Method

Subjects. The subjects are all students in a course in research paper writing at a medium-sized, public university in the midwest. The course is the second semester of a standard two-term writing requirement for most students in the institution. All students have given written permission for their work to be used anonymously in research and to disclose their Myers-Briggs Type Indicator results and other details of their cases. They are all traditional-age college students, and all are native speakers of English. The papers address some aspect of career exploration, broadly defined, consistent with issues under discussion in the classes for which these papers were written. The assignment usually occurs in the second half of the semester, after the students have had formal library instruction and have worked on other writing tasks to develop research skills and strategies for argumentation. Four students who voluntarily provided the initial draft of their research report, a full set of peer responses, and a copy of the final draft were included in the data set.

Materials and Procedure. The materials available for analysis for the purposes of the study include the students' drafts of their research papers, peer feedback on an informal questionnaire sheet in which the respondents' personality types are known, and the final draft of the paper. These materials were analyzed in terms of both the role of personality type in presentation of the ideas in the paper and organizational and editorial changes. Changes from draft version to final version were analyzed in terms of the two hypotheses under study. The procedure for analysis involved considering the personality type of the writer and the typical writing behavior of that type as described by Jensen and DiTiberio (quoted earlier). On each dimension, the data were examined in terms of changes from the draft to the final version.

Results on Hypothesis 1

The student papers were examined first to see if they showed that personality type shapes the revising processes of student writers. There is some evidence from these cases to suggest support for this hypothesis. The evidence is limited, as previously noted, due to students' general concerns with grades and correctness. Jensen and DiTiberio describe the typical strategies of each type, and these strategies do appear in limited ways in the revising behavior of these writers.

Student 1, for example, whose type preference is ENFP, has a draft that shows some deletion of extraneous material, typical of an extraverted writer. One such change, in the section dealing with preparation to be a teacher, is the deletion of the sentence "During these years, general education requirements are being finished, while introductory courses in education are begun." The writer also asked about some technical points, typical of an intuitive type. She needed help with organization and worked on this in response to a listing of her main points by a thinking reader by marking the draft with several different colors of highlighter. Finally, all readers told this writer her summary was too long (more than one typed double-spaced page) and that she needed to cut and refocus it, a typical problem of the perceiving writer.

Student 2, ESFJ, does not show much deletion of extraneous material but did ask for help with technical points from the readers of her draft. She shows many corrections of grammar, mechanics, and other technical problems on the draft. This writer shows few changes to organizational structure, a typical need of feeling writers, but she did expand the opening in a substantive way by adding definitions of key terms, consistent with her judging preference. The sentences she added are as follows: "RNs work with a variety of people and have a broad field to decide from. On the other hand, midwives work mainly with expectant mothers and their families, helping them before, during and after their pregnancy."

Student 3, INFP, seems to have kept her revising processes more private. In this case, there are very few changes written on the draft (all students were using word processing to some degree), perhaps consistent with the introverted preference of Student 3. Typical of intuitives, this writer left behind numerous technical errors and spelling problems, despite the availability of spell check. This writer did make a substantive change in her opening from draft to final version, clarifying her overall presentation by adding a list of issues to be discussed and by saying that she was unsure if the career she researched was a sound choice for her. This clarification is the kind of change Jensen and DiTiberio say intuitive writers typically need to make. Also in this case, there was a problem with the ending being too long and somewhat unfocused, consistent with the writer's perceiving preference.

Student 4, ISFJ, shows the typical sensing ability to produce a clean draft in terms of technical matters. This writer did some reorganization of her draft to create the final version, consistent with her feeling preference. The paper also shows the writer's judging preference in that she expanded the draft by one full page to create the final version, and as part of the expansion, this writer lengthened her opening and strengthened her thesis. Her thesis in the draft was as follows: "In this paper, I will discuss the rights parents have now, what Europe offers compared to the United States, what steps U.S. companies have taken towards a national policy, and the job options available." By the final version, the thesis had become: "If the government would make more progress towards a policy [for parental leave], parents would not have to work as hard in the debate with their employers about a leave." The final version of the thesis much more clearly reflects the writer's point, chiefly because it goes beyond listing the issues to be discussed to state the main idea the writer wants to convey.

In each case discussed, then, there is some limited evidence to suggest that these student writers go about revising in ways consistent with their personality types. Yet, type does not control the process, nor is there evidence of revision consistent with every dimension of personality in every case. In fact, what seems to be driving much of the change in the student papers from draft to final version is the students' perception of the need for correctness and their perceptions of instructors' priorities. Thus, there is limited support for the first hypothesis among the student writers.

Results on Hypothesis 2

The student papers were examined a second time to see if student writers show an ability to shift their revising strategies and use nonpreferred strategies effectively. Because the research papers under study do not appear to raise emotional issues for students, it is difficult to see whether such shifts in strategy occur when students work on this type of task. Because students usually respond favorably to type descriptions in terms of both their lives outside school and in terms of their writing, they can approach revising tasks more easily if they are offered strategies that come from the opposite end of each dimension than where their preference lies. So, for instance, sensing types may be so focused in revising on the details of the text that they do not pay enough attention to their meaning. On the other hand, intuitive types do not attend enough to the details of the text. Each can profit from working at the other end of the dimension and/or from getting feedback from readers who are their opposites on one dimension or another.

Collaborative work in a personality preference context becomes highly valuable when writers can get responses from readers with differing preferences and see how to use alternative, nonpreferred strategies to improve their writing. However, students need to be told about this specifically because, at least in these data, they do not make much use of nonpreferred strategies or advice from readers of opposite type. Student 1, ENFP, for instance, had three readers of her draft, ESFJ, ENTJ, and ESTP.

All of them agreed that the last paragraph of the draft was too long, even the perceiving reader. In response to the suggestions, however, the writer still ended up with a summary paragraph that is more than one full typed page in length. Similarly, both thinking readers suggest to Student 1 that she reorganize the paper, and she was able to make some changes, although not enough to create a clear structure for her discussion. Finally, the two sensing readers both ask for a listing in the opening of the main issues to be discussed in the body. Although the writer was able to add an opening paragraph, and although she went through the draft to see the points she had covered, she was not able to provide such a list of points to be discussed.

Student 2, ESFJ, had all extraverts reading her paper, and all were perceiving types. In this case, though, the most interesting response came from the NT reader, who went through the draft and reworded many awkward sentences and rephrased them at a number of points. In the draft, for instance, the writer had said: "Now with becoming a midwife there are a few more obstacles the student must go through." The NT reader revised this to read: "Becoming a midwife presents a few more obstacles for the student to overcome." The writer took this change and incorporated it into the final draft. The NT reader noted on the peer response sheet that she understood the issues discussed in the paper and offered a list of these on the response sheet, but said the paper needed "wording changes," which she made on the draft. The writer incorporated virtually all the wording changes offered by the NT reader and also made more clear her preference for one career (registered nursing) over another (midwifery) in the opening paragraph. These revisions suggest that the writer was able to take suggestions from readers and work to some extent in a nonpreferred way. However, it is not at all clear that the writer could have made these changes on her own, without peer assistance. That is, the shift to nonpreferred strategies is not one that this writer would have made without outside input. By contrast, expert writers can and do make such changes, calling on nonpreferred strategies and using them effectively.

Student 3, INFP, responded to her peer readers but ended up with a paper that reflects her preferences and an unsuccessful conclusion. Two of her readers prefer sensing and told her to add some missing items to her summary. In following this advice, she ended up with a summary paragraph of almost a page and a half, typed double space. This suggests the NP tendencies to want to be inclusive and avoid closure. It is true that the writer was able to respond to reader critique but not very effectively. It is also true that readers are not always helpful, even if their preferences are opposite those of the writer: The two sensing readers did not point out numerous technical errors and spelling problems on the draft, and only some of these were corrected on the final version (chiefly, it appears, by running spell check). Thus, again, the writer is not able to use the advice of readers with other preferences.

Student 4, ISFJ, had only two readers, ESTP and ENTP. Both of these readers told her that her opening was misleading, or at least inconsistent with her ending. The result of this was an important change to the thesis, as noted earlier, along with some expansion of the opening paragraph to provide a fuller introduction to the discussion. In this case, the student was able to make changes in response to suggestions from thinking readers that were truly helpful to the draft and resulted in a more effective paper. This case differs markedly from the other student cases in the study. I speculate that this student case is the only one that resembles the expert writers' cases. The student was looking ahead to a business career and hoped to have a family, so leave policies and related issues were a matter of substantive and emotional concern to her. This speculation may help to account for why she was better able to make use of suggestions from readers of opposite type on the TF dimension.

The overall picture on hypothesis 2 does not provide strong evidence of students' consistent abilities to shift to nonpreferred strategies when needed to improve their writing. They can sometimes use advice from readers of differing personality preferences but not always or usually, and even when they do, the resulting changes do not always produce an effective piece of writing. Expert writers, in the second study, differ markedly from the students in this regard. Unlike the students, they can, with or without outside critique, shift strategies as necessary to produce highly readable writing.

STUDY 2: EXPERT WRITERS REVISING

In the present study, two writers with considerable experience working with documents were chosen for study and were asked to provide detailed background prior to an observation of two revising sessions on two different documents, accompanied by think-aloud protocols. The resulting data provide support for both hypotheses under study here and suggest clear pedagogical strategies that may help move student writers into the expert category. What distinguishes expert writers is their ability to balance their writing preferences with strategies from the opposite of their dominant function, that is, from their inferior function (Quenk, 1993).

METHOD

Subjects. The subjects in this study are all adult females, working in jobs that involve substantial amounts of document preparation. Their work is expressly not secretarial in nature, as each holds at least a Master's degree in a field and each has some supervisory responsibility in her work setting. Although one subject has recently had a formal academic course in writing, in general, neither subject has specific training in workplace writing so that both subjects appear to be drawing on writing skills developed over time without direct instruction. The documents they worked on are in general typical work-related kinds of writing, including a letter of recommendation, a performance appraisal, a memo, and a section of a dissertation. Each subject had completed the Myers-Briggs Type Indicator at an earlier time in a context unrelated to the study, and each was asked to furnish a report of her type and the numerical score on each dimension. Each subject was also asked to read the section of this report summarizing the observation of her revising processes and to comment on its accuracy.

Materials and Procedure. Each subject was asked to provide a first draft of any document being worked on in the context of this project. The subjects were given completely free choice as to which documents they worked on for the purposes of the study. In one case, the writer revises as she goes along, and so I watched both the text generation and the revision process in this case. The subjects also provided intermediate drafts if they had printed copies of them during the observation, as well as the last version of the document generated at the end of the think-aloud protocol. Finally, subjects provided a finished version of the document, including additional revisions made after the observation, if any. Each subject revised two different documents for the study; thus, a total of four documents comprise the expert writers' data set.

The use of an oral interview and think-aloud protocol is not necessarily the best or only way to get information about writers as they work. However, as Odell, Goswami, and Herrington (1983) have noted, discourse-based interviews and oral composing do give researchers access to writers' tacit knowledge about writing. They found that their interview procedures, which are similar to the ones being followed here, revealed that writers can discuss the basis for writing decisions reliably. They also point out that the way in which the interview process is used makes some difference:

> We are using interviews to identify the kinds of world knowledge and expectations that informants bring to writing tasks and to discover the perceptions informants have about the conceptual demands that functional, interactive writing tasks make on them. (p. 228)

The use of an interview and think-aloud protocol in this study similarly attempts to capture the knowledge and strategies writers bring to a task.

Peter Smagorinsky's (1994) collection of articles considers the nature of think-aloud protocols and the various difficulties in using them. He and other writers in his collection suggest that the data be considered more exploratory than confirming, and that users of think-aloud protocols rely on case studies. The articles point out the ways in which think-alouds can influence how writers behave, making writing with thinking aloud somewhat different than writing without it. Also, they advocate the use of think-aloud data along with other kinds of data to investigate aspects of the writing process. Despite the various challenges to using this methodology, Smagorinsky concludes that think-aloud studies can "be a remarkably illuminating research methodology" (p. 16).

Each subject was asked a series of background questions on her language ability, formal training in writing and questions about her current position, amount of time spent working on writing, and related matters (see Appendix A). Each subject was then asked a series of questions relevant to the document being worked on during the observation, including title, length, audience, purpose, focus of revision, and readability of the document (see Appendix B). Each writer was next presented with a short paragraph about the weather and asked to read it and briefly discuss revisions that she might make to improve it, to give a sense of what was needed in the think-aloud process. Finally, an audiotape recorder was set up with the writer's permission, and the writer began working on the document and talking while working. During the actual revision, my role was only to watch the screen as the document developed (both writers work at word processors) and take some notes. If the writer made a substantive change without comment, I asked for an explanation, but such questions were rare. The session ended when the writer said she was through with the current draft of the document. Each writer was given a copy of the section of this report pertaining to her revision processes to read and comment on prior to completion of the report. Any comments have been incorporated here.

Results on Hypothesis 1

The expert writers' documents and think-aloud protocols were examined first to see if their revising strategies were consistent with their personality type's revising characteristics as described by Jensen and DiTiberio (1989) and discussed earlier. In each case, the expert writers show fairly high consistency with the strategies described. Each writer worked on two different documents during two separate revising sessions, and, although the documents were of very different types, the strategies applied are consistent for each writer and her type preferences.

Expert 1, INTJ, is a faculty member in the writing program at a medium-sized public university in the midwest. She is the writer for whom drafting and revising occur simultaneously. However, during my first observation, which lasted about one hour, this expert generated three different drafts of the first document. This document was a letter of recommendation for a former student. In her running commentary on her process, this writer said that she sometimes likes to leave a few days from the draft version to a final version of a document, typical of an introvert. In the course of her work on this task, she let a number of details of mechanics and formatting go until near the end of the process. This and her focus on clarifying her ideas is consistent with her intuitive preference. Although she had inserted headings to structure and organize her ideas early in the process, by the final version, she had formed four clear paragraphs, each with a firm focus. The first draft was quite unfocused despite the headings. This pattern is typical of feeling types, not thinking types, and so is one example of revision work not consistent with type. She clarified and improved the transitions over the course of her work, as many judging types do in revising.

In her second document, Expert 1 was dealing with what she described as a complex rhetorical situation. The document is a report of a teaching discussion and observation as part of an ongoing peer review process in her department (the department that teaches writing). In her work on this document, Expert 1 had difficulty integrating audience, topic, and purpose in a way she thought appropriate, saying at one point, "It's not writing itself very well," and at another, "I don't know where I'm going with this." She struggled to relate her ideas to her experience, consistent with introverts' revising strategies, but had problems with this because of the situation. At one point in the work, she said she was going to create the draft and then consult with a colleague who was part of the observation team to generate a revised version. It was clear that she had a number of complex ideas to sort out, as intuitive types frequently do, partly because the purpose of the document was to describe what happened; however, the writer also felt a need to provide evaluation and was trying to keep this out of the document.

She tried to put in examples of the teacher's behavior but again ran into difficulty with this because her negative evaluation was overriding her attempt to provide objective description. Thus, although she was trying to work on the document using her preferred thinking strategy, it was problematic. As a judging type, Expert 1 was clearly trying hard to modify or qualify or more thoroughly analyze her statements in her review of the draft as it appeared on the screen. But again, she was in great difficulty given the complex nature of the document. She had started in a planful way, consistent with judging, setting a general organizational structure of describing the preliminary teaching discussion followed by the classroom visit, but the organizational structure did not seem to help her much. At the end, she said that she would consult with the second observer before generating another draft. I discuss this further later but it is another instance in which Expert 1 deviated from her type preference as an introvert for working alone. Expert 1, then, shows much of her revising behavior, although not all of it, to be generally consistent with her type preferences.

Expert 2, INFP, is an academic administrator at a medium-sized public university in the midwest. This expert also shows revising behavior consistent with her type preferences. The first document she worked on was a memo to a former employee in her office who had requested an internship in the office in connection with academic coursework. The draft document she had at the beginning of the observation had been begun as an e-mail response to the applicant. Subsequently, Expert 2 decided that the response needed to be longer and in written memo form. She had a printed copy of the memo, and a day or two had elapsed since her initial attempt to write the document. Ultimately, I was given four versions of the document: the initial draft I have just described, a second draft resulting from my observation session, an intermediate draft reviewed by two colleagues, and the final draft. The writer noted that usually she does more revising while drafting but had restrained herself with an eye toward my observation.

The allowance of time elapsing from the initial draft is typical of introverted writers in revising, and the very complex ideas of the document are typical of intuitive writers. At the beginning of the working session, this writer is very focused on the tone of the document and mentions tone several times over the course of the revision. This reflects Expert 2's dominant feeling preference and concern for how this document is going to impact the reader. At one point, she says of her own phrasing, "I need to temper this," and at another, "This seems a bit strong but it is the message I want to convey," both of which suggest her concern with how the reader will respond to the document, a typical concern of feeling writers.

In her work, the most interesting changes occur in the third paragraph of the document. In its draft form, the paragraph reads as follows:

> First, as you know [another intern] is currently interning with us. Her internship will not be complete until sometime in August. At the end of last summer, I made the decision that I would not again have two interns at the same time. As I told [the internship director], I felt it affected the experience of both [intern 1] and [intern 2], although they might not have been aware of it. However, I was aware of it, and I know it was not fair to either one of them.

By the time Expert 2 generated the final draft, this paragraph has changed substantially:

> First of all, as you know, [another intern's] internship will not be complete until sometime in August. I learned from our experience last summer that having two interns does not work well. Both of them get short-changed. I had indicated to [the internship director] at the end of the last summer that I would not again choose to have two interns at the same time. We can only do justice to one intern at a time. I felt that the experiences of both [intern 1] and [intern 2] were negatively affected by the dual situation, although they might not have been aware of what they missed. However, I was aware of it, and I know it was not fair to either one of them.

This example shows the complex nature of the document and Expert 2's consistent effort to clarify her ideas and revise extensively. These patterns are those described for introverted and intuitive writers according to Jensen and DiTiberio (1989).

The data from Expert 2 generally support the first hypothesis, even though this writer does not show strategies in revising that are consistent with her perceiving preference. The first draft of this document was a single sheet, and the final draft was a full page and a half. However, much of her revision process is consistent with her introverted, intuitive, and feeling preferences. In particular, her dominant feeling preference causes her to rethink, soften, temper, and otherwise adjust phrasing with an eye toward the likely impact of the document on her reader. At the very end of the revising session, Expert 2 commented that she was not pleased with either the document or having to produce it at all.

Expert 2's second document was quite different. This document was a portion of her proposal for her doctoral dissertation, then undergoing revision prior to an oral defense. In a session with her adviser prior to revision, the writer had prepared an addendum specifying procedures for her study. The addendum and handwritten notes based on the adviser's comments were to be incorporated into the draft proposal. The sections to be reworked focused on subjects in the study and the method of data collection. Expert 2 was generally following the American Psychological Association style for her presentation.

The focus of her revision in this case is on organization and once again is consistent with her feeling preference as described by Jensen and DiTiberio (1989). Feeling writers may need to clarify content and improve organization according to Jensen and DiTiberio. She looks first at the overall organization of the section on the subjects and observes that "these are all going to be out of order and this is going to be difficult to do." She is working off two documents, the draft and the addendum, and also has handwritten notes from the meeting with her adviser.

In the draft version, the opening of the Subjects section is "The subjects of the case study will be a total of 3 children of average intelligence in grades 3 and 4." In the revised version, the opening reads as follows:

> Students in grades 3, 4 and 5 who have been referred for the first time to the reading clinic at [X] University for tutoring in reading will be screened for learned helplessness, reading problems and intelligence prior to the onset of tutoring.

From this, the writer goes on in the remainder of the opening paragraph to specify the method for the screening on each dimension and the criteria for eligible subjects. The section consists of four tightly focused paragraphs in its revised form, expanded from three in the draft. The reorganization of components is not done with an eye toward impact on the reader, as was the case in the first document, but is done with considerable emphasis on organizational issues, consistent with her feeling preference. A similar revision is made to the opening of the section on Data Collection, setting up the organizational structure of the section.

Throughout her work on the Subjects section, it is clear that the writer has a sense of the complexity of what she is planning, and she tries to sort out the complexity of her ideas. This work is consistent with her intuitive type and is similar to some of her revising of the first document. The overall process is one of teasing out the major points to be made and reorganizing them for clarity because of their initial complexity. In the work on this document, Expert 2 worked much more in her head so that the process was more private, consistent with her introverted preference.

When she moved on to the section on Data Collection, Expert 2 became very concerned with the overall organization and her use of headings in the document. She made a note in the revised draft to check her use of headings against the APA's suggested format. Again, this focus on organization is consistent with revising efforts by people with a feeling preference. In general, then, Expert 2 works at revising in ways mostly consistent with her introverted, feeling, and intuitive preferences.

Both Expert 1 and Expert 2 provide data that support Hypothesis 1, because both engage in revising using strategies consistent with their personality types.

Results on Hypothesis 2

The expert writers' documents and think-aloud protocols were examined a second time in connection with the second hypothesis under study here. The second hypothesis states that by contrast to student writers, expert writers revise more effectively because they can shift to nonpreferred strategies more easily and effectively and do so especially when there are emotional issues at stake. Although the results on the first hypothesis suggest that expert writers prefer to draw on strategies consistent with their types when revising, when they confront a difficult document or one in which they have emotional involvement, they are adept at using techniques from the opposite of their dominant type for revising. Not all the documents produced in connection with the study fit this category, so the discussion of the data on hypothesis 2 is more selective.

Expert 1, INTJ, seemed to be in distress generating her report of the teaching observation discussed previously. One common feature of the revising of introverts is their preference to work alone, but this expert said that she would share her draft with the colleague who observed the teacher with her and ask for feedback and response before revising further. In this way, this writer, whose dominant type is introverted intuitive, chose to use her inferior, extraverted sensing, for revision purposes. Subsequently, she abandoned the draft generated during my observation and produced a different document collaboratively with her colleague. Collaborative revising is a more likely choice of extraverts, so this is one instance in which Expert 1 confirms the hypothesis.

In her struggles on this document, Expert 1's chief difficulty was in trying to avoid evaluation because this report is supposed to be description only. As noted earlier, very complex and tangled ideas are quite typical of intuitive writers. However, evaluative remarks kept creeping into the text, despite her wish to avoid them. Thus, for instance, a comment on the preliminary meeting with the teacher comments about the syllabus: "Since the syllabus is not dated either, but both documents are similar but are labeled XXX [writing course number], I assume that you use the same material year in and year out." Later, in the discussion of the classroom observation, she writes: "Unfortunately, you had left your text and lesson plan in the office when you were talking with [other observer] and me, so you were unable to refer to them [during class] except by memory."

The difficulty has something to do with the fact that this introverted intuitive writer is trying to work from a sensing perspective. She was trying to get at the implications of her draft, in the way that Jensen and DiTiberio (1989) suggest that sensing types should, in revision and also trying to keep away from evaluation. Thus, although Expert 1 did not have great success revising the early draft of this document, it appears that she was trying to make use of her inferior function in grappling with this difficult document.

In the revised, collaboratively developed alternative version of this document, Expert 1 takes on a considerably more objective and focused tone. The document is much more purely descriptive in nature and also much more focused on the details of the observations and discussion. The number of headings used expands, for example, from two to five, and instead of the personal "you" the teacher is now referred to by name and with the third-person pronoun.

Expert 1's work on this document, thus, shows her moving away from her preferred introverted intuitive strategies when they failed to help her produce the document she needed. Partly, they failed because her intuition tells her that the subject of the document needs more evaluation than the writing situation allows. In her reading of a draft of this paper, Expert 1 confirms this analysis. She is able to shift to her inferior functions, extraversion and sensing, using these in combination both to seek outside, collaborative assistance in the writing and also to focus more objectively on the facts and details of her observations. The result is a complete and detailed document that is appropriate as a description of the teacher she observed. Expert 1's work on this document appears to provide strong evidence supporting the second hypothesis.

Expert 2, INFP, ran into a similar difficulty to that of Expert 1 with her first document, in which she adopted the persona of a writer with different preferences than her own. The document is Expert 2's response to the applicant for an internship in her office. The applicant had previously worked in the office and had some conflicts with Expert 2, specifically in terms of supervision. In general, the writer perceives the task to call for a response contrary to the writer's type. In this case, the writer's dominant is introverted feeling, but she is forced to make use of extraverted thinking, her inferior, to produce a document to serve her needs.

As she worked on this memo, Expert 2 tried out at least one phrase, "good fit," in her text and subsequently rejected it as too conversational in tone. This choice demonstrates her awareness of the extravert's conversational style and her unwillingness to use it. In addition, following my observation, Expert 2 shared her draft with two colleagues for feedback and made some additional changes based on the responses that she got. Like Expert 1, also an introvert, this writer prefers to work alone but chose in this case to get some collaborative help on this difficult document.

In the first draft, she tried an organizational structure in the openings of the paragraphs using "first . . . second . . . " and subsequently rejected this also. However, in another part of the document, she writes about the issue of supervision: "Quite frankly, that is a problem." This statement, which she described in her protocol as clear and to the point, is not what a feeling type would prefer but is what she put in. At still another point, she describes a part of the applicant's behavior as "inappropriate and unprofessional." About this, she remarked that it seemed a bit strong but it was the message she wanted to convey. This strong phrasing and the addition, among the drafts, of a number of examples of other internship possibilities for the applicant are both instances of thinking strategies applied by this feeling dominant writer. In this case, then, there is also considerable evidence to support hypothesis 2.

In a number of ways, then, Experts 1 and 2 both show an ability to draw on writing strategies other than their preferred ones. When they work on revision, they normally call on preferred techniques that are consistent with their type preferences. However, when the document presents difficulties, they can shift to their opposite, inferior functions and make use of nonpreferred approaches to produce a well-written document. Thus, both of these writers confirm the second hypothesis.

DISCUSSION

Study 1

The work of the student writers in this research shows that they make use of the revising strategies of their type when they engage in revising. Many changes noted in the students' final versions of their research reports show revisions from the draft that are consistent with their personality types. As Jensen and DiTiberio (1989) point out, it is useful for students to develop as fully as possible their natural preferences for working at writing. This view is also consistent with psychologists' view of type development. However, when student writers run into difficulty with their writing, their ability to shift strategies and especially to capitalize on strategies from their inferior function is quite limited, at least in these data.

These students seem fairly typical of traditional American college students, and it is reasonable to think that a broader study of revising strategies would show similar results. Student writers can benefit substantially from instruction on the relevance of personality type for writing and from instruction to help them develop both preferred and nonpreferred strategies for writing.

Study 2

The expert writers present data that also support the first hypothesis under study here. These writers are quite capable of making use of the strategies for revising consistent with their personality type. They make good use of these strategies and can revise effectively. However, when a document presents difficulties for expert writers, they show their distinction from student writers quite clearly. The expert writers studied here show a marked ability to make use of their inferior functions, resorting to strategies quite different from those they prefer, to produce a well-written and effective document. Thus, the expert writers strongly confirm the second hypothesis in a way that the student writers do not.

CONCLUSIONS AND IMPLICATIONS

There are both theoretical and pedagogical implications to be drawn from this study. In terms of the first hypothesis, the data from these cases show that revising behavior is generally consistent with personality type. Both student and expert writers approach revising constrained by their preferences. The second hypothesis shows a key difference between the students and the expert writers. The data show that at least part of what makes experts expert is their ability to use nonpreferred strategies and to do so particularly when there are emotional factors involved in the writing. The findings, then, suggest that type plays a role in revising behavior and may have a much greater influence than has previously been suggested.

From a pedagogical standpoint, the usefulness of the findings lies in helping students learn to become more effective revisers. Edward White (1994) noted that students are known to avoid much revising:

> The unwillingness of students to revise is really an odd paradox: no professional writer would dream of publishing work without many revisions, but the least skilled writers in America, the students, almost invariably hand in first drafts, usually produced the night before the due date. Writing teachers constantly implore students to revise, without much effect. . . . But no real revision of writing can take place unless the *writer* sees what needs to be changed and how to change it. Professionals revise all the time because they are careful readers and evaluators of their own work and therefore know how to make it better. In contrast, most students do not revise because they have not learned how to evaluate what they write; they have not internalized any consistent set of criteria or standards to which they can hold themselves. (pp. 9-10; emphasis in original)

The results discussed earlier suggest that White understands only part of the problem. The problem is not only that students need to learn more evaluative techniques, but also that they need to learn a wider array of revising strategies so that they can become more effective revisers.

Revising's importance is growing, particularly as portfolios for grading and assessment grow in use. Students need to become more effective and efficient revisers. Applying concepts of personality preference to revising shows that student writers do work at revision in ways consistent with their personalities, as do expert writers. However, the experts demonstrate a capacity to approach revising with a great deal more flexibility, thus offering a clear insight for teaching. The difference between student and expert writers is that the experts know about, and are capable of shifting to, nonpreferred strategies when their most comfortable and preferred strategies do not work. If teachers want students to revise at all and especially want them to revise and make their papers better, teachers should discuss the influence of type and help students develop nonpreferred as well as preferred strategies for revising papers.

REFERENCES

Couture, B., & Rymer, J. (1993). Situational exigence: Composing processes on the job by writer's role and task value. In R. Spilka (Ed.), *Writing in the workplace: New research perspectives* (pp. 4-20). Carbondale: Southern Illinois University Press.

Gebhardt, R. C. (1983). Writing processes, revision, and rhetorical problems: A note on three recent articles. *College Composition and Communication, 34,* 294-296.

Horning, A. S. (1993). *The psycholinguistics of readable writing: A multidisciplinary exploration.* Norwood, NJ: Ablex.

Jensen, G., & DiTiberio, J. (1989) *Personality and the teaching of composition.* Norwood, NJ: Ablex.

Keirsey, D., & Bates, M. (1984). *Please understand me: Character and temperament types.* Del Mar, CA: Prometheus Nemesis Book Company.

Mulderig, G. P. (1995). *The heath handbook* (13th ed.). Lexington, MA: D.C. Heath.

Myers, I. B. (1980). *Gifts differing.* Palo Alto, CA: Consulting Psychologists Press.

Odell, L., Goswami, D., & Herrington, A. (1983). The discourse-based interview: A procedure for exploring the tacit knowledge of writers in nonacademic settings. In P. Mosenthal, L. Tamor, & S. Walmsley (Eds.), *Research on writing: Principles and methods* (pp. 221-236). New York: Longman.

Quenk, N. (1993). *Beside ourselves: Our hidden personality in everyday life.* Palo Alto, CA: Consulting Psychologists Press.

Smagorinsky, P. (1994). Think-aloud protocol analysis: Beyond the black box. In P. Smagorinsky (Ed.), *Speaking about writing: Reflections on research methodology* (pp. 3-19). Thousand Oaks, CA: Sage.

Smith, F. (1994). *Writing and the writer* (2nd ed.). Hillsdale, NJ: Erlbaum.

Sommers, N. (1980). Revision strategies of student writers and experienced adult writers. *College Composition and Communication, 31,* 378-387.

White, E. M. (1994). *Teaching and assessing writing: Recent advances in understanding, evaluating and improving student performance* (2nd ed.). San Francisco: Jossey-Bass.

Woodruff, J. (Ed.). (1993). *A piece of work: Five writers discuss their revisions.* Iowa City: University of Iowa Press.

APPENDIX A

Revising Study Subject Background Questionnaire

1. TAPING: OK? Y N
2. SUBJECT NAME AND TODAY'S DATE:
   MBTI TYPE PREFERENCES AND SCORES:
   SELF-ID PREFERENCES IF DIFFERENT:
3. LANGUAGES SPOKEN OR KNOWN AND LEVEL OF ABILITY:
4. POSITION/OFFICIAL JOB TITLE:
5. LENGTH OF TIME IN JOB:
6. HIGHEST DEGREE AND YEAR OF AWARD:
7. APPROXIMATE AMOUNT OF TIME SPENT PREPARING DOCUMENTS:
   per day? per week?
8. SPECIFIC TRAINING IN WRITING IN OR BEFORE PRESENT JOB/WHEN?:
   courses
   seminars
   workshops
   other
9. HOW MUCH COLLABORATIVE WORK DO YOU DO IN DOCUMENT PREPARATION?
10. DESCRIBE YOUR WRITING STRATEGIES OR HABITS....
    paper vs. wp
    use of dictaphone
    do you have an editor or typist or other person who looks at your writing?
11. DESCRIBE YOUR APPROACH OR PROCESS FOR WRITING GENERALLY....
    prewriting
    drafting
    final copy preparation
    use of spell check/machine-based editor

APPENDIX B

Revising Study Questionnaire for Revising Tasks

1. NAME AND DATE:
2. TASK 1/ TASK 2—if task 2, any thoughts about process since task 1 or observations, comments, etc.?

3. TITLE OF DOCUMENT OR DOCUMENT TYPE/to be read silently, speech, ad, manual (directions)...:
4. IS THERE RESEARCH INVOLVED IN THIS DOCUMENT, AND IF SO HOW MUCH AND WHAT KIND?
5. IS THERE A MODEL FOR THIS DOCUMENT OR A PATTERN FOLLOWED? (If so, ask for copy of model or pattern document.)
6. LENGTH PARAMETER (# OF WORDS, PAGES OR TIME):
7. TIME SPENT ON THIS DOCUMENT TO.DATE:
8. AUDIENCE FOR DOCUMENT:
9. AUDIENCE NEEDS/WRITER'S ASSUMPTIONS ABOUT AUDIENCE:
10. TOPIC OF DOCUMENT/THESIS/POINT/MAIN IDEA:
11. PURPOSE/USE OF DOCUMENT:
12. FOCUS OF REVISION (RHETORICAL, TECHNICAL, DESIGN/MECHANICS):
13. GENERAL DEFINITION OF READABILITY:
14. WHAT WILL MAKE THIS A READABLE DOCUMENT?

Chapter 10

Personality and Writing Process Preferences of Teachers Related to the Use of Computers

Dianne Swenson Koehnecke
Southern Illinois University

Preliminary classroom observations of students in college composition classes showed differences in word processing methods and computer anxiety about word processing. Later observations noted that teachers enrolled in a graduate course on professional writing displayed similar differences. Some of the teachers appeared anxious about using the computer, whereas others, similar to subjects studied by Selfe (1989), saw it as a welcome tool that could actually improve their writing. Some teachers, based on various surveys, including one by Atwell (1987), had problems getting started, whereas others began their task immediately. Some teachers asked to go to the library, sit quietly and think first, or do other "prewriting" exercises, whereas others began their writing assignments immediately.

Some of the teachers needed to write everything out in longhand before they keyboarded the words onto the computer screen, whereas others wrote directly on the keyboard. Some teachers were anxious about learning the software package, whereas others appeared to view this exercise as a necessary step for using the computer effectively. Some teachers used the menu-driven commands to move chunks of their writing around, whereas others wrote their thoughts in a sequential order and had no interest in the cut-and-paste revision commands. Some teachers printed out copies of their drafts for editing and revision purposes, whereas others made most of their corrections directly on the screen. Some teachers rewrote their versions many times, whereas others did little or no rewriting. Some teachers struggled with the endings of their papers, whereas others originated endings that gave fresh insight or effective review.

These differences in the way teachers used the computer to write their papers led to the first of two formal studies on personality in word processing. The 11 teachers who were subjects in the first study completed interviews, written surveys, questionnaires, and evaluations, as well as daily written anxiety logs. Many teachers seemed to be following a writing style process taught to them, rather than their natural personality preferences. Earlier observations of teachers in a pilot study writing course suggested that some of them were writing in a forced, artificial style they had been taught, even when they were not comfortable with it. This observation led to the first study of 11 teacher subjects in 1991. Additional observations of over 80 teachers enrolled in the professional writing course during the summers of 1992-1995 provided data for a second study. Combined results of both studies are described in this chapter.

Many differences writers utilize when writing on the computer are clear from even cursory observation. Writers need to discover what strategies could be most effective when utilizing word processing and what methods could be used to overcome various writing problems that occur while using word processors.

The study addresses several interrelated questions. Could personality preferences be a factor in how writers utilize the computer to write their manuscripts? If so, in what ways could writers use computers to understand their natural writing style, to enjoy writing more, and to write more effectively? If subjects in the study were not following natural preferences, were they using a style that had been learned? Could they discover their true style and find ways to overcome writing and word processing difficulties by using their preferred preferences in the service of the unpreferred? This five-year study attempted to discover answers to these questions.

The study draws on data from several different sources. Subjects involved took the Myers-Briggs Type Indicator (Myers & Myers, 1977) to help them assess their natural personality preferences. An informal, unpublished inventory, the Writing Process Inventory (WPI), designed by George Jensen and John DiTiberio (1986a), was also given to the subjects in an attempt to help them understand and utilize their writing preferences as they wrote on the computer. The WPI was used because its questions relate specifically to the writing process. The WPI, a 76 forced-choice item survey, was given to see how the subjects in the study approached the writing process. These items look at writing traits as separate entities and do not attempt to present a personality profile.

In addition, to help subjects assess personality type and writing processes, information from Jensen and DiTiberio's (1989) book, *Personality and the Teaching of Composition*, was provided. Jensen and DiTiberio's text focuses on writing processes that may or may not be related to personality type preferences. Additional information from DiTiberio and Jensen (1995) was used to review the preferred process subjects in the study said they used as they composed. Some terms defined by the authors (Jensen & DiTiberio, 1986b) aligned with functions and attitudes of the Myers-Briggs: action (extraversion) or reflection (introversion), realism (sensing) or imagination (intuition), analytical (thinking) or personalized (feeling), decisive (judging) or inclusive (perceiving). Writing Process descriptors were delineated to help subjects relate their personality preferences with their preferred writing processes. Different terms were used to describe different approaches to the writing process. Profile descriptions of these approaches were utilized from writing process information provided by Jensen and DiTiberio (1986b). To avoid duplication of MBTI descriptors and to differentiate between personality preferences and writing, the author of this study created her own writing preference words and definitions. Reflective writers were defined as those who preferred to consider what they would write about before putting anything on paper or into the computer. Active writers preferred to talk about their ideas before writing. Writers who preferred a specific approach preferred to write sequentially, whereas creative writers preferred to look for new, original ways to say things and often looked for hidden meanings to complex issues. Objective writers were organized, logical, and could remain detached from their writing, whereas writers who preferred a personalized approach needed to care about their topics and liked to write in the first person about their experiences. Decisive writers liked deadlines and liked to plan what they would write about, whereas writers with flexible approaches could handle several writing projects at the same time and allowed deadlines to motivate them to complete writing assignments.

Why was this study important? Student writers' frustration is clear as they move from their beginning drafts to their finished products. K-12 instructors in a computer lab setting show similar frustration to that of student writers. If personality and writing process are related, an understanding of this relationship could benefit those involved in teaching writing as they work with their students to overcome writing difficulties with the help of useful word processing strategies.

METHOD

For this study, subjects were expected to learn a computer software program and use it to write a variety of papers. These assignments included journals, a paper about their own writing style, a critical abstract, and a professional manuscript. Data utilized in the study were the MBTI and WPI and their accompanying report forms, subject interviews and observations, and a variety of written responses subjects made on daily journals, questionnaires, surveys, and evaluations. Subjects also shared writing anxieties and concerns through a computer network or e-mail system.

Specific written data involved a demographic survey, a beginning writing survey, a writing style inventory (Sudol, 1991a), a computer inventory, daily questionnaires, anxiety logs, and a series of evaluation forms. Subjects' written responses, oral responses in personal interviews, and observations were reviewed to analyze how they utilized word processing in relationship to their personality preferences. To allow adequate time for observation and interviews, a teaching assistant was hired to help with the class sessions.

Follow-up studies included a telephone interview and a written survey. The phone interview was conducted by the investigator with each subject two weeks after the course ended; the written response survey was sent to participants four months later. These instruments were used to see how subjects utilized word processing concepts in their writing that had been taught in the course. During the course, subjects were paired each day with similar and opposite types to alleviate writing blocks (DiTiberio, 1990; Jensen & DiTiberio, 1983), to view similarities and differences in word processing and writing approaches, and to edit one another's works. Speakers included writers and MBTI experts (John DiTiberio in 1992; Pat Otto in 1991 and 1993-95). The original course on professional writing was taken by 11 teacher subjects the first year (1991). Follow-up studies were conducted the following four successive summers (1992-1995) with over 80 additional teacher subjects. All but three of these subjects agreed to participate in the study.

After completing the MBTI, subjects were given their report forms indicating their reported type. Research statistics (Carskadon, McCarley, & McCaulley, 1987) on MBTI reliability studies were reviewed. Each subject also reviewed Gordon Lawrence's (1993) checklists for individual preferences in order to help them assess the accuracy of their MBTI report. The networking or e-mail system that was developed was based on a suggestion (Hawisher, 1991) that involved having subjects write and respond to one another daily about their writing. This system helped the subjects share frustrations and successes. Subjects could use pseudonyms if they wished. Networking was entirely subject-centered; the instructor/investigator did not participate in this activity.

After required writing assignments were completed, subjects filled out surveys that included questions about their writing concerns in utilizing the computer as well as their concerns about beginning and ending each assignment. Only one assignment required answering an inventory (Sudol, 1991a) before starting the task. This inventory asked subjects to analyze their writing styles. Additional material on personality type and the writing process (DiTiberio, 1983; Jensen & DiTiberio, 1983, 1984, 1989; Sudol, 1991b) was provided to the subjects at this time.

Subjects were interviewed about their individual writing preferences related to writing on the computer. These interviews were recorded by the investigator on a word processor. Based on suggestions from Zinsser (1983), subjects wrote daily journals or response logs, describing how they felt about writing on a computer. After writing journal entries, subjects ranked their anxiety level on a scale ranging from low to high.

Different methods were used to establish triangulation, (three different types of observation) or verification of the data, including written responses to a variety of materials, personal interviews, and investigator observations. During this time, information from Jensen and DiTiberio's (1989) text, the WPI, and Sudol's (1991a) inventory was reviewed with each subject. When the data were collected, an analysis of the different ways subjects used the computer was compared with personality and writing process preferences to determine if subjects used their writing process differently on the computer from their natural preferences as measured from their MBTI scores.

In light of Halio's (1990) study, IBM computers were used by the subjects during the first four years because they were available in the computer lab. In 1995, however, Macintosh computers were selected because of the availability of new computers and laser printers, subject preference, and use of Macs outside the lab, as well as the availability of the user-friendly Claris Works word processing package in the computer lab. Professional Write software on the IBM was replaced with Claris Works on the Macintosh. The IBM/Macintosh debate about which machine was superior did not appear significant, because both brands appeared to be user friendly, and professional laser printers were offered by both brands. No attempt in this study was made to compare personality preferences between the IBM and the Macintosh. Primarily because the majority of the subjects studied from 1991-1994 used the Macintosh, this machine was selected for the 1995 study.

RESULTS

Results on First Two Questions

The first two questions under study concerned whether personality preferences are a factor in how writers utilize the computer to write their manuscripts. If so, in what ways could writers use computers to understand their natural writing style, to enjoy writing more, and to write more effectively? Results of the study indicate that computer use in the writing process appears to be related to personality preferences. Subjects with the most confidence about their writing had MBTI personality preferences that related to at least one corresponding area in their WPI writing process preferences of realistic/specific or imaginative/creative, as well analytical/objective or personalized choices. Subjects who had at least one corresponding MBTI and WPI preference numbered 69 subjects, or 74.19%. Those whose MBTI and WPI preferences corresponded in all areas numbered 17 subjects, or 18.28%. These subjects said they felt confident in using the computer to write their papers compared with subjects who had differing preferences. Subjects who struggled the most with both writing and word processing either differed in at least one natural preference compared with writing process preference or indicated that they preferred sensing on the MBTI.

Yet even subjects who struggled with the writing process indicated a more positive attitude about writing and computers on their final evaluation forms. They said they found the computer useful in enhancing writing strengths and in providing compensatory word processing aids that helped them improve and sometimes even overcome particular writing difficulties.

MBTI profiles of all subjects in the study are summarized in Table 10.1. Results for the subjects on the WPI are summarized in Table 10.2. Subjects whose MBTI and writing process preferences showed corresponding differences in their E/I (Action/Reflection) and J/P (Decisive/Inclusive) attitudes and processes did not appear to have difficulty in utilizing opposite writing processes in these areas.

Results on Questions Three and Four

The results show that subjects have writing difficulties if they use approaches they learned rather than ones consistent with their natural preferences, another of the questions under study. In addition, findings address the question of whether subjects can discover their true style and find ways to overcome writing and word processing difficulties by using their preferred preferences in the service of the unpreferred.

Table 10.1. MBTI Profiles of Teachers Enrolled in a Computer Writing Class, 1991-1995 (Total = 93).

| Sensing Types | | Intuitive Types | |
with Thinking	with Feeling	with Feeling	with Thinking
ISTJ	ISFJ	INFJ	INTJ
n=10	n=13	n=4	n=3
%=10.75	%=13.98	%=4.30	%=3.23
XXXXXXXXXX	XXXXXXXXXXXXX	XXXX	XXX
ISTP	ISFP	INFP	INTP
n-0	n=4	n=7	n=1
%=	%=4.30	%=7.53	%=1.11
	XXXX	XXXXXXX	X
ESTP	ESFP	ENFP	ENTP
n=2	n=10	n=6	n=3
%=2.15	%=10.75	%=6.45	%=3.23
XX	XXXXXXXXXX	XXXXX	XXX
ESTJ	ESFJ	ENFJ	ENTJ
n=7	n=8	n=6	n=9
%=7.53	%=8.60	%=6.45	%=9.68
XXXXXXX	XXXXXXXX	XXXXX	XXXXXXXXX

n = 93
x = % of n
I = 42 (45.16%)
E = 51 (54.84%)
S = 54 (58.06%)
N = 39 (41.94%)
T = 35 (37.63%)
F = 58 (62.37%)
J = 60 (64.52%)
P = 33 (35.48%)

When dominant and auxiliary MBTI functions were accompanied by opposite writing processes in the realistic/imaginative and analytical/personalized categories, subjects appeared to struggle more with assignments and to be under greater stress.

Table 10.3 summarizes the comparison of MBTI and WPI profiles for all subjects. Subjects with opposing preferences in the two middle letters of both the MBTI and WPI profiles numbered 8 subjects. Of these 8 subjects, 7 agreed to participate in the study. These subjects complained more about assignments, asked for more help with both writing

Table 10.2. WPI Profiles of Teachers Enrolled in a Computer Writing Class, 1991-1995 (Total 93).

Objective	Personalized	Personalized	Objective
RSOD	RSPD	RCPD	RCOD
n=11	n=12	n=4	n=2
%=11.83	%=12.90	%=4.30	%=2.15
XXXXXXXXXXX	XXXXXXXXXXXX	XXXX	XX
RSOF	RSPF	RCPF	RCOF
n=5	n=12	n=9	n=1
%=5.38	%=12.90	%=9.68	%=1.11
XXXXX	XXXXXXXXXXX	XXXXXXXXX	X
ASOF	ASPF	ACPF	ACOF
n=4	n=12	n=8	n=0
%=4.30	%=12.90	%=8.60	%=0
XXXX	XXXXXXXXXXXX	XXXXXXXX	
ASOD	ASPD	ACPD	ACOD
n=0	n=9	n=4	n=0
%=0	%=9.68	%=4.30	%=0
	XXXXXXXXX	XXXX	

n = 93
x = % of n
R= 56 (60.22%) reflective
A = 37 (39.75%) active
S = 65 (69.89%) specific
C = 28 (30.11%) creative
O= 23 (24.73%) objective
P = 70 (75.27%) personalized
D= 42 (45.16%) decisive
F = 51 (54.84%) flexible

assignments and computer functions, listed their stress level as higher on their daily anxiety logs, and were not as satisfied with their writing compared with subjects whose middle two functions and accompanying writing processes corresponded. No subjects differed in all four of the MBTI and WPI profile descriptors.

Further analysis of the data involved comparison of MBTI and WPI scores of subjects who had both opposite dominant and auxiliary MBTI functions corresponding with the middle two WPI descriptors (S/N, with corresponding realistic/specific or imaginative/creative writing processes; and T/F, with analytical/objective or personalized writing processes). Of the 93 subjects who were studied, the 7 who had opposing

Table 10.3. MBTI Profiles Compared to WPI Profiles of Teachers Enrolled in a Computer Writing Class, 1991-1995 (Total = 93).

Sensing Types	Intuitive Types		
with Thinking	with Feeling	with Feeling	with Thinking
ISTJ	ISFJ	INFJ	INTJ
n=10	n=13	n=4	n=3
%=10.75	%=	%=4.30	%=3.23
XXXXXXXXXX	XXXXXXXXXXXXX	XXXX	XXX
WPI	WPI	WPI	WPI
RSOD- 2 2.15%	RSOD- 2 2.15%	RCPD-1 1.08%	RSOD- 2 2.15%
RSPD- 3 3.23%	RSPD- 4 4.30%	RSOF- 1 1.08%	ASOF- 1 1.08%
RSPF- 1 1.08%	RCOD- 1 1.08%	RSPF- 1 1.08%	
RCPF- 1 1.08%	RSOF- 1 1.08%	RCPF- 1 1.08%	
ASPD- 2 2.14%	RSPF- 2 2.15%		
ACPD- 1 1.08%	ASOF- 1 1.08%		
	ASPF- 1 1.08%		
	ASPD- 1 1.08%		
ISTP	ISFP	INFP	INTP
n=0	n=4	n=7	n=1
%=0	%=4.30	%=7.53	%=1.11
	XXXX	XXXXXXX	X
	WPI	WPI	WPI
	RSOD- 1 1.08%	RSPD- 1 1.08%	RSOD- 1 1.08%
	RSPD- 1 1.08%	RCPD- 1 1.08%	
	RSOF- 1 1.08%	RSPF- 1 1.08%	
	RCPF- 1 1.08%	RCPF- 2 2.15%	
		RCOF- 1 1.08%	
		ACPF- 1 1.08%	
ESTP	ESFP	ENFP	ENTP
n=2	n=10	n=6	n=3
%=2.15	%=10.75	%=6.45	%=3.23
XX	XXXXXXXXXX	XXXXXX	XXX
WPI	WPI	WPI	WPI
ASPF- 2 2.15%	RSPF- 3 3.23%	RCPF- 2 2.15%	RCPD- 1 1.08%
	ASPF- 2 2.15%	ACPF- 4 4.30%	RSOF- 1 1.08%
	ACPF- 2 2.15%		RSPF- 1 1.08%
	ASPD- 3 3.23%		

Table 10.3. MBTI Profiles Compared to WPI Profiles of Teachers Enrolled in a Computer Writing Class, 1991-1995 (Total = 93) (cont.).

ESTJ		ESFJ		ENFJ		ENTJ	
n=7		n=8		n=6		n=9	
%=7.53		%=8.60		%=6.45		%=9.68	
XXXXXXX		XXXXXXXX		XXXXX		XXXXXXXXX	
WPI		WPI		WPI		WPI	
RSPD- 1	1.08%	RSOD- 1	1.08%	RSOD-1	1.08%	RSOD-1	1.08%
RCOD- 1	1.08%	RSPD- 1	1.08%	RSPF- 1	1.08%	RCPD- 1	1.08%
RSPF- 1	1.08%	RSOP- 1	1.08%	RCPF- 1	1.08%	RSOF- 1	1.08%
ASOF- 2	2.15%	RSPF- 1	1.08%	ASPF- 3	3.23%	RCPF- 1	1.08%
ASPF- 1	1.08%	ASPF- 2	2.15%			ASPF- 1	1.08%
ASPD- 1	1.08%	ASPD- 2	2.15%			ACPF- 1	1.08%
						ACPD- 3	3.23%

n = 93
x = % of *n*

R = reflective
A = active
S = specific
C = creative
O = objective
P = personalized
D = decisive
F = flexible

Of the 93 subjects:
69 (74.19%) had one MBTI preference that was the same as the WPI preference.
17 (18.28%) had MBTI and WPI preferences that were exactly alike.
7 (7.53%) had MBTI and WPI middle preferences opposed.
None of the subjects had all four MBTI and WPI preferences opposed.

MBTI and WPI preferences in both of the middle two descriptors were assessed. Of these 7, the first subject did not appear to have serious writing anxieties, 2 of the subjects did not think their scores were accurate, and a fourth subject did not appear to have difficulty with the writing process, as indicated by her daily anxiety logs, interviews with the investigator, and the quality of writing demonstrated in her manuscripts. This subject also suspected that her MBTI preferences actually aligned more closely with her writing process preferences. A fifth subject did have anxiety about her writing but was reluctant to share her concerns with the investigator. The 2 remaining subjects are discussed in detail later.

Results on "At-Risk" Writers

The data were also examined to review all the subjects who had been referred by their advisors as having major writing difficulties or who had described themselves as having problems with writing or who experienced difficulty writing on the computer. A writing difficulty list was prepared, including the following criteria, to describe at-risk writers:

1. Difficulty with basic writing skills, such as writing in complete sentences, indenting for new paragraphs, knowing and applying appropriate grammar and punctuation rules
2. Difficulty with higher-level writing skills such as clarity, focus, coherence, synthesis, analysis, and evaluation
3. Little understanding of audience
4. Dislike of writing/computers
5. Writing/computer anxiety

The group of at-risk subjects who had difficulty with writing and/or word processing made up a larger list than the previous inventory of subjects with opposite personality and writing process preferences. In addition to Beatrice (who is studied in detail later), 10 subjects were profiled as "at-risk" writers in the master's program during this five-year study. Of these 10 subjects, 7 were eliminated from the study because of a lack of keyboarding or English language skills, departure from the course for personal reasons, and related factors. The 3 remaining subjects had the following MBTI profiles: ISFJ, ISFP, and ESTJ.

All 3 had matching writing process preference scores on the WPI in the middle two descriptors: The first and second subjects preferred to write realistic/specific and personalized papers, whereas the third subject preferred a realistic/specific and analytical writing style. The first subject (ISFJ) preferred an active inclusive/flexible writing process, diametrically opposed to her introverted, judging personality preference. The second subject (ISFP) preferred a reflective writing approach, but her decisive writing process was the opposite of her perceiving personality preference. The third subject (ESTJ) differed in her thinking personality preference compared with her inclusive/flexible writing process preferences.

All 3 struggled with writing in both content and context, in audience perception, and in the most basic of writing skills. Yet all 3 put forth great effort to improve in these areas throughout the entire course; one is now completing her master's degree, whereas another has just begun. All 3 experienced high writing anxiety, however, as measured by their investigator interviews and observations and from their written responses. All 3 also stated, in their writing styles assignment, that they found the computer to be a useful tool to help them with basic writing skills, such as spelling, punctuation, and sentence fragments. All 3 also learned how to utilize software commands in the revision process to move material around, delete text, and add material to their drafts.

Based on a review of the 10 at-risk subjects described, the major significant finding from this part of the study was that all 10 preferred the sensing function on the MBTI. In their informal writing process surveys, all except Beatrice and the nonnative speaker also described their writing process preference as realistic/specific. Of the two subjects who preferred an imaginative/creative approach, one subject was the nonnative speaker, whose scores on both indicators were not necessarily accurate because of the language barrier; the other subject was Beatrice, who is described in an in-depth profile later. Five of the at-risk subjects reported a preference for thinking on the MBTI, with the other 5 preferring feeling. On the WPI, 6 reported a preference for a personalized writing process, whereas 4 preferred an analytical/objective approach.

Case Studies: Sally and Beatrice

Profiles of Sally and Beatrice are given in the following paragraphs to help readers see the significance of opposite personality and writing process preferences in the middle two descriptors of the MBTI and WPI. The first subject, Sally, had an ST personality preference with an imaginative/creative and a personalized writing process preference. Sally wrote well; the education director recommended her as a possible teaching assistant for the course. Although Sally was a good writer, she appeared to struggle with the process, as evidenced by her manuscript on her personal writing style, her spoken comments, observations by the investigator, and her written responses to surveys and other questionnaires.

The second subject, the previously mentioned Beatrice, was an SF with imaginative/creative and analytical/objective writing processes. Beatrice was classified as an "at-risk" student by her advisor, by herself, and by her peers. She told the investigator she needed a great deal of help with her writing.

These subjects have been chosen because they:

1. agreed to participate in the study
2. provided useful data about word processing preferences related to personality and writing process preferences
3. represented similar findings compared with data, including Sudol's (1991a) inventory, which was collected on other participants in the study, particularly the at-risk writers described in the preceding paragraphs.

Sally was one of the subjects described with opposite MBTI functions and WPI descriptors in the middle two components of these two inventories. Sally was also the only subject with opposing preferences who displayed superior writing skills, as demonstrated by her writing assignments, by her advisor's recommendations, and by her past performances on writing assignments for other professors. Beatrice was the only at-risk subject profiled in this study with opposite personality and writing process preferences in both of the middle two descriptors as reported from her MBTI and the WPI scores.

Sally

Sally, an ISTJ, preferred an imaginative/creative and personalized writing process preferences. In her journal, she described herself as "a gardener who labors with purpose, constantly observing her garden." She added, "A gardener recognizes she did not create the goodness of her garden, but works quietly to preserve it. She is serious." Sally then switched to a first-person point-of-view and continued using the gardener metaphor to describe her ISTJ preferences. "I have always been a diligent worker," she wrote. "As I grow older, I recognize my need to have a purpose to my work. If there is no practical outcome to a task, I become unsettled and will make the task meaningful intrinsically." This description coincides with the ISTJ characteristic described by Myers (1993): "They work with steady energy to fulfill commitments as stated and on time. They go to almost any trouble to complete something they see as necessary, but balk at doing anything that doesn't make sense to them" (p. 8).

Sally's third journal paragraph reviewed her childhood and described her introverted attitude: "As a young girl I began watching people around me. I rarely spoke about what I saw, but catalogued it all. Still, I am constantly soaking up the world around me." Her next paragraph described "virtues" of "self-discipline, faith, and compassion," all important characteristics to ISTJs. Sally's introverted preference was shown in her description of herself as a gardener who did not require an audience and could "enjoy the preparation as well as the presentation." She continued to downgrade her creative side and believed her role was merely to "preserve" her garden.

Family was important to Sally. In her next paragraph, she described her husband and young daughter. "These things make me rich," she wrote. Her loyalty to her family and her strong sense of responsibility to them was apparent in this paragraph.

Sally's serious SJ temperament was also described in her journal entry. "Sometimes I am too serious and overlook the fruits of my work," Sally admitted. "It is probably the quality I have always used to keep myself private and protected. I desire to relax and take time to smell my roses."

Sally's sentences were sequential, short, and to the point, all characteristics of a sensing, analytical writer. She also wrote with logic as she analyzed her life in metaphorical terms. The only writing she mentioned in this personal description was an interest in "writing letters to old friends," which reinforced her loyalty to thoroughly established relationships.

In her personal interviews with the investigator and in various surveys and questionnaires, Sally reiterated her need to find a purpose in what she wrote. She had no difficulty accepting the word processing program, because it was the same one she had used for some time. Yet she was often hesitant to help other subjects who were having difficulty with the commands. Only when the investigator or teaching assistant asked her for assistance did she provide it. In addition, she continued to prematurely judge all the writing assignments as insignificant and told the investigator, "If I cannot find a purpose for these assignments, they are worthless to me." As Myers (1993) noted: "If they have not developed their Sensing, they may rush into premature judgments and actions without considering new information" (p. 8). She was sometimes seen by other subjects as rigid, critical, and inconsiderate of the needs of others who needed her service by refusing to help them with the software package.

All students who were familiar with Claris Works, the software package utilized during the final year of the study, were encouraged by the investigator to help those who were unfamiliar with this program. When she was willing to take time to help others, subjects said Sally gave them useful advice in a straightforward manner, and they quickly learned the new commands. Sally, however, appeared to concentrate heavily on her current assignment and did not appear to consider the impact her actions had on other subjects who asked her for help. In these cases, Sally appeared to be neglecting her nonpreferred intuitive and feeling parts and, as described by Myers (1993), did not appear to "respond appropriately to others' needs for connections and intimacy" (p. 8).

When Sally felt rushed, during the last research paper assignment, she ignored the requests of others and moved away from those who asked her for help as she worked on her manuscript on a different computer in a more secluded area of the lab. When asked by the investigator about why she intended to attempt a massive research project in the few remaining days left of the class, she appeared to be quite defensive and said, "I know I will be able to do this assignment, and if I don't do it my way, it won't mean anything to me." True to her word, she did complete a 10-page research paper that incorporated major evaluation methods for her elementary school students. Although her writing continued to look professional, she did not appear to enjoy her task and later told her advisor she was "bored with the course." Her need to have structure and purpose to her assignments, her consistent and orderly papers, and the calm approach taken in her personal journal entries all exemplified her ISTJ preferences.

On the WPI, Sally reported imaginative/creative and personalized writing process preferences. The writing anxiety Sally experienced did not appear to be related to using the computer but rather to her opposing preferences. In fact, Sally entitled her paper about writing, "On a Collision Course." She explained, "As I write, impressive style plays dodge ball in my head; when my ideas collide with style, it's no happy accident. Right now, the two are separate bouncing balls; it takes my deliberate effort to bring these together and express my thoughts in a clear way." This significant description of her difficulty meshing her imaginative, creative writing process preference with her serious, sensing personality preference was viewed by Sally as a "bouncing ball." She was able to come up with imaginative, creative ideas, but it took her sensing side to take "deliberate effort" in making things clear to the reader.

Sally's imaginative writing process preference originated a creative way to improve her writing through revision. "Right now I am concentrating on eliminating redundant words," she wrote. "The delete button is going to get quite a work out!" She carried this effective strategy for revision into a creative assignment for helping her students become better writers: "After identifying and teaching one element, I can post on a reminder chart: HOW'S YOUR STYLE? DID YOU _____." Sally hoped the results of her strategy would help beginning writers use "identified parts of style as a natural expression of ideas." Once again, Sally mixed the orderly, neat, sensing preference of identifying established elements of style with the creative expression of ideas.

Sally personalized her writing in her next paragraph, in which she explained the importance of the computer. "The writing process, especially using computers, encourages the use of good style because it enables the writer to go back to make deletions and changes," she says. She continued to elaborate on the importance of personalizing her writing, while noting the importance of a clear, logical final product: "As a writer it [the computer] frees me to let my ideas and style bounce along separate paths until I go back for revisions, grab hold of both of them, and toss them together." The dichotomy in personality and writing process preferences created stress for Sally. "The process of writing drains me while the product of my writing floods me with satisfaction," she wrote. "As a writer, causing my thoughts to collide with style will always be exhausting, but I hope, for my reader, my writing will be clearly refreshing." Again, Sally's conflict with her analytical, objective, and thoughtful ideas about style appeared to "collide" with her personalized need for her readers to find her writing "refreshing."

In her writing style paper, Sally continued to juxtapose her ST personality preferences with her imaginative/creative and personalized writing approach. In this paper, as before, Sally used a metaphor as she compared her writing style to a river that "flows, meanders, dams up, transports, builds pressure, evokes feeling, changes the banks around it, and travels with purpose." She admitted she was a writer with characteristics that made writing either "fulfilling and easy" or, conversely, a "burden."

In both her MBTI and WPI scores, Sally revealed a strong tendency for reflection. "I require quiet time to list my ideas and map out my plan before letting my words flow on the page," Sally wrote. She added that the word processor was an effective tool for her because it allowed her to easily change her path as she expressed her ideas. Once she determined her "source, tributaries, and mouth" of her ideas, she said her thoughts would "flow onto the paper." Subjects in this study with a feeling preference in the MBTI who preferred a personalized writing approach told the investigator they were able to stay on course once their writing began to flow. Sally too used the word flow to express the output of ideas, but she went through a logical, practical elimination process, using the computer to "change her path" until she was free to use her personalized preference as her thoughts were finally released and "flowed onto the paper."

Sally continued to verify her WPI preference as she added, "My writing style is personal. I tend to use writing to communicate my values." Her personalized writing process preference was also apparent when she said she liked to make her writing original and communicate her ideas with subtleties. As an experienced writer, she realized her writing tended "to be complex and often wordy" and found the computer "saves me tremendous time, as I revise my drafts so my thoughts are more clearly expressed."

The greatest difficulty Sally faced in her writing was her conflict with her natural personality preferences and her writing process preferences, which she felt were accurate. This conflict created the most stress for her when asked to write for an assigned audience. "When I am assigned a piece, I must understand the objectives and goals for my writing," she said. According to Jensen and DiTiberio (1983), "If not given a logical rationale for an assignment, they are likely to regard it as a meaningless academic exercise" (p. 14). Sally supported this idea, as she wrote, "Although I am able to follow assigned criteria when composing and can make the writing meaningful in some way, writing under specific guidelines with deadlines is most difficult for me. I prefer to write spontaneously, when a topic becomes meaningful to me."

The entire course was structured in assignments with set deadlines; this criterion continuously created conflict for Sally, as she wrote: "When deadlines, strict criteria, and meaningless topics stand in my way, pressure builds and I shut down." Sally's difficulty with assignments she did not believe were important continued to create stress for her. She sometimes refused to share her work with her peers, continuously questioned the investigator and assistant about the purpose of the assignments, and concluded that the papers were "boring" for her to write. Fortunately, Sally realized the importance of the computer in helping her ideas "flow onto the paper" and also, in the revision stages, by eliminating and deleting her "wordy writing." Unfortunately, the juxtaposition of personality and writing process preferences in three of the four categories, appeared to create a negative attitude towards each of the writing assignments. Yet Sally optimistically concluded her writing style manuscript with hopeful insight, as she stated, "I will always write. It is a part of who I am."

During a telephone interview (personal communication, October 22, 1995), Pat Otto reviewed Sally's profile with the investigator. According to Otto, it appeared that Sally, when writing, had flipped over into her inferior function and was using feeling to assess values. For example, not considering some assignments as relevant, not wanting to help others in the class, and voicing her frustration in a childlike manner indicated Sally's use of her inferior feeling function. The more stress she was under, the more she appeared to withdraw, such as moving away from others to her own private computer. When stressed, Otto said a typical reaction for ISTJs is to cut off anything that does not appear absolutely essential to them. Otto suspected Sally might be willing to help others more when not as stressed. Otto said it appeared that Sally's voice, in all the investigator's data, spoke from her values when her logic was actually her strength. Bringing her back to her strength, Otto added, could have been helpful to Sally.

Beatrice

Unlike Sally, Beatrice, an ISFJ who preferred an imaginative/creative and analytical/objective writing process on the WPI, acknowledged her writing difficulties. Beatrice's own admission of her weakness in writing appeared in an initial written survey. When asked what she considered her strengths as a writer, she wrote, "I do not have any strengths when it comes to writing." She added that she considered herself a "weak writer" because she had "a hard time gathering thoughts and organization [organizing] them." In a preliminary writing inventory (Atwell, 1987), when asked how she learned to write, Beatrice said: "I learn [learned] to write by the teacher modeling what is to be written."

This statement indicated that her writing processes had been learned and if the processes reported on her WPI profile were accurate, Beatrice's teachers had modeled imaginative/creative and analytical/

objective writing processes. Beatrice reinforced her belief that writing was a learned activity when she reiterated that people learned to write "by the teacher modeling the written assignment." When asked why people wrote, she stated, "People write because it is necessary to complete their work. Some write because they enjoy it." She continued to reinforce a preference for a learned, objective writing process when she said that a good writer "need[s] to have organization, use good grammer [grammar], puncutation [punctuation] and stick to the topic." No mention was made of personalizing writing in this inventory. Beatrice admitted, "When I write, I get negative thoughts about my writing. It [is] never good enough."

From the initial surveys and interviews with the investigator, before Beatrice had even been shown her MBTI or WPI scores, she appeared to have a strong negative feeling about her writing. From her initial written and spoken comments, her practical and realistic natural personality preferences seemed to conflict with a learned writing process.

On the first day of class, on a scale from low to high, she rated her anxiety level about writing on the computer as high. She expressed her anxiety by writing: "I feel a little overwhelmed . . . about having to do my writing on the computer. . . . I still do not feel comfortable using it." According to Myers (1993), the introverted sensing type with extraverted feeling is uncomfortable with confrontation. During an interview with the investigator, Beatrice said she felt threatened by the computer. As the course continued, she said her concerns centered on being able to recall information about how to use computer commands, and she worried about work "disappearing for [from] the screen." Another day, midway through the course, she wrote, "I still find move [moving] around on the screen to do different things on the computer to be scary."

Beatrice added that her biggest fear was not writing on the computer but "sitting and trying to think of something to write about." As an introvert on the MBTI who preferred reflection in her writing process on the WPI, Beatrice followed the quiet, serious, conscientious description Myers (1993) gives: "ISFJs are unassuming and quiet in their interactions, often putting the needs of others . . . ahead of their own" (p. 9).

Throughout the course, other subjects in the class described Beatrice as quiet and unassuming while working in their peer groups. Several commented that Beatrice did not interact with others but preferred to work alone. They did not consider her unfriendly, however, but used words such as "quiet" and "doesn't talk much" to describe her interaction with the group. Several also commented on Beatrice's conscientious, considerate attitude. Unfortunately, Beatrice was unable to get sufficient help in peer group consultations because she did not voice her anxieties about writing and word processing to other subjects. Fortunately, she did state her concerns to the investigator and assistant, who attempted to address Beatrice's writing anxiety and major computer concern about losing material that had been keyboarded and saved on her computer disk.

In her third anxiety log, Beatrice indicated in her journal that she did not use spell check and was anxious about "whether I am writing correctly." In this example, she exemplified her need for structure and expected the investigator to tell her if her writing was "correct." As Myers (1993) noted: "If ISFJs do not find a place where they can use their gifts . . . they usually feel frustrated and may become rigid in supporting hierarchy, authority, and procedures" (p. 9).

Yet by the fourth day of the class, Beatrice's frustrations appeared to have decreased; on this day she ranked her anxiety as *medium,* as she wrote, "I learned how to turn the computer on and how to open up my folder, how to do spell check. Oh, I think I am become [becoming] an expert . . . well I still have the same concerns as before . . . that the work would disappear from the screen." On this day she added that she did not know whether the WPI assessed her writing process accurately.

Midway through the course, Beatrice wrote that she felt she was "progressing," and the software package was becoming easier for her to use. She added, "I suppose that the computer enhance [enhanced] my journal writing." She ranked her anxiety level as *medium.*

During the final days of the course, Beatrice continued to rank her anxiety level as *medium* but said she was feeling more "confidence about using the computer" because she "did not lose" any of her work. She continued to worry about her work "disappearing from the screen" and added that when she had used the computer to write before she "was not sure" about what she was doing. She appeared to be consistently under great anxiety about losing her work. As Myers (1983) wrote: "Under great stress, ISFJs can get caught up in "catastrophizing"-imagining a host of negative possibilities" (p. 9). The investigator, the assistant, and other subjects in the class repeatedly assured Beatrice that her work was safe. She was told that the computer would automatically save what she had written every fifteen minutes, as long as she answered "yes" to the command that appeared on the screen about saving her works. Yet these assurances did not appear to change her anxiety about the computer mysteriously erasing everything she had written.

On a journal questionnaire Beatrice reiterated her concern that "all my work will disappear from the screen." She said she wrote her assignments out in longhand first, typed her work into the computer, and then had "some [one] edit it." On a computer inventory given on the first day of class, Beatrice repeated that she wrote almost everything out in longhand first. At this time she indicated that she did not think her writing improved through word processing but said she "sometimes" liked using the computer to write her papers. She also said she used the computer to do her report cards.

When Beatrice described her writing style in an unpublished inventory (Sudol, 1991a), her conflicting SF preferences appeared to juxtapose with an imaginative/creative and analytical/objective writing processes. Yet she did not feel she had developed her preferred imagination or analytical writing processes. She said she was not good at condensing ideas into a natural formal style and felt her writing seemed too formal. She wrote that she was reluctant to express feelings and ideas. She preferred to write factual reports but said she had trouble showing her reader the idea behind the facts. She thought her writing was too abstract and flighty and was often unsupported by examples and background. She did not think she could organize well or write logically and objectively. She said she was not good at using personal experiences to express her beliefs and personality. She had difficulty choosing topics and said writing was a slow, tedious process for her. She did admit that her writing could be arbitrary, opinionated, and underdeveloped; in both the MBTI and the WPI, Beatrice showed a preference for a planned lifestyle (J) and a decisive (D) writing process. Beatrice concluded Sudol's (1991a) inventory by stating that she did not think she was able to write thoroughly, or that her ideas were well developed and supported.

In her writing style paper, she wrote her paper out in longhand first and said she did not like having to type it onto the word processor. She did, however, think that her paper had improved as a result of word processing. Again, her major fear in writing this paper was that her work would "disappear from the screen."

Beatrice utilized information from Jensen and DiTiberio's (1989) text when writing her paper about her individual writing style. Instead of personalizing her paper, she took terms directly from the authors' descriptions of personality and writing and said that they applied to her own writing style. For example, when describing her creative writing process preference, she said that in her writing she tended to "conceptualize topics in a different way." From her analytical writing process preference, she said she preferred to write "based on objective points of view. I need clear understanding and organization of the content when I write. I seem to guide writing decisions by using certain standards."

Beatrice never developed Jensen and DiTiberio's ideas about writing and personality with personal examples. Instead, she merely gave definitions already detailed by the authors, without support or anecdotal evidence. Her introversion on the MBTI and reflective writing process she said allowed her "to anticipate ideas and plan before I start to write." As a J on the MBTI who preferred a decisive writing process, she said she liked to make decisions on her topic and needed to set a schedule to complete assignments. She added that she felt she "should" (J) work on her projects until she completed them. Unfortunately, Beatrice was unable to give specific examples about when or how Jensen and DiTiberio's descriptions about writing and personality applied to her own style. She did not think it was unusual that the middle two descriptors were different on her MBTI and WPI. "Of course, my MBTI was different from my WPI inventory," she wrote. She added, "It is wonderful to be different. It would be sad if we all had the same personality *and* the same writing style."

She did not appear to realize the problems her opposing personality and writing process preferences created for her in this paper, although she consistently discussed them with the investigator. Unfortunately, the difference in Beatrice's natural personality preference functions and apparent learned writing processes appeared to cause her great anguish about her writing, as described in her journals, inventories, and interviews with the investigator. As an undeveloped, at-risk writer, Beatrice struggled with her assignments throughout the course. On the last day of the class she admitted, in a final survey, that she was still concerned about her work "disappearing from the screen." In an evaluation of the course, however, she said she thought her writing and use of word processing had improved.

Pat Otto (telephone interview, October 25, 1995) also reviewed the investigator's assessment of Beatrice. Otto remarked on Beatrice's need for harmony. "She's going to agree to almost anything as long as you don't get too upset with her," Otto explained. The discussion about Beatrice's need for clear understanding and content as well as the strong need for standards was natural for a dominant sensor, such as Beatrice. Otto summarized Beatrice's responses as quite simple. Although Beatrice stressed the need for value and harmony, what she really required was the structure.

CONCLUSIONS

Based on five years of action research on the relationship between personality, writing process, and word processing, the MBTI and writing process inventories provided useful information for analyzing this relationship. Both Jensen and DiTiberio's (1989) and Sudol's (1991a) unpublished informal inventories on writing process were also assessed by participants as being useful in this analysis. The major finding from this study is that an understanding of personality type theory could provide participants with useful individual strategies for writing with word processors.

In *Gifts Differing* Myers (1980) summarizes good type development as having four major principles:

  1. Discovering and accepting preferred functions and attitudes
  2. Learning to make expert use of these preferences

3. Developing at least minimal comfort with the unpreferred
4. Use of the unpreferred in the service of the preferred. (pp. 181-188)

Myers's summary is a good beginning strategy for teachers to use with all types. Although all teachers may not be qualified to give the MBTI, an understanding of Jungian theory can be applied to incorporate useful strategies in the teaching of writing with word processors. Encouraging students to use preferred writing processes develops confidence in both the writing process and in word processing. The majority of subjects in this long-term study chose to use word processing for their assignments, no matter what their type, because it saved them time, offered them opportunities to revise more often and more effectively, and produced a more professional product. An understanding of their personality type was an added benefit subjects listed in developing and refining their word processing skills.

In this study, the MBTI, information on writing process taken from Jensen and DiTiberio (1989), from Sudol (1991b) and informal response from surveys, questionnaires, and inventories served as useful predictors for subjects' responses and use of word processing. Anxiety about word processing lessened when subjects used their natural preferences effectively, particularly in their dominant functions, and developed at least minimal ease with their less preferred side. In addition, writing strengths were enhanced with the use of the computer for all personality types. Software commands such as spell check and cut and paste often compensated for writing difficulties related to personality type. Understanding their writing preferences proved particularly useful to subjects who experienced difficulty in writing when the middle two descriptors in their writing processes differed from their MBTI dominant and auxiliary functions.

After collecting follow-up data on how personality affects the writing process, it is clear that when type differs from process with no apparent writing difficulties, subjects in this study appeared to continue to follow whatever writing process worked well for them. For those with writing difficulties, when type differed from process, an understanding of personality theory and the writing process helped these subjects analyze and improve their writing. In addition, these subjects, including Sally and Beatrice, agreed that word processing was a useful tool for enhancing writing strengths and improving writing difficulties.

The implications of this study indicate that personality type combined with an analysis of one's writing style can lead to a greater understanding and application of writing processes. Various computer techniques helped writers of all types in all stages of the writing process. In addition, when writing on the computer, using preferred preferences in the service of the unpreferred was found to be effective. For example, a feeling dominant writer who preferred to write personal pieces was assigned a research project. This writer learned how to use her thinking side to analyze and form objective conclusions because she valued an organized, thoughtful piece of research. Perhaps the most important finding from this study relates directly to the previous example: Teachers, students, and others who learn about personality theory can use all sides of their personalities to accomplish a task successfully.

Further implications indicate that writing anxiety can be reduced through the use of word processing, even when the middle two descriptors in the MBTI and the writing process differ, as they did for Sally and Beatrice. An understanding of the use of computers in the writing process as it relates to personality theory helped by providing strategies for diverse types.

Although this study indicated that the writing process may not become easier as writers develop in their competence, the majority of subjects said computers helped lessen anxiety in all of the writing process stages, from prewriting to the final printed hard copy. The speed, multiple functions, and ease of the computer in addition to the various formatting choices in fonts and styles, as well as in laser printouts, gave subjects less anxiety about their writing, as measured by personal surveys, investigator interviews, and anxiety logs. Knowledge of type theory and the writing process was found to be useful to participants. Subjects of all types found in the study indicated, in a final evaluation form, that this knowledge, combined with word processing techniques, helped them improve their writing in prewriting, drafting, revising, editing, and rewriting.

REFERENCES

Atwell, N. (1987). *In the middle: Writing, reading, and learning with adolescents.* Upper Montclair, NJ: Boynton/Cook.

Carskadon, T. G., McCarley, N. G., & McCaulley, M. H. (Eds.). (1987). *Compendium of research involving the Myers- Briggs Type Indicator.* Gainesville, FL: Center for Applications of Psychological Type.

DiTiberio, J. K. (1983, Autumn). The person behind the student: The Myers-Briggs approach to learning styles. *Learning Styles Network Newsletter,* pp. 4-5.

DiTiberio, J. K. (1990, June). *Teaching writing through personality.* St. Louis: Summer Institute, Saint Louis University.

DiTiberio, J. K., & Jensen, G. H. (1995). *Writing & personality: Finding your voice, your style, your way.* Palo Alto, CA: Davies-Black.

Halio, M. P. (1990, January). Student writing: Can the machine maim the message? *Academic Computing,* pp. 16-19.

Hawisher, G. E. (1991, March). *Emerging connections: Research, electronic conferences, and the writing class.* Paper presented at the Conference on College Composition and Communication, Boston.

Jensen, G. H., & DiTiberio, J. K. (1983). The MBTI and writing blocks. *MBTI News, 5,* 14-15.

Jensen, G. H. & DiTiberio, J. K. (1984). Personality and individual writing processes. *College Composition and Communication, 35*(3), 285-300.

Jensen, G. H., & DiTiberio, J. K. (1986a). *Writing process inventory.* Unpublished inventory.

Jensen, G. H., & DiTiberio, J. K. (1986b). *Writing process inventory profile.* Unpublished manuscript.

Jensen, G. H., & DiTiberio, J. K. (1989). *Personality and the teaching of composition.* Norwood, NJ: Ablex.

Lawrence, G. (1993). *People types and tiger stripes.* Gainesville, FL: Center for Applications of Psychological Type.

Myers, I. B. (1980). *Gifts differing.* Palo Alto, CA: Consulting Psychologists Press.

Myers, I. B. (1993). *Introduction to type* (5th ed.). Palo Alto, CA: Consulting Psychologists Press.

Myers, P. B., & Myers, K. D. (1977). *Myers-Briggs Type Indicator Form G.* Palo Alto, CA: Consulting Psychologists Press.

Selfe, C. (1989). Redefining literacy: The multilayered grammars of computers. In C. Selfe & G.E. Hawisher (Eds.), *Critical perspectives on computers and composition instruction* (pp. 3-15). New York: Teachers College Press.

Sudol, R. A. (1991a, March). *Inventory on writing strengths and weaknesses.* Unpublished inventory.

Sudol, R. A. (1991b, March). *Personality influences on student use of word processing.* Paper presented at the College Conference on Composition and Communication, Boston.

Zinsser, W. (1983). *Writing with a word processor.* New York: Harper and Row.

Chapter 11

Psychological Type and Extremes of Training Outcomes in Foreign Language Reading Proficiency

Madeline E. Ehrman
Foreign Service Institute

At the Foreign Service Institute (FSI), the training branch of the U.S. Department of State, U.S. government personnel and adult members of their families preparing for overseas assignments study over 60 foreign languages on an intensive basis. Their programs put equal emphasis on speaking (including interactive comprehension) and reading for foreign affairs purposes, particularly the local press. FSI language programs tend to have strong communicative orientation and at the same time promote inductive and analytic learning. All teachers are native speakers of the languages they teach. Most students have a goal equivalent to ACTFL "superior."

In an ongoing study with over 1,000 subjects, I have been investigating the relationship of individual difference variables (personality, cognitive, and affective) to learning success in both speaking and reading. Unlike earlier articles, which addressed these multiple variables, including psychological type, this report is limited to psychological type alone. Success is measured by results on oral and reading proficiency tests. The reading test requires students to skim, scan, and read in depth.

As part of the larger ongoing study, I reported on learners who did either extremely well or extremely poorly in long-term intensive training, as reflected in their scores on the *speaking* portion of the interactive end-of-training proficiency test (Ehrman, 1994b). The weakest and strongest speakers were best differentiated from all the others by the Modern Language Aptitude Test (MLAT; Carroll & Sapon, 1959). Personality variables also came into play, in general suggesting a considerable disadvantage for students who do not easily tolerate ambiguity. Among the major indicators of tolerance of ambiguity were the Jungian sensing-intuition dimension of personality and, to a lesser degree, the judging-perceiving dimension on the Myers-Briggs Type Indicator (MBTI; Myers & McCaulley, 1985).

This report addresses *reading* proficiency outcomes, focusing on the psychological type aspects of the strongest and weakest 3% to 4.5% of readers. In two earlier articles (Ehrman, 1994a; Ehrman & Oxford, 1995), I reported on correlations of psychological type with both speaking and reading proficiency for the entire sample; in this report, I treat the extremes of reading.

Although the participants in this study were not university students, they were nearly all at least college graduates. They thus represent the future of university students, especially those in university concentrations that lead to careers in foreign affairs, such as international relations or foreign language and culture. (Readers of this study in college and university settings are encouraged to seek comparisons and contrasts with their students.)

REVIEW OF LITERATURE

The Myers-Briggs Type Indicator (Myers & McCaulley, 1985) has been used to investigate reading for several decades. The following sections attempt to provide an overview of the findings.

Differential Performance

As the purpose of this chapter is to examine the relationship between foreign language reading proficiency and personality type in the Myers-Briggs model, I do not address the almost overwhelming literature in reading in general, particularly in reading foreign languages. Instead, I briefly review literature on the MBTI and reading.

Sensing and Intuition. The findings for research in reading and the MBTI consistently find a clear correlation between a preference for intuition and reading proficiency in the native language (English, because most studies were conducted with American students). This finding is usually attributed to speed of mental processing (especially on speeded tests), comfort with abstractions, orientation to meaning, and interest in conceptual material.

Several authors suggest reasons for intuitive success in reading. Lochhead and Whimbey (1987) clearly show that verbal reasoning skills are essential to reading comprehension. Such verbal reasoning is probably another important component of the intuitive "advantage" in reading. Hanson (1987b) suggests what he calls "visual literacy," or the ability to notice, visualize, make visual discriminations, and perceive abstractly in terms of symbols and images. Although noticing may be associated with sensing, the others are more likely to be linked with intuition. Visual discrimination, for instance, is almost certainly a factor in success on the usual measure of field independence, the ability to find a geometric figure in a complex design. Indeed, a number of studies have found a correlation between intuition and this kind of field independence (e.g., Holsworth, 1985), as well as with other psychological type dimensions. Gordy and Thorne's (1994) counterintuitive findings about the superiority of intuitives as proofreaders also support the perceptual strengths of intuition for verbal material.

Intuitives tend to outperform sensing types on verbal measures in general. The MBTI manual (Myers & McCaulley, 1985) reports a variety of findings that support this result, both for verbal tasks in general and for reading in particular. Studies cited in the manual that address reading directly report the usual strong correlation of intuition with reading (content and speed) and lower correlations for introversion and perceiving. For adult learners, Roberts and Butler (1982) found that intuition (and no other MBTI preference) significantly predicted success in vocabulary, reading comprehension, and total reading, and Fourqurean, Meisgeier, and Swank (1988) found similar results among fourth and fifth graders.

SN sometimes interacts with EI. In the earliest reference I have found to the MBTI and reading (Guttinger, 1977), ES was overrepresented in remedial students, and intuitives were overrepresented among the high achievers in reading among middle school students. Low performance among ES types also appears in the MBTI manual (Myers & McCaulley, 1985). Myers (1962) found an interaction effect of introversion with intuition on the untimed Concept Mastery Test (measures high levels of vocabulary and verbal reasoning). Hester (1990) reports a significant main effect for SN and for an SN-EI interaction. (These findings disappeared when academic aptitude was statistically controlled.) These results are interpreted as being affected by habits of mind that draw people differentially to activities that involve ideas and symbols.

Closely related to reading is vocabulary. In the MBTI Manual (Myers & McCaulley, 1985), researchers plotted distributions of IQ score and vocabulary for a large high school sample, based on strength of preference on the four MBTI scales. For the EI, TF, and JP scales, the stronger the preference in either direction, the greater the advantage in both vocabulary and IQ over weak preferences on the criteria. However, on the SN scale, for both IQ and vocabulary, the distribution was almost a straight line, in which high preference for sensing was related to lower IQ and vocabulary than low preference for sensing, and high preference for sensing was related to worse IQ and vocabulary results than low preference for intuition. High preference for intuition also meant high IQ and vocabulary. Intuitives' vocabulary was also found to be much stronger in the combination NP versus SJ in a more recent study (Hester, 1990).

Other MBTI Scales. Roberts and Butler (1982) point out that reading is both a perceptual and a cognitive process, so we should expect that differences in an individual's preferences for perception (sensing or intuition) and judgment (thinking or feeling) would make a difference to reading. The evidence is overwhelming for the relevance of the perceiving function (SN); it is less clear for extraversion-introversion and for the judgment function (TF).

Some studies indicate a relationship between reading and preference for introversion. Reading was associated with introversion in Martray (1971) and with introversion and intuition in McCaulley and Natter (1974/1980). In contrast, extraverts outperformed introverts in Singer's (1989) study of reading comprehension among university students in developmental reading courses.

Results are mixed for thinking and feeling. A number of studies favor feeling. Hanson (1987a) cites performance on language achievement test scores that very significantly differentiate in favor of intuitives and then in favor of intuitive feeling types over intuitive thinking types (sensing feeling types also outperform sensing thinking types). The overrepresentation of thinking types addressed in the MBTI manual (Myers & McCaulley, 1985) among poor readers and the greater gain by feeling types in remediation that included reading training and personal consultation suggest a disadvantage for thinking. Singer (1989) found an advantage for feeling when testing with narrative text.

Some studies show strength for thinking. Singer (1989) reports that thinking types outperformed feeling types on expository material and received higher scores on expository than narrative texts (whereas all other preferences did better with narrative material than expository). Intuitives, thinking types and perceiving types recalled variously more idea units and relationships from subordinate levels of prose text (Dunn, Raney, & Infield,

1989). In a related vein, Dunn, VanCleave, and Hymes (1984) found thinking to be significantly related to closure speed on gestalt completion, a characteristic hypothesized to be related to field independence and inductive reasoning, which are also probably related to reading success.

What Kind of Criterion? Although perceiving types outperform judging types on aptitude measures, judging types consistently get higher grades than the similar perceiving type, for example. INTJ vs. INTP (Myers & McCaulley, 1985). This fact is important when considering the criterion variable in studies of reading or any other skill. Thus, if grades are the criterion variable, judging types are likely to be advantaged in a way they might not be in a performance test. Of course, the type of test makes a difference, too. Sensing types are likely to do better on a discrete point test seeking mastery of facts, whereas intuitives will probably show better performance on one that emphasizes concepts. Nisbet, Ruble, and Schurr (1981) suggest that intuitives may be hindered on tests with convergent answers, in that they may make inferences unintended by the item writer and may be dissatisfied with the multiple-choice options provided. The nature of the criterion thus affects interpretation of the results of the study. The criterion measure in the study reported on later is an attempt to simulate realistic reading tasks.

Summary of Literature on Reading Achievement. Much of the material on reading and verbal achievement that is cited here is also found in Lawrence (1984). Lawrence also summarizes the research on psychological type and reading as of 1984 as follows: "Studies on type and reading consistently report that intuitive types have higher scores on speed and comprehension, with the IN_ _ types scoring higher than the EN_ _ types, and the ES_ _ types usually scoring lowest. Intuitive types also tend to be more interested in reading, and they read more books" (p. 5).

Personality Type and the Practice of Reading

Most of the studies cited earlier address performance on tests. Personality type also plays a role in more everyday reading behaviors. Hicks (1984) found sharp distinction between Ss and Ns in the number of books read in a year. Following a study in which these results were not confirmed (Hammer, 1985), Hicks (1989) again found a highly significant relationship between the amount of reading and intuition. Hicks' findings are similar to those of Golanty-Koel (1977), who found that sensing types reported a preference for television over reading and appeared to do little or no association of what is read to their own life or other books, in contrast to intuitives. An investigation of preferred learning media

(Roberts, 1982) showed that seven of the eight intuitive types included reading as one of their top two or three media, and none of the sensing types selected reading.

Jensen (1987) cites characteristics associated with each of the eight preferences. He states that sensing types may need help breaking the symbolic "code" and may ignore concepts in favor of facts, whereas intuitives are more facile with reading and may favor concepts over facts. Thinking types may ignore "tone" in their focus on the content and may tolerate impersonal presentation; feeling types are much more influenced by tone and the relationship of the content to their own values.

Personality Preference and Foreign Language Learning

Application of personality type to foreign language learning is relatively recent. Perhaps the earliest such reports were articles on personality type and language learning strategies (Ehrman & Oxford, 1989; Oxford & Ehrman, 1988), in which intuitives were found to significantly prefer searching for and communicating meaning, hypothesis formation, and authentic language use. Feeling types tended to endorse social strategies and general study strategies (practice), judging types significantly chose general (practice) strategies, and introverts and perceiving types significantly used communicative meaning strategies. Although this study did not address reading specifically, these findings suggest that intuitives will make use of induction and pattern seeking approaches in foreign language reading just as in native-language reading.

A very fine-grained qualitative study of preferred learning strategies (Ehrman & Oxford, 1990) found intuitives and perceiving types to use strategies that compensate for missing information. Intuitives liked multiple alternatives and complexity. Thinking types endorsed cognitive strategies, especially analysis; feeling types rejected them. Judging types (and introverts) sought to plan and reported difficulty with compensation strategies. In addition to the use of compensation strategies cited earlier, perceiving types used cognitive strategies such as analyzing and recombining but tended to avoid planning. Again, these findings suggest approaches that make a difference to reading success.

Later studies using a large adult sample in intensive long-term language training have found advantages for intuition in both speaking and reading tested by oral interview, in which both speaking and reading are tested interactively (Ehrman, 1993, 1994a, 1994b; Ehrman & Oxford, 1995). Intuition (and less consistently perceiving) are found to correlate to tolerance for ambiguity and ability to discriminate stimuli. Although the TF main scale did not appear to make a difference in speaking or in reading, thinking correlated significantly with end-of-training reading proficiency on four of the subscales for TF on the Type Differentiation Indicator (Ehrman, 1994a). The thinking poles of these subscales were critical, tough-minded, questioning, and logical.

Carrell and Monroe (1993) addressed the MBTI and writing, finding that intuition, thinking, and judging are related to the highest rated foreign language essays. Moody (1988) reported the SN and TF scales distinguish between liberal arts and non-arts students, which would also suggest differential approaches to reading.

WORKING HYPOTHESES

A list of commonly recognized component skills for reading seems to relate to the issue of perception and judgment. This list comes from Grabe (1991):

1. Automatic recognition skills
2. Vocabulary and structural knowledge
3. Formal discourse structure knowledge
4. Content/world background knowledge
5. Synthesis and evaluation skills/strategies
6. Metacognitive knowledge and skills monitoring.

The first four are probably related to perception; the last two are probably influenced by the judgment function. In terms of time sequence, it seems likely that 1-4 precede 5-6 and to some degree may be prerequisite to them. If this sequence is the case, it makes sense that the perceiving function (sensing or intuition) should prove highly important in reading, perhaps more than the judgment function.

My working hypotheses, based on this observation and previous findings, are as follows:

1. The perception function will play a major role in reading success. Based on previous research, both that cited earlier and my own previous findings for FSI training, intuition will characterize the strongest readers, and sensing will characterized the weakest.
2. The judging function will play a role at the extremes. Thinking, with its link to field independence, will characterize stronger readers. Feeling readers may do less well with the expository material used for training and testing at FSI, perhaps because they are less motivated to engage with them.

METHODOLOGY

Sample

The 40 very weak and 55 very strong FSI students whose characteristics
are addressed here were drawn from a subsample of 1,325 students who
entered intensive long-term language training at the U.S. State
Departments Foreign Service Institute (FSI) and for whom MBTI scores
were available. The mean age was 39 (SD=9), and the median educational
level was between BA and MA. The sample was 55% male; the median
number of languages previously studied was 2. Most of the group (71%)
were from the Department of State, whereas 10% were from the Defense
Department, 8% were from the U.S. Information Agency, 7% were from
the Agency for International Development, and the rest (4%) were from
other government agencies. English was the native language of more than
99% of the students. These students spent an average of 20 weeks in full-
time intensive training, with a range of 8-44 weeks. Slightly less than one
third each were learning Spanish (29.6%) and French (28.5%).

Filter Variables

The extreme student groups were designated by two dichotomous filter
variables, one for the *weak students versus all others,* and one for the
strong students versus all others. Both variables were determined through a
combination of difficulty of language category, number of weeks of study,
and end-of-training reading score (EOTR). Language categories are
established on the basis of relative difficulty for English speakers to learn;
normal maximum training lengths differ among categories as follows:
Category 1 (Western European languages)-24 weeks; Category 2 (Swahili,
Indonesian, Malay)-36 weeks; Category 3 (all others except Category 4)-44
weeks; Category 4 (Arabic, Chinese, Japanese, Korean)-88 weeks. EOTR is
the score from the FSI end-of-training interactive proficiency test, which is
described in Appendix A under "Measures of Student Language
Proficiency."

     Weak Student Variable. Cases were selected if (a) start-of-training
speaking score was S-0 or S-0+ (beginners) and (b) number of weeks was
equal to or greater than 12, AND:

Category of Language	Number of Weeks	End-of-Training Speaking >=
1	> =20	1+
2	>= 28	1+
3	>= 40	1+
4	>= 40	1

Strong Student Variable. Cases were selected if (a) start-of-training speaking score was S-0 or S-0+ (beginners) and (b) number of weeks was equal to or greater than 12, AND:

Category of Language	Number of Weeks	End-of-Training Speaking >=
1		3+
1	<= 22	3
2		3+
2	<=30	3
3		3+
3	<= 41	3
4		2+
4	<= 41	2

The numbers of extremely weak and strong subjects in the results cited here vary because not every participating student completed every instrument. Thus both total numbers of those for whom end-of-training data and any given instrument are available vary, as do the numbers of extreme (strong or weak) students whose scores are available for each instrument. Some of the numbers are low but are included because they are at least suggestive and appear to be consistent with trends indicated for other instruments.

The very strong students represent about 4.5% of their various subsamples; the weak students represent about 3% of the sample. The difference in proportions is attributable to two factors. The first is an artifact of the cutting scores for number of weeks of training and level of end-of-training speaking proficiency that were used in the formulas given earlier used for selecting members of each category. The second reflects a certain amount of screening of students that takes place before they are ever sent to training: Students with a poor track record in language learning or with poor language aptitude test scores may never be selected for training in the first place.

Individual Difference Variables

Data Collection and Instrumentation. Data collection was done through questionnaires. No measures were repeated. Instruments addressed in this report are described in Appendix A.

All students were asked to take the MBTI in either the short version (Form G) or its longer version (Form J, with the Type Differentiation Indicator (TDI) scoring system) at the beginning of their training. Many of them also completed one or more of five other instruments. The one of these of interest in this chapter is the Modern Language Aptitude Test (MLAT), for which many students had scores on record when they entered training. The other instruments were administered on a random-sample basis. That is, student identification codes were selected at random to receive one, two, or three questionnaires in addition to the MBTI. The number for the MBTI (TDI) is much larger than the others because it was also administered at the beginning of training to all French and Spanish students entering the classes beginning 10 times a year from October 1991 through September 1992. End-of-training proficiency ratings in speaking and reading are available for many of the students. For some there are also faculty ratings on overall effectiveness as learners, effort, and other factors. The number of students with complete end-of-training data differ from instrument to instrument.

Data Analysis Procedures

Each of the two variables derived from the formulas for finding the weakest and strongest learners was used to compare means for the various individual difference variables through T-tests.

Type distributions are compared using the chi-square-based Selection Ratio Type Table program (SRTT; McCaulley, 1985). Symbols (", #, *) used to indicate significance levels in Tables 11.3-11.5 follow SRTT conventions. The convention in Tables 11.6-11.7 is that * indicates the .05 level, ** indicates the .01 level, and *** indicates the .001 level.

For correlational results referred to in this chapter, I used Spearman's rho, a correlation statistic usually used for rank-order data. When used with interval or ratio data, Spearman's rho provides a more conservative result than Pearson product-moment correlations. All tests of correlational significance were two-tailed. Correlations of at least .15 are reported. Although .15 is very low, findings at this level are reported so that later research can further examine them with other populations.

For all statistical tests reported in this study, the acceptable significance level was set at $p < .05$ level. Some subsignificant results are also mentioned because the number of extremely weak and strong students was so small that a moderate increase in the number could well make the results significant and because they tended to pattern with other results that reached significance.

RESULTS

This report of results is organized by a set of questions about each group of students. Each question is answered first for the weakest students then for the strongest. The questions include: (a)What are they like (demographics and personality)? Includes analysis of type table distributions; (b) How do they learn?; and (c) What do the different types do to learn to read (strategies)?

Details of the number of subjects, means and standard deviations for the criterion group and the remainder of the sample, T-statistics, degrees of freedom, and significance levels are provided in Tables 11.1 (Weakest Students) and 11.2 (Strongest Students). These data are therefore not ordinarily provided in the following text, unless required to make a special point. MBTI type distributions of the whole group (Table 11.3) and the two criterion groups (Tables 11.4 and 11.5) are presented in the conventional array called a "type table."

What Are They Like?

Weakest Students. These students have significantly less previous language learning experience than other students, in terms of number of languages previously studied and in highest previously attained speaking and reading proficiencies. Male students are overrepresented among the weakest students. They are also significantly older than the others. On the biographic background questionnaire, the weakest students indicated some self-knowledge by significantly indicating that languages were less easy for them than their classmates did. They are more likely to be in category 1 languages and less likely to be in category 3 or 4 languages. These assignments are in part a result of differential assignment to training based on MLAT scores, which are indeed lower: The index score (a T-score version of the total score) in Table 11.1 represents the five part scores, which all very significantly distinguish the bottom 4.5% of readers.

These students spent more weeks in training. Finally, their teachers give them lower ratings after training on both how good a student they were and on observed aptitude.

On the MBTI, the three type tables (Tables 11.3-11.5) show the whole sample, the weakest students, and the strongest students. We can see that the weakest students show a preference for taking in information through sensing: These people prefer practical, sequential, fact-oriented learning, with a desire to control risk in the classroom. On the TDI scoring system, which provides subscales for each of the main MBTI scales plus seven comfort-discomfort scales, weakest readers significantly report themselves as concrete (vs. abstract), realistic (vs. imaginative), pragmatic (vs. intellectual), and traditional (vs. original). These are four of the five TDI subscales for sensing-intuition, and the students tend to report themselves at the sensing pole on all four subscales.

Table 11.1. Weakest Students.

Category	Non-weakest Students			Weakest Students			T	df	Signif.
	N	Mean	(SD)	N	Mean	(SD)			
Background Variables									
Age	827	38.44	(7.4)	32	42.44	(9.2)	2.95	34.80	.006
Gender (female high)	967	1.46	(.499)	40	1.28	(.452)	-2.50	43.02	.016
Highest prev. rd score	403	2.46	(1.1)	10	1.40	(1.350)	-2.99	411	.003
Highest prev. spk score	410	2.39	(1.1)	12	1.33	(1.435)	-3.18	420	.002
Numb. of prev. langs.	716	1.75	(1.0)	37	1.30	(.845)	-3.15	41.5	.003
Languages easy fr you?	909	.42	(.5)	34	.15	(.36)	-4.33	37.83	.000
Genl posthoc tchr ratg	254	61.59	(25.5)	14	42.14	(25.9)	-2.78	266	.006
Posth. tchr aptitude rtg	252	59.24	(25.8)	14	35.36	(28.6)	-3.35	264	.001
Numb. weeks of training	995	23.17	(12.6)	40	25.45	(5.892)	2.25	54.47	.028
Language category	805	2.05	(1.2)	38	1.21	(.741)	-6.57	46.72	.000
Modern Language Aptitude Test									
Index (T-score of tot.)	477	63.61	(9.8)	13	46.00	(10.6)	6.46	488	.000
Myers-Briggs Type Indicator									
Sensing-Intuition	974	105.3	(29.7)	38	88.7	(29.9)	-3.46	1010	.001
Concrete-abstract	914	5.9	(3.3)	35	4.7	(3.5)	-2.19	947	.029
Realistic-imaginative	914	6.2	(3.2)	35	5.1	(3.1)	-2.08	947	.038
Pragmatic-intellectual	914	6.3	(2.7)	35	4.3	(2.7)	-4.25	947	.000
Traditional-original	914	6.3	(3.0)	35	5.3	(3.0)	-1.91	947	.056

Table 11.1. Weakest Students (cont.).

			End of Training Proficiency Scores						
Reading	901	1.99	(.933)	40	1.23	(.480)	-9.35	53	.000
Speaking	903	2.05	(.880)	40	1.33	(.594)	-7.37	47	.000
End-of-Training Class Activities Questionnaire									
Correct to clarify mng.	120	2.6	(0.7)	4	3.0	(0.0)	7.36	119	.000
Risk-taking encour.	121	2.8	(0.5)	4	3.0	(0.0)	5.52	120	.000
Listen to NS before spk	119	2.5	(0.7)	4	1.8	(1.0)	-2.36	121	.020
End-of-Training Study Activities Questionnaire									
Study Grammar	99	2.6	(0.6)	3	3.0	(0.0)	6.24	98	.000
Written homework	103	2.7	(0.6)	3	3.0	(0.0)	6.39	102	.000
Self-designed activities	99	2.8	(0.5)	3	3.0	(0.0)	5.32	98	.000
Vocabulary list	86	2.7	(0.6)	3	2.0	(1.0)	-1.95	87	.054

Table 11.2. Strongest Students.

Category	Non-strongest Students			Strongest Students			T	df	Signif.
	N	Mean	(SD)	N	Mean	(SD)			
Background Variables									
Age	724	38.92	(9.3)	54	34.8	7.6	-3.73	65.34	.000
Education years	865	3.40	(1.093)	55	3.76	(.88)	2.96	65.05	.004
Languages easy fr you?	791	.40	(.49)	46	.65	(.48)	3.37	835	.001
Highest prev. rd score	358	2.36	(1.1)	35	3.03	(1.04)	3.41	391	.001
Highest prev. spk score	367	2.30	(1.2)	35	2.77	(1.1)	2.34	400	.020
Numb. of prev. langs.	683	1.67	(1.0)	42	2.19	(.862)	3.25	723	.001
Genl posthoc tchr ratg	247	57.94	(25.4)	20	80.70	(19.8)	3.91	265	.000
Posth. tchr aptitude rtg	245	55.11	(26.2)	20	80.35	(16.9)	-6.10	27.8	.000
Numb. weeks of training	872	22.98	(13.1)	55	27.42	(9.5)	2.48	926	.013
Modern Language Aptitude Test									
Index (T-score of tot.)	389	62.09	(10.5)	34	68.56	(6.2)	-3.55	421	.000
Myers-Briggs Type Indicator									
Sensing-Intuition	848	102.9	(29.3)	53	117.6	(25.3)	3.58	899	.000
Thinking-Feeling	848	95.5	(24.7)	53	87.2	(23.5)	-2.40	899	.017
Concrete-Abstract	794	5.7	(3.3)	46	7.0	(3.2)	2.75	838	.006
Realistic-Imaginative	794	6.0	(3.2)	46	7.4	(2.7)	2.94	838	.003
Pragmatic-Intellectual	794	6.1	(2.7)	46	7.6	(2.2)	4.68	54	.000
Experientl-Theoretical	794	6.1	(2.7)	46	6.9	(2.5)	2.14	838	.033
Traditional-Original	794	6.2	(3.0)	46	7.3	(2.5)	2.51	838	.012

Table 11.2. Strongest Students (cont.).

Tough-Tender	794	6.2	(2.7)	46	5.4	(2.4)	-1.53	838	.054
Questioning-Accomm.	794	4.1	(2.7)	46	2.9	(2.3)	-3.01	838	.003
Logical-Affective	794	4.6	(3.1)	46	3.4	(2.7)	-2.70	838	.007
Defiant-Compliant.	794	5.7	(2.2)	46	4.9	(2.1)	-2.47	838	.014
End of Training Proficiency Scores									
Reading	869	1.79	(.879)	55	3.17	(.474)	11.60	922	.000
Speaking	870	1.88	(.847)	55	3.04	(.460)	10.06	923	.000
End-of-Training Class Activities Questionnaire									
Relevant to life/work	102	2.0	(0.8)	8	2.5	(0.6)	-2.19	108	.031
Risk taking encouraged	104	2.8	(0.5)	8	3.0	(0.0)	5.19	103	.000
Take it step by step	105	2.0	(0.8)	7	1.4	(0.5)	-1.94	105	.055
Observe nat. spkrs	103	2.2	(0.7)	6	2.8	(0.4)	2.20	107	.030
Teacher at center.	103	3.0	(1.0)	7	2.1	(0.7)	-2.21	108	.029
End-of-Training -Study Activities Questionnaire									
Study alone	91	85.1	(21.2)	7	95.7	(4.5)	3.78	37	.001
Study at home	83	2.8	(0.5)	6	3.0	(0.0)	4.37	.82	.000
Hours talking to self	66	2.8	(2.4)	7	4.9	(4.6)	1.91	71	.060
Self-designed activities	81	2.8	(0.4)	7	3.0	(0.0)	4.78	80	.000
Listen to radio	40	2.3	(0.7)	5	3.0	(0.0)	6.39	39	.000
Tell stories to self	54	2.5	(0.7)	8	3.1	(0.8)	2.46	60	.017
Talk to self	63	2.4	(0.7)	7	2.9	(0.4)	2.69	11	.022
Watch TV	44	2.3	(0.8)	3	3.0	(0.0)	6.93	43	.000
Use videotapes	59	2.3	(0.7)	6	2.8	(0.4)	2.78	8	.023

Table 11.3. Type Table of the Participants in the Language Learning Profiles Project (N = 1325 + = 1% of N).

The Sixteen Complete

ISTJ	ISFJ	INFJ	INTJ
n = 181	n = 86	n = 58	n = 137
13.7%	6.5%	4.4%	10.3%
+++++	+++++	++++	+++++
+++++	++	+++++	
++++			

ISTP	ISFP	INFP	INTP
n = 40	n = 29	n = 65	n = 89
3.0%	2.2%	4.9%	6.7%
+++	++	+++++	+++++)
++			

ESTP	ESFP	ENFP	ENTP
n = 24	n = 28	n = 129	n = 95
1.8%	2.1%	9.7%	7.2%
++	++	+++++	+++++
+++++	++		

Types Dichotomous Preferences

E	n = 640 (48.3%)
I	n = 685 (51.7%)
S	n = 554 (47.8%)
N	n = 771 (52.2%)
T	n = 782 (59.0%)
F	n = 543 (41.0%)
J	n = 826 (62.3%)
P	n = 499 (37.7%)

Pairs and Temperaments

IJ	n = 462 (34.9%)
IP	n = 223 (16.8%)
EP	n = 276 (20.8%)
EJ	n = 364 (27.5%)
ST	n = 354 (26.7%)
SF	n = 200 (15.1%)
NF	n = 343 (25.9%)

Table 11.3. Type Table of the Participants in the Language Learning Profiles Project (N = 1325 + = 1% of N) (cont.).

ESTJ	ESFJ	ENFJ	ENTJ
n = 109	n = 57	n = 91	n = 107
8.2%	4.3%	6.9%	8.1%
+++++	++++	+++++	+++++
+++	++	+++	

NT	n = 428 (32.3%)
SJ	n = 433 (42.7%)
SP	n = 112 (8.5%)
NP	n = 378 (28.5%)
NJ	n = 393 (29.7%)
TJ	n = 534 (40.3%)
TP	n = 248 (18.7%)
FP	n = 251 (18.9%)
FJ	n = 292 (22.0%)
IN	n = 339 (25.6%)
EN	n = 422 (31.9%)
IS	n = 336 (25.4%)
ES	n = 218 (16.5%)
ET	n = 335 (25.3%)
EF	n = 305 (23.0%)
IF	n = 238 (18.0%)
IT	n = 447 (33.7%)

Jungian Types (E)	n	%
E-TJ	216	16.3
E-FJ	148	11.2
ES-P	52	3.9
EN-P	224	16.9

Jungian Types (I)	n	%
I-TP	129	9.7
I-FP	94	7.1
IS-J	267	20.2
IN-J	195	14.7

Dominant Types	n	%
Dt. T	345	26.0
Dt. F	242	18.3
Dt. S	319	24.1
Dt. N	419	21.6

Madeline E. Ehrman
Psychological Type and Extremes of Training Outcomes in Foreign Language Reading Proficiency.

Table 11.4. Type Table of the Weakest Readers (N = 38, + = 1 person I = selection index: ratio of percent of type in group to % in sample).

The Sixteen Complete Types

ISTJ	ISFJ	INFJ	INTJ
n = 5	n = 4	n = 0	n = 2
13.2%	10.5%	0%	5.3%
I=0.96	I=1.62	I=0.00	I=0.51
+++++	++++	++	++
++++			

ISTP	ISFP	INFP	INTP
n = 2	n = 2	n = 0	n = 2
5.3%	5.3%	0%	5.3%
I=1.74	I=2.4	I=0.00	I=0.78
++	++	++	++

ESTP	ESFP	ENFP	ENTP
n = 0	n = 1	n = 6	n = 1
0%	2.6%	15.8%	2.6%
I=0.00	I=1.25	I=1.62	I=0.37
	+	+++++	+
		+	

Dichotomous Preferences I

E	n = 21 (55.3%) 1.14
I	n = 17 (44.7%) 0.87
S	n = 26 68.4%) 1.64 *
N	n = 12 31.6%) 0.54 *
T	n = 20 (52.6%) 0.89
F	n = 18 (47.4%) 1.16
J	n = 24 (63.2%) 1.01
P	n = 14 (36.8%) 0.98

Pairs and Temperaments

IJ	n = 11 (29.0%) 0.83
IP	n = 6 (15.8%) 0.94
EP	n = 8 (21.1%) 1.01
EJ	n = 13 (34.2%) 1.25
ST	n = 15 (39.5%) 1.48
SF	n = 11 (29.0%) 1.92 "
NF	n = 7 (18.4%) 0.71

Table 11.4. Type Table of the Weakest Readers (N = 38, + = 1 person I = selection index: ratio of percent of type in group to % in sample) (cont.).

ESTJ #	ESFJ	ENFJ	ENTJ
n = 8	n = 4	n = 1	n = 0
21.1%	10.5%	2.6%	0%
I=2.56	I=2.45	I=0.38	I=0.00
+++++	++++	+	
+++			

NT	n = 5 (13.1%) 0.41 "
SJ	n = 21 (55.3%) 1.69 #
SP	n = 5 (13.2%) 1.44
NP	n = 9 (23.7%) 0.83
NJ	n = 3 (7.9%) 0.27
TJ	n = 15 (39.5%) 0.98
TP	n = 5 (13.2%) 0.70
FP	n = 9 (23.7%) 1.25
FJ	n = 9 (23.7%) 1.07
IN	n = 4 (10.5%) 0.40 "
EN	n = 8 (21.1%) 0.66
IS	n = 13 (34.2%) 1.35
ES	n = 13 (34.2%) 2.08 #
ET	n = 9 (23.7%) 0.94
EF	n = 12 (31.2%) 1.36
IF	n = 6 (15.6%) 0.87
IT	n = 11 (29.0%) 0.86

* implies significance at the .001 level
" implies significance at the .05 level
implies significance at the .01 level

Jungian Types (E)	n	%
E-TJ	8	21.1
E-FJ	5	13.1
ES-P	1	2.6
EN-P	7	18.4

Jungian Types (I)	n	%
I-TP	4	5.3
I-FP	2	5.3
IS-J	9	23.7
IN-J	2	5.3

Dominant Types	n	%
Dt. T	12	26.4
Dt. F	7	18.4
Dt. S	10	29.3
Dt. N	9	23.7

Madeline E. Ehrman
Psychological Type and Extremes of Training Outcomes in Foreign Language Reading Proficiency.

Table 11.5. Type Table of the Strongest Readers (N = 53, + = 1 person I = selection index: ratio of percent of type in group to % in sample).

The Sixteen Complete Types				Dichotomous Preferences I	
ISTJ	ISFJ	INFJ	INTJ	E	n = 25 (47.2%) 0.98
n = 4	n = 2	n = 2	n =10	I	n = 28 (52.8%) 1.02
7.6%	3.8%	3.8%	18.9%		
I=0.55	I=0.58	I=0.86	I=1.82	S	n = 12 22.6%) 0.54 #
++++	++	++	+++++	N	n = 41 77.4%) 1.33 #
			+++++		
				T	n = 33 (62.3%) 1.05
				F	n = 20 (37.74%) 0.92
ISTP	ISFP	INFP	INTP		
n = 0	n=0	n = 5	n = 5	J	n = 20 (6.6%) 0.91
0%	0%	9.4%	9.4%	P	n = 23 (43.4%) 1.15
I=0.00	I=0.00	I=1.92	I=1.40		
++	++	+++++	+++++		*Pairs and Temperaments*
ESTP	ESFP	ENFP	ENTP	IJ	n = 18 (34.0%) 0.97
n = 0	n = 0	n = 6	n = 7	IP	n = 10 (18.9%) 1.12
0%	0%	11.3%	13.2%	EP	n = 13 (24.5%) 1.18
I=0.00	I=0.00	I=1.16	I=1.84	EJ	n = 12 (22.6%) 0.82
+	+	+++++	+++++		
		+	+	ST	n = 7 (13.2%) 0.49 "
				SF	n = 5 (9.43%) 0.61
				NF	n = 15 (28.3%) 1.09

Table 11.5. Type Table of the Strongest Readers (N = 53, + = 1 person I = selection index: ratio of percent of type in group to % in sample).

ESTJ #	ESFJ	ENFJ	ENTJ		
n = 3	n = 3	n = 2	n = 4	NT	n = 26 (49.1%) 1.52 #
5.7%	5.7%	3.8%	7.6%	SJ	n = 12 (22.6%) 0.69
I=0.69	I=1.32	I=0.55	I=0.93	SP	n = 0 (0.0%) 0.00 "
+++	+++	++	++++	NP	n = 23 (43.4%) 1.52 "
				NJ	n = 18 (34.0%) 1.15
				TJ	n = 21 (39.6%) 0.98
				TP	n = 12 (22.6%) 1.21
				FP	n = 11 (20.8%) 1.10
				FJ	n = 9 (17.0%) 0.77
				IN	n = 22 (41.5%) 1.58 "
				EN	n = 19 (35.6%) 1.13
				IS	n = 6 (11.3%) 0.45 "
				ES	n = 6 (11.3%) 0.59
				ET	n = 14 (26.4%) 1.04
				EF	n = 11 (20.8%) 0.90
				IF	n = 9 (17.0%) 0.94
				IT	n = 19 (35.9%) 1.07

" implies significance at the .05 level
implies significance at the .01 level
* implies significance at the .001 level

Jungian Types (E)			Jungian Types (I)			Dominant Types		
	n	%		n	%		n	%
E-TJ	6	13.3	I-TP	10	18.8	Dt. T	22	32.1
E-FJ	5	9.4	I-FP	5	9.4	Dt. F	10	18.8
ES-P	0	0.0	IS-J	6	11.4	Dt. S	6	11.4
EN-P	13	24.5	IN-J	12	22.7	Dt. N	25	47.2

Madeline E. Ehrman
Psychological Type and Extremes
of Training Outcomes in Foreign
Language Reading Proficiency.

Strongest Students. These students show superiority in education level (somewhat beyond the bachelors degree vs. not quite graduated), number of languages previously studied, and highest speaking and reading scores in previously learned languages, relative to those who are not in this group. They also tend to be younger (by about four years) than all other students and considerably younger than the weakest students (by over seven years). Unlike the weakest readers, there is no difference with respect to gender. After training, their teachers perceive them as substantially better students overall and as having higher observed language learning aptitude. Their tested aptitude very significantly differentiates them from the other students, but some of the MLAT part scores do not distinguish the strongest readers from the others as clearly as they do the weakest.

On the MBTI, the strongest students report themselves as preferring intuition and thinking. On the TDI version of the MBTI, they also prefer the intuitive pole on all five SN subscales, the thinking pole on three of the five TF subscales on the TDI subscales, and the thinking/discomfort pole of one comfort subscale. In effect, they describe themselves as abstract, imaginative, intellectual, theoretical, original, tough, questioning, logical, and defiant.

Analysis of Type Distributions

The overall type table (Table 11.3) shows that the modal type is ISTJ, but all the T-types along with ENFP and ENFJ are relatively well represented. EI and SN are more or less balanced, but there are 6 Ts to every 4 Fs, and nearly two thirds of the sample are judging types. Because of the large number of ISTJs, SJ is the best represented temperament, and, as is usual in samples from organizations, SP is the smallest group. EN is the most populous of the "quadrants" (IS, IN, ES, EN); ES is the least. There are somewhat more dominant thinking types and fewer dominant feeling types. Females are significantly more extraverted and males more introverted (female EI continuous score-104.5, SD-26; male score-96.9, SD-26; T = 4.99, df = 1190, p level .000). Both sexes favor thinking, but males more so (female TF continuous score 98.6 SD 25, male score 91.6 SD 23, T = 4.89, df = 1076, p level .000).

Among the weakest readers (Table 11.4), the most striking fact is the highly significant overrepresentation of sensing types, ES, SJ, SF, and ESTJ in particular. Intuition, NT, and IN are significantly underrepresented. Numerically there a greater percentage of dominant sensing types and, as before, a smaller percentage of dominant feeling types. No significant type differences appear between the genders among the weakest learners.

As for the strongest readers (Table 11.5), intuition is significantly overrepresented, especially among NTs, NPs, INs, and INTJs. Sensing, ST, and IS are significantly underrepresented. Even more striking is the fact that there are no SPs in this group at all. The percentage of dominant intuitives is very high; that of dominant sensing types is very low. As with the weakest readers, there are no significant type differences between the genders.

In summary, the weakest readers have less language learning background than other students; they are older and more frequently male. Their MLAT scores are substantially lower, they spend more time in training, and their teachers rate them lower. Sensing and sensing judging types are overrepresented. The strongest readers, in contrast, have more education than other students, previous language background, and higher MLAT scores. They are younger, get better teacher ratings, and among them intuitives are overrepresented. They tend to prefer thinking.

How Do They Learn?

Information on how useful students think various classroom and study activities are is taken from an end-of-training questionnaire. The weakest readers endorsed correction to help clarify their message and a classroom that encourages risk taking. They rejected listening to native speakers before speaking. The weakest readers also found studying grammar, written homework, and study activities they thought up themselves to be most useful. They rejected use of vocabulary lists.

The strongest readers wanted the content of their training to be relevant to their lives and work, appreciated a classroom in which risk taking is encouraged, and found it helpful to observe native speakers using the language. They clearly rejected step-by-step learning and a teacher-centered classroom. They also endorsed study alone; study at home; self-designed activities; using radio; television and videotapes; telling themselves stories; and talking to themselves. They reported significantly more hours talking to themselves in the target language than did all other students, although at a near significant level.

In summary, weakest readers tend to seek relatively structured training. Strongest readers indicate more independence as learners.

What Do Representatives of the Different Types Do To Learn?

Tables 11.6 and 11.7 show correlations between the MBTI scales and the TDI subscales on the one hand, and selected classroom and study activities that are more or less related to reading on the other. On the classroom activities questionnaire, Table 11.6 tells us that introverts prefer to build a secure base and work in a controlled, apparently low-risk way. This finding is in contrast to extraverts, who are willing to guess at unknown words and want all meanings of a new word. Sensing types seek a regular routine in

Table 11.6. MBTI/TDI and Classroom Activities, N=97-159; Correlations for the TDI subscales follow the main scales to which they are related. (* .05, ** .01, *** .001 levels; near significant: p level of .051-.060).

EXTRAVERSION		INTROVERSION	
Guess meaning of what is read	.16*	Learn skills first, then apply	.17*
S1: Gregarious		Intimate	
		none related to reading	
S2: Enthusiastic		Quiet	
Get all meanings for a new word	.16*	Read aloud & get corrected	.16 near sig.
Guess meaning of what is read	.24**	Translate readings into English	.20*
S3: Initiator		Receptor	
		Learn skills first, then apply	.21**
S4: Expressive		Contained	
		none related to reading	
S5: Auditory		Visual	
		none related to reading	
SENSING		INTUITION	
Regular routine for each lesson	.18*	Correction for formal features	.20*
Learn vocabulary	.17*	Risk-taking encouraged	.22**
in context		Read without dictionary	.22**
		Read silently	.16 near sig.
S8: Concrete		Abstract	
		no significant correlations	
S9: Realistic		Imaginative	
Regular routine for ea. lesson	.24**	Correction for formal features	.21**
		Risk-taking encouraged	.24**
S10: Pragmatic		Intellectual	
Regular routine for each lesson	.21**	Risk-taking encouraged	.16*

Table 11.6. MBTI/TDI and Classroom Activities, N=97-159; Correlations for the TDI subscales follow the main scales to which they are related. (* .05, ** .01, *** .001 levels; near significant: p level of .051-.060) (cont.).

Translate readings	.20 near sig.	Guess meaning of what is read	.19*
		Read material over one's head	.16 near sig.
S11: Experiential		Theoretical	
Direct relevance to life, work	.17*	Risk-taking encouraged	.23**
		Read without dictionary	.19*
S12: Traditional		Original	
Regular routine for each lesson	.23**	Correction for formal features	.17*
Learn vocabulary in context	.17*	Risk-taking encouraged	.27***
		Read without dictionary	.21*
		Read material over one's head	.20*
THINKING		FEELING	
		Regular routine for each lesson	.20*
		Direct relevance to life, work	.15 near sig.
S14: Critical		Accepting	
		Direct relevance to life, work	.18*
		Explicit objectives- program, lesson	.20*
		Read authentic mater. frm start	.18*
S15: Tough		Tender	
		none related to reading	
S17: Questioning		Accommodating	
Read silently	.16 near sig.	Read aloud & get corrected	.16 near sig.
Get new word when ask for it	.18*		

Table 11.6. MBTI/TDI and Classroom Activities, N=97-159; Correlations for the TDI subscales follow the main scales to which they are related. (* .05, ** .01, *** .001 levels; near significant: p level of .051-.060) (cont.).

S19: Logical		Affective	
		Go step by step	.16*
		Read aloud & get corrected	.15 near sig.
		Read authentic mater. frm start	.21**
S20: Reasonable		**Compassionate**	
Risk-taking encouraged	.16*	Explicit objectives-program, lesson	.16*
		Go step by step	.18*
		Regular routine for each lesson	.21**
JUDGING		**PERCEIVING**	
Read only known material	.17*	Direct relevance to life, work	.17*
		Read without a dictionary	.18*
S21: Stress-Avoider		**Polyactive**	
Read only known material	.16*	Read without a dictionary	.22**
		Read authentic mater. frm start	.19*
		Learn vocabulary in context	.19*
S22: Systematic		**Casual**	
		Direct relevance to life, work	.20*
		Go step by step	.17*
S23: Scheduled		**Spontaneous**	
Regular routine for ea. lesson	.18*	Formal presentation of culture	.19*
S24: Planful		**Open-ended**	
Read only known material	.21**	Direct relevance to life, work	.17*
		Read material over one's head	.16*

Table 11.6. MBTI/TDI and Classroom Activities, N=97-159; Correlations for the TDI subscales follow the main scales to which they are related. (* .05, ** .01, *** .001 levels; near significant: p level of .051-.060) (cont.).

S25: Methodical		Emergent	
Read aloud & get corrected	.15 near sig.	Direct relevance to life, work	.18*

COMFORT-DISCOMFORT (CD) SCALES

S13: Guarded (T/D)		Optimistic (F/C)	
Correction for formal features	.19*	Risk-taking encouraged	.17*
Understand every word/detail	.26**	Get all meanings for new word	.16*
Read only known material	.16 near sig.		

S16: Defiant (T/D)		Compliant (F/C)	
Risk-taking encouraged	.20*	Regular routine for each lesson	.16*
Read without a dictionary	.19*		
Read material over one's head	.20*		

S18: Carefree (T/C)		Worried (F/D)	
Get all meanings for new word	.20*	Formal presentation of culture	.18*

S26: Decisive (J/C)		Ambivalent (P/D)	
Risk-taking encouraged	.23**		

S6: Intrepid (E/C)		Inhibited (I/D)	
Risk-taking encouraged	.26***	Direct relevance to life, work	.16 near sig
Get all meanings for new word	.20*		
Communicate with limited language	.16*		

S7: Leader (E/C)		Follower (I/D)	
Risk-taking encouraged	.27***		
Read material over one's head	.18*		

Table 11.6. MBTI/TDI and Classroom Activities, N=97-159; Correlations for the TDI subscales follow the main scales to which they are related. (* .05, ** .01, *** .001 levels; near significant: p level of .051-.060) (cont.).

S27: Proactive (J/C)		Distractible (P/D)	
Get all meanings for new word	.17*	Read without a dictionary	.19*

Strain (composite discomfort scale):	
Risk-taking encouraged	-.27***
Get all meanings for new word	.21**

Note: TDI subscales are reported on a 10-point continuum, in which 0 is at the E, S, T, and J poles, and 10 is at the I, N, F, and P poles. Each comfort-discomfort scale also occurs in a major type category. For instance, S6 (intrepid-inhibited) is primarily a comfort-discomfort scale but is also an E-I scale. This fact is why Intrepid is labeled E/C (extroversion/comfort).

each lesson and want vocabulary in context. Intuitive readers value risk-taking, will read without a dictionary, are comfortable with reading material with a lot of unfamiliar matter, and want to be corrected (in speaking) for grammar and other elements of accuracy. Feeling types want direct relevance to their life and work and value risk taking; on the other hand, in the TDI TF subscales, feeling types indicate a desire for external support in the form of regular lesson routines, formal correction, explicit lesson objectives, step-by-step learning, and getting corrected when reading aloud. Thinking shows many fewer correlations among the classroom activities. Judging types report disruption when they have to read material that includes only material they are familiar with. Activities associated with perceiving are something of a mixture, but the tendency is for them to be relatively open-ended and require tolerance of ambiguity. On the comfort scales, with the exception of defiant-compliant, the tendency is for those who endorse the "comfort" pole of each subscale to also endorse the encouragement of risk taking, getting wide range of meaning for a new word, and in general valuing ambiguous activities. Anxiety (represented by the "Strain" scale) is negatively correlated with risk taking but positively linked with getting all the meanings of a new word.

On the questionnaire addressing study outside class, extraverts find it useful to read magazines and newspapers, whereas introverts use interactive video and the radio. There are very few correlations with the SN scale. Thinking types regularly endorse audio- and videotapes; feeling types undertake reorganization of notes, use of vocabulary lists, and the

Table 11.7. MBTI/TDI and Study Activities, N=27-136; Correlations for the TDI subscales follow the main scales to which they are related. (* .05, ** .01, *** .001 levels; near significant: p level of .051-.060).

EXTRAVERSION		INTROVERSION	
Magazines & newspapers	.18 near sig.	Interactive video	.55**
		Vocabulary lists	.24*
S1: Gregarious		Intimate	
Magazines & newspapers	.20*	Interactive video	.49*
		Radio	.26*
S2: Enthusiastic		Quiet	
Interactive video	.39*		
S3: Initiator		Receptor	
Magazines & newspapers	.18 near sig.	Interactive video	.42*
S4: Expressive		Contained	
Television	.25*		
S5: Auditory		Visual	
none related to reading			
SENSING		INTUITION	
Read books about the language	.29*		
S8: Concrete		Abstract	
none related to reading			
S9: Realistic		Imaginative	
none			
S10: Pragmatic		Intellectual	
Reorganize class notes	.22 near sig.		
S11: Experiential		Theoretical	
no significant correlations			
S12: Traditional		Original	
Read books about the language	.30**	Audiotapes	.19*

Table 11.7. MBTI/TDI and Study Activities, N=27-136; Correlations for the TDI subscales follow the main scales to which they are related. (* .05, ** .01, *** .001 levels; near significant: p level of .051-.060) (cont.).

THINKING		FEELING	
Audiotapes	.19*	Vocabulary lists	.23*
Videotapes	.28**	Make up tests for self	.34 near sig.
S14: Critical		**Accepting**	
Audiotapes	.17*		
Written homework	.23**		
S15: Tough		**Tender**	
Videotapes	.23*		
S17: Questioning		**Accommodating**	
Videotapes	.24*		
S19: Logical		**Affective**	
Videotapes	.28**	Study grammar	.18*
		Reorganize notes	.25*
		Vocabulary lists	.27**
S20: Reasonable		**Compassionate**	
Audiotapes	.26**		
Videotapes	.25*		
JUDGING		**PERCEIVING**	
		none related to reading	
S21: Stress-Avoider		**Polyactive**	
		Magazines & newspapers	.31***
		Learn vocabulary in context	.19*
		Television	.25*
S22: Systematic		**Casual**	
		none related to reading	
S23: Scheduled		**Spontaneous**	
		none related to reading	
S24: Planful		**Open-ended**	
		Audiotapes	.20*
		Videotape	.21 near sig.
S25: Methodical		**Emergent**	
		none related to reading	

Table 11.7. MBTI/TDI and Study Activities, N=27-136; Correlations for the TDI subscales follow the main scales to which they are related. (* .05, ** .01, *** .001 levels; near significant: p level of .051-.060) (cont.).

COMFORT-DISCOMFORT (CD) SCALES

S13: Guarded (T/D)		Optimistic (F/C)	
Interactive video	.40*		
S16: Defiant (T/D)		Compliant (F/C)	
Audiotapes	.17*		
S18: Carefree (T/C)		Worried (F/D)	
		Interactive video	.46*
S26: Decisive (J/C)		Ambivalent (P/D)	
Read books in the	.28**		
target language			
Use flashcards	.24*		
S6: Intrepid (E/C)		Inhibited (I/D)	
	no significant correlations		
S7: Leader (E/C)		Follower (I/D)	
Magazines &	.24**	Interactive video	.63*
newspapers			
Radio	.32**		
S27: Proactive (J/C)		Distractible (P/D)	
Read books about	.25 near sig.	Reorganize	.22 near sig.
the language		notes	
		Television	.27*
Strain (composite discomfort scale):			
Interactive video	.56**		

Note: TDI subscales are reported on a 10-point continuum, in which 0 is at the E, S, T, and J poles, and 10 is at the I, N, F, and P poles. Each comfort-discomfort scale also occurs in a major type category. For instance, S6 (intrepid-inhibited) is primarily a comfort-discomfort scale but is also an E-I scale. This fact is why Intrepid is labeled E/C (extroversion/comfort).

like. No learning activities are associated with judging; perceiving types indicate finding a wide range of sources and resources of use. Interactive video and other nonprint media seem to be preferred by those whose scores on the comfort scales indicates discomfort, including the composite anxiety score "strain."

To summarize, the extraverts, intuitives, and perceivers appear to endorse more risky, ambiguous learning activities. Although feeling types value risk taking, they also seek external structure. Patterns for out-of-class study preferences are not entirely clear.

Summary of Results

Table 11.8 summarizes the findings of this study, as do the following paragraphs. The weakest readers relative to all other learners in the sample are older, more male, and less likely to be assigned to a "hard" language. They have less previous language learning experience. They report fewer learning activities than the strongest readers. They manifest a clear preference for sensing on the MBTI sensing-intuition scale and four of its TDI subscales and much lower cognitive aptitude.

Table 11.8. Summary of Results.

Weakest Students Older	Strongest Students Younger
Less language learning experience	More language learning experience
	Higher education level
Enter training considering language difficult.	Enter training considering language relatively easy
MBTI Sensing preference, i.e., sequential, preorganized, concrete and discrete-point learning	MBT weak preferences for imaginative and, emergent learning, i.e., more random, unplanned, or ambiguous learning
Substantially lower cognitive aptitude (ca. 1.7 SD) as measured on the MLAT	More cognitive aptitude (ca. .6-.7 SD) as measured on the MLAT
Report fewer study strategies	Report more study strategies
Self-study strategies tend to be closed-ended	Self-study activities tend to be open-ended
	Reject teacher-centered, sequential classroom activities

The strongest learners relative to all others appear to enjoy more learning resources, including more years of education, and more language learning experience to higher levels. They report more learning strategies. They are younger and show greater tested cognitive aptitude. They indicate strong preferences for intuition (on the main scale and on all five TDI subscales) and for thinking (main scale and three of the five TDI subscales, plus a TDI comfort scale associated with thinking).

DISCUSSION

An earlier paper (Ehrman, 1994b), addressed the extremes of achievement for end-of-training speaking proficiency. The present chapter looks at some of the same variables associated with extremes of reading performance. A number of the findings are very similar, most notably the demographics (except gender), the MLAT, intuition on the MBTI, and a preference by stronger students for more open-ended learning in contrast to the opposite preference by the weakest students. The most notable difference is the importance of thinking judgment to reading proficiency, in contrast to speaking proficiency, where the TF dimension played no role.

Both hypotheses presented earlier are supported. The perception function is very important to reading success: Intuition characterizes the strongest readers, and sensing characterizes the weakest. The judging function plays a role at the extremes; thinking characterizes stronger readers in this group, but weaker readers do not prefer either feeling or thinking.

Student Characteristics

The differential level of previous language learning experience by the two extreme groups relative to the other students is striking. However, the direction of causality is uncertain. People who have learned more languages previously and to a higher level of proficiency tend to learn how to learn. On the other hand, those who find learning easy may well undertake more learning of the same kind. In that way, language learning ability could well set a kind of chain reaction going, in which many of the best keep getting better.

As in the speaking study, the mean age for the strongest readers is almost 35. Although they are younger than all the other students, they are still well beyond the age when most others believe that adults can no longer learn languages to high levels. Even more encouraging for the older among us is the fact that 35 is an average. This finding means that there are plenty of learners who are well into middle age in the best reader group.

Other findings in the Language Learning Profiles Project indicate no gender difference in learning success (e.g., Ehrman, 1994b, 1995, 1996b). This investigation is the first to find a performance difference between the sexes. The difference is only among the weakest readers. It may be a result of the fact that largely males show up in occupations that are also overrepresented among those with consistent difficulty with language learning in FSI classrooms, for example, security personnel or technical equipment operators. Reading, with its strong link with educational background, may also disadvantage members of these groups because they tend to be less well educated than the foreign service officers for whom much of the curriculum is designed.

As suggested in Ehrman (1994b, 1996b), the MBTI findings for weakest learners suggest a focus on surface learning and a relative lack of orientation to deep processing. The pragmatic sensing students are often interested in mastering only what is immediately useful or shows promise of being useful soon. Other studies have indicated a preference by sensing students for structured, well-defined learning situations that required little in the way of making inferences or what-if imagining (Ehrman, 1989; Ehrman & Oxford, 1990). Inasmuch as many sensing students do very well in language training, it is likely that some kind of moderating variable is at work. Perhaps the active variable is flexibility and finding ways to adapt. Ability to adapt, in turn, is probably related to tolerance of ambiguity. This latter construct is addressed at length in Ehrman (1993, 1996b).

Strongest readers show a much greater preference for intuition (on the main scale and all five TDI subscales) and for thinking (on the main scale and three TDI subscales plus the comfort scale defiant-compliant, in the defiant direction). Intuitive students enjoy abstractions, like to work out underlying systems (especially if intuitive and thinking), tend to use learning strategies characterized by the use of meaning, are often responsive to discovery learning procedures, and may experience boredom with routine and thus welcome some unpredictability in their learning experiences (Ehrman & Oxford 1990).

Thinking is associated in particular with analytic processing, metacognitive and affective self-regulation (Ehrman, 1989; Ehrman & Oxford, 1990), and depth and accuracy of content (Lawrence, 1993). It is my guess that the use of analytic strategies, which particularly characterize intuitive thinking learners, makes the difference for reading. It may therefore be most accurate to say that intuitive thinking types in this sample are better readers, rather than that intuition and thinking separately enhance reading. This conclusion is supported by the usual finding that a strongly favored learning strategy for NTs is reading (Lawrence, 1993). In addition, the SRTT analysis of the best readers (Table 11.5) shows the NTs as significantly overrepresented but the SFs, although underrepresented, not significantly so.

Instead, it was the STs who were found in significantly smaller proportion. These findings suggest that either NT is more relevant than N and T, or that sensing preference is a more powerful variable than the TF dimension in determining reading success, or both. In fact, the consistency of findings for SN in other studies and the inconsistency of findings for the TF scale lend support to the latter interpretation. Support for the former comes from the fact that SF is significantly overrepresented among the weakest readers (Table 11.4). It is likely that both interpretations can contribute to our understanding of the NT reading phenomenon.

The absence of findings for EI and JP are somewhat surprising. For EI, if nothing else, one might expect that the introversion pole of the TDI scale auditory-visual would have shown a relationship to reading. My interpretation is that this group of students—mature, well-educated, and achievement-oriented—may have a sufficient level of type development that they have learned to operate effectively in the less preferred domain, which for extraverts when reading would usually be introversion. Additionally, these students are extremely strongly motivated by both upcoming overseas job requirements and more immediately by classroom competition and the end-of-training proficiency test (Ehrman, 1996), which may also override the comfort factor and push these relatively flexible extraverts into developing their reading skills.

It seems likely that judging and perceiving cancel each other out. Judging types tend to be organized and disciplined in their study, which is probably an important factor in their greater academic achievement relative to perceiving types, who tend to have higher tested aptitudes (Myers & McCaulley, 1985). On the other hand, perceiving types, despite their less predictable study habits, tend to be more tolerant of ambiguity (Ehrman, 1993, 1996b), both by the nature of the construct itself (open-ended, flexible) and by the consistent correlation found in study after study between perceiving and intuition (Myers & McCaulley, 1985).

Learning Strategies and Techniques

The weakest readers endorse a classroom that permits them to take risks and offers correction to clarify meaning, which suggests that they are aware of the areas in which they need to improve. The need for improvement is suggested by the third classroom strategy that is significant for them: They reject listening to native speakers before speaking, suggesting a tendency to come to premature closure (or not to open up at all), thus becoming stuck in erroneous usage. On their own, weakest students like to study grammar and do written homework, both of which tend to be relatively concrete and defined. They reject use of vocabulary lists, perhaps indicating that analytic strategies do not work well for them. Finally, they say that self-designed study activities have been helpful to them, which may indicate that many of them, with relatively little previous language learning experience, have had to learn to cope as well as they can.

The strongest readers appear to seek open-ended learning and reject activities that constrain their freedom. They want the opportunity to take risks in class and to observe native speakers using the language. They reject a limitation to language that is relevant, as well as step-by-step curricula and teacher-centered classrooms. On their own, they study alone and at home; during this time they use a variety of media, including their own self-generated material (telling stories to themselves, talking to themselves). The absence of print among the media used is surprising; I understand this absence to be a result of the fact that all students make very heavy use of print sources as part of their training thus reducing the distinctiveness.

The fact that both weakest and strongest readers find self-designed activities significantly useful deserves a look. I have noted earlier that for the weakest, this endorsement may indicate necessary efforts to develop coping strategies. For the strongest, it may suggest expertise in learning strategies such that the student finds the best ways for him or herself, not necessarily the best ways for all.

In general, the importance of intuition for reading is supported by findings reported in Ehrman (1995) that suggest that proficiency in both speaking and reading is related to use of a variety of unstructured input situations, especially those that involve interaction with native speakers, and that such proficiency is negatively linked to techniques that reduce risk (e.g., not moving on until a grammar point is mastered, strict routine in lessons, or making the teacher responsible for ones learning). Thus, these strong students seem to reject a number of the more limiting items that are negatively correlated with proficiency.

Teacher Ratings

The differential teacher ratings for overall quality as a student and observed aptitude provide no surprises. Weakest readers as measured by the end-of-training proficiency test are also rated significantly lower after training by their teachers, and the best readers on the test get significantly higher ratings from the teachers.

MBTI CATEGORIES AND READING

This study adds further weight to the stream of evidence linking intuition and reading. It shows that the findings for English as a native language described in the literature review earlier also apply to foreign language learning. They also strengthen the case for the contribution of the thinking function to the reading of complex expository text (the kind of material used in the end-of-training reading test), in a setting where there is strong extrinsic motivation. (There might have been less of an effect for TF if there had been more emphasis on the reading of imaginative material under conditions promoting primarily intrinsic motivation.)

The operative characteristic seems to be an optimum combination of tolerance for ambiguity (intuition) with well-developed analytic skills (thinking) to simultaneously do top-down, meaning-oriented processing and a more analytic parsing of text. Intuition and thinking work together to promote "deep" cognitive processing of material, which does not arouse the personal dimension that energizes feeling types. It remains to be seen if thinking types would retain their reading advantage if fictional material of an emotion-arousing nature were part of the test. (Examinees have some choice of reading topic area, including cultural themes, but the material is almost exclusively expository.)

As described in Ehrman (1994b), tolerance of ambiguity and tested language learning aptitude distinguish among learners in spite of student preselection and often intense efforts to get students to their training goals at FSI. (Students are seldom taken out of training because they are not learning well; instead, they tend to be given more time in training.) The strength of the T-test findings for extremes in reading relative to rather low overall correlations between personality variables and end-of-training proficiency for the sample as a whole (Ehrman & Oxford, 1995) suggests some sort of nonlinear relationship for which correlations are not the best measure. (A similar pattern was found for end-of-training speaking proficiency, as described in Ehrman, 1994b.)

Important abilities that relate to reading as well as speaking include associating new material with existing knowledge (intuition) and organizing and elaborating it cognitively (thinking) rather than simply adding it into a storage bin (Jones, Palincsar, Ogle, & Carr, 1987). The correlations between the MLAT and intuition in particular suggest a disposition to use one's cognitive resources to go beneath the surface and that establish elaborated knowledge structures. This tendency is likely to lead learners to be open to new material, cope with contradictions, treat their perceptions of input as hypotheses to be tested, be interested in meaning, and find ways to associate new input with previous knowledge structures. These are all mental activities that surely enhance reading proficiency, especially once the basics of unfamiliar writing systems and new language characteristics are no longer obstacles.

The weakest ignore complexity or are overwhelmed by it; the strongest appear to embrace it. The preference for thinking among the strongest readers suggests that they are able to make use of "field-independent" strategies for setting priorities and finding the salient points in what they read and then use these to organize the rest of the material in the passage. It remains to be seen if the same skills apply to listening comprehension, which is complicated by the need to process in "real time." Speed of processing associated with intuition and the tolerance of open-endedness that characterizes perceiving suggests an advantage for these two preferences. It is my guess that neither thinking nor feeling will strongly distinguish listeners: Thinking types will still have their analytic skills, and feeling types may be more attuned overall to the speaker to whom they are listening.

Various writers have suggested factors that affect reading. The reading field has had much discussion of top-down and bottom-up processing (e.g., Bernhardt, 1991a, 1991b; Hulstijn, 1991). Top-down processing is almost certainly the intuitives' playground. One might expect that bottom-up processing is the sensing types' domain, and focus on details and facts certainly plays a role. However, research on the most effective proofreaders (Gordy & Thorne, 1994) indicates that intuitive pattern recognition also probably plays a role at this level.

Automaticity of recognition and processing is probably enhanced by intuitive pattern recognition and quickness and may be interfered with by sensing reflectivity, in which perceptions are checked (sometimes repeatedly) for accuracy. Intuitives are relatively comfortable with informed guessing, another component of effective reading, and using "global redundancy," that is, additional information from the text beyond the sentence level (McDonough, 1981). Intuition probably helps with not getting bogged down and keeping the "big picture"; thinking probably contributes to the formation of a conceptual hierarchy, together with intuition. Various writers on second language reading have addressed a threshold of linguistic knowledge before which effective reading is very difficult (e.g., Hulstijn, 1991); perhaps the abilities described earlier contribute to reducing the level of the threshold for readers who can tolerate more ambiguity.

Also consistent with the role of intuition in reading is connectionist theory. For example, Stanovich (1991) describes connectionism as a model in which, as a result of activation of networks of (neural) connections and associations, information generates patterns of activation and reinforces connection strengths. Stanovich thinks this process is important in reading; it also seems to be related to the kind of pattern processing that characterizes intuition.

Bernhardt (1991b) says that "literacy variables" include such "intrapersonal variables" as the purpose for reading, the reader's intention, and the reader's preferred level of understanding. The last of these, level of understanding, is likely to be strongly influenced by intuition and possibly by the NT temperament, with its constant search for competence (Keirsey & Bates, 1978). On the other hand, Bernhardt (1991b) also describes reading as a "social process," in which "texts are social and cultural artifacts reflecting group values and norms" (p. 14). This aspect of reading is likely to appeal to feeling types.

Alderson (1984) makes two hypotheses about the causes of poor second language reading. The first is poor reading skills in the first language. Although the MBTI literature suggests that this proposed cause may be true for sensing types in the general population, the effects of this phenomenon are probably muted in the FSI sample. It is true that FSI intuitives are very significantly better educated (Ehrman, 1994a), but the sensing types in the sample are almost all college graduates and thus not weak readers in their native language. The second hypothesis is that insufficient knowledge of the second language affects the ability to read. (This hypothesis is the foundation of the threshold model mentioned earlier.) For the FSI population, the second hypothesis is certainly valid. The role of psychological type is, as described earlier, to lower the threshold and give access, through intuitive tolerance of ambiguity and related strategies, to print media at lower levels of linguistic proficiency and to give access to more meaning at every level through the same strategies. Indeed, another reading scholar specifically mentions the importance of tolerance of ambiguity in reading (Clarke, 1979).

CONCLUSIONS

We have seen a combination of individual difference factors that appears to differentiate extremely weak and strong readers in intensive language training. The SN scale is the most powerful of the psychological type variables; thinking-feeling appears to play a secondary role that may be determined by purpose of reading, nature of reading material, and context of learning, thus helping account for the inconsistency of findings for thinking and feeling and reading in the literature. However, certain cautions are in order in applying these findings.

Although individual capacities and developed skills seem to be important, some of the influence may go the other way: FSI curricula and classroom techniques have evolved over the years to meet the requirements of a certain type of student who is common among our clients. The students in this sample closely resemble others who have entered in the past; they surely benefit from training that has been developed to fit their predecessors. That is, there may be a set of attributes that characterize good classroom readers, but at the same time, FSI classrooms may have evolved to fit a certain learner profile, thus enhancing the "edge" of those who most have the features of the profile. We do know that intuition advantages readers in almost every other setting studied so far, but we do not know yet what profile describes those who can best learn to read in natural settings.

How well can we generalize from this sample to students in other settings? FSI students are older, better educated, generally high functioning, and intensely motivated. They are relatively experienced learners and have already demonstrated an interest in foreign languages and cultures by their very choice of career. On the other hand, perhaps the characteristics that help FSI students might contribute to success in high school and college language classes; this relationship in turn might lead the stronger students to be attracted to a career involving other languages and cultures.

Investigations remain to be done. Other statistical tests could be done. This study focused primarily on the MBTI; the other individual difference variables addressed in the study of extremes in speaking (Ehrman, 1994b) should also be included. The two end-of-training learning activity questionnaires need validation. Different cut points in the population than the bottom 3% and the top 4.5% might yield additional enlightenment. At some point, we should examine interaction effects as well as main effects.

It is vital not to overgeneralize to individuals. The fact that one personality style appears to have a statistical advantage in a certain learning situation does not exclude those without it from the ranks of successful learners. These statistics expose trends but they in no way describe an individual's drive, maturity, intelligence, or coping skills. Furthermore, statistics such as these may be highly specific to this population and situation. These findings can be constructively used to make hypotheses about individuals, but the hypotheses must be tested against the reality of each individual's abilities, type development, and motivation.

REFERENCES

Alderson, J. C. (1984). Reading in a foreign language: A reading problem or a language problem? In J. C. Alderson & A. H. Urquhart (Eds.), *Reading in a foreign language* (pp. 1-24). London: Longmans.

Bernhardt, E. B. (1991a). How is reading in a second language related to reading in a first language? In *Reading in two languages. AILA Review 8*, 5-14.

Bernhardt, E. B. (1991b). *Reading development in a second language: Theoretical, empirical, & classroom perspectives.* Norwood, NJ: Ablex.

Carrell, P., & Monroe, L. B. (1993). Learning styles and composition. *The Modern Language Journal, 77,* 148-162.

Carroll, J., & Sapon, S.M. (1959). *Modern Language Aptitude Test.* New York: Psychological Corporation.

Clarke, M. A. (1979). Reading in Spanish and English: Evidence from adult ESL students. *Language Learning, 29,* 121-150.

Dunn, B. R., Raney, G., & Infield, S. (1989). Personality type and free recall from text. *Journal of Psychological Type, 19,* 45-47.

Dunn, B. R, VanCleave, R., & Hymes, D. (1984). The relation of the Myers-Briggs Type Indicator to closure speed. *Journal of Psychological Type, 8,* 45-47.

Ehrman, M. E. (1989). *Ants and grasshoppers, badgers and butterflies: Quantitative and qualitative investigation of adult language learning styles and strategies.* Ann Arbor, MI University Microfilms International.

Ehrman, M. E. (1993). Ego boundaries revisited: Toward a model of personality and learning. In J. E. Alatis (Ed.), *Strategic interaction and language acquisition: Theory, practice, and research* (pp. 331-362). Washington, DC: Georgetown University Press.

Ehrman, M. E. (1994a). The Type Differentiation Indicator and adult foreign language learning success. *Journal of Psychological Type, 30,* 10-29.

Ehrman, M. E. (1994b). Weakest and strongest learners in intensive language training: A study of extremes. In C. Klee (Ed.), *Faces in a crowd: Individual learners in multisection programs* (pp. 81-118). Boston: Heinle and Heinle.

Ehrman, M. E. (1995). Personality, language learning aptitude, and program structure. In J. E. Alatis (Ed.), *Linguistics and the education of second language teachers: Ethnolinguistic, psycholinguistic, and sociolinguistic aspects.* Washington, DC: Georgetown University Press.

Ehrman, M. E. (1996a). An exploration of adult language learner motivation, self-efficacy, and anxiety. In R. Oxford (Ed.), *Language learning motivation: Pathways to the new century.* Honolulu: University of Hawaii Press.

Ehrman, M. E. (1996b). *Understanding second language learning difficulties: Looking beneath the surface.* Thousand Oaks: CA: Sage.

Ehrman, M. E., & Oxford, R. L. (1989). Effects of sex differences, career choice, and psychological type on adult language learning strategies. *The Modern Language Journal, 72,* 1-13.

Ehrman, M. E., & Oxford, R. L. (1990). Adult language learning styles and strategies in an intensive training setting. *The Modern Language Journal, 74,* 311-327.

Fourqurean, J., Meisgeier, C., & Swank, P. (1988). The Murphy-Meisgeier Type Indicator for Children: Exploring the link between psychological type preferences for children and academic achievement. *Journal of Psychological Type, 16,* 42-46.

Gordy, C. C., & Thorne, B. M. (1994). Proofreading ability as a function of personality type. *Journal of Psychological Type, 28,* 29-36.

Grabe, W. (1991). Current developments in second language acquisition research. *TESOL Quarterly 25,* 375-406.

Guttinger, H. I. (1977). Patterns of perceiving: Factors which affect individualized reading instruction at the high school level. *Bulletin of Research on Psychological Type, 1,* 78-79.

Hammer, A. L. (1985). Psychological type and media preferences in an adult sample. *Journal of Psychological Type, 10,* 20-26.

Hanson, J. R. (1987a). *Learning and teaching styles: A review of the research.* Moorestown, NJ: Hanson, Silver, Strong, & Associates.

Hanson, J. R. (1987b). *Learning and visual literacy: Connections and actions.* Moorestown, NJ: Hanson, Silver, Strong, & Associates.

Hester, C. (1990). The differential performance of MBTI types on learning tasks. *Journal of Psychological Type, 19,* 21-26.

Hicks, L. E. (1984). Conceptual and empirical analysis of some assumptions of an explicitly typological theory. *Journal of Personality and Social Psychology, 46*(5), 1118-1131.

Hicks, L. E. (1989). Bookishness and the null hypothesis. *Journal of Psychological Type, 17,* 14-19.

Holsworth, T. E. (1985). Perceptual style correlates for the MBTI. *Journal of Psychological Type, 10,* 32-35.

Hulstijn, J. (1991). How is reading in a second language related to reading in a first language? *Reading in two languages. AILA Review 8,* 5-14.

Jensen, G. H. (1987). Learning styles. In J. A. Provost & S. Anchors (Eds.), *Applications of the Myers-Briggs Type Indicator in higher education* (pp. 181-208). Palo Alto, CA: Consulting Psychologists.

Jones, B. F., Palincsar, A. S., Ogle, D. S., & Carr, E. G. (1987). *Strategic teaching and learning: Cognitive instruction in the content areas.* Alexandria VA.: Association for Supervision and Curriculum Development.

Keirsey, D., & Bates, M. (1978). *Please understand me: Character and temperament styles.* Del Mar, CA: Prometheus Nemesis.

Lawrence, G. (1984). A synthesis of learning style research involving the MBTI. *Journal of Psychological Type, 8,* 2-15.

Lawrence, G. (1993). *People types and tiger stripes* (3rd ed.). Gainesville FL: Center for Applications of Psychological Type.

Lochhead, J., & Whimbey, A. (1987). Teaching analytical reasoning through thinking aloud pair problem solving. In J. E. Stice (Ed.),

Developing critical thinking and problem-solving abilities (pp. 73-92). San Francisco: Jossey-Bass.

Martray, C. R. (1971). An empirical investigation into the learning styles and retention patterns of various personality types. (Doctoral dissertation, University of Alabama). *Dissertation Abstracts International*, 1972, *32*, 5043A. (University Microfilms No. 72-8446).

McCaulley, M. H. (1985). The selection ratio type table: A research strategy for comparing type tables. *Journal of Psychological Type, 10,* 46-56.

McCaulley, M. H., & Natter, F. L. (1980). *Psychological (Myers-Briggs) type differences in education.* Gainesville, FL: Center for Application of Psychological Type.

McDonough, S. H. (1981). *Psychology in foreign language learning.* Boston: George Allen & Unwin.

Moody, R. (1988). Personality preferences and foreign language learning. *The Modern Language Journal, 72,* 389-401.

Myers, I. B., & McCaulley, M. (1985). *Manual: A guide to the development and use of the Myers-Briggs Type Indicator.* Palo Alto, CA: Consulting Psychologists.

Nisbet, J. A., Ruble, V. E., & Schurr, K. T. (1981). Predictors of academic success with high risk college students. *Journal of College Student Personnel, 23*(3), 227-235.

Oxford, R. L., & Ehrman, M. E. (1988). Psychological type and adult language learning strategies: A pilot study. *Journal of Psychological Type, 16,* 22-32.

Roberts, D. Y. (1982). Personality and media preferences of community college students. *Journal of Psychological Type, 5,* 84-86.

Roberts, D. Y., & Butler, L. G. (1982). Relationship of personality type and reading ability among pre- and in-service teachers. *Journal of Psychological Type, 5,* 80-83.

Saunders, D. (1989). *Type Differentiation Indicator Manual: A scoring system for Form J of the Myers-Briggs Type Indicator.* Palo Alto, CA: Consulting Psychologists Press.

Singer, M. (1989). Cognitive style and reading comprehension. *Journal of Psychological Type, 17,* 31-35.

Stanovich, K. E. (1991). The psychology of reading: Evolutionary and revolutionary developments. *Annual Review of Applied Linguistics, 12,* 3-30.

APPENDIX A: INSTRUMENTATION

The Myers-Briggs Type Indicator (MBTI; Myers & McCaulley, 1985) Form G.

This instrument is a 126-item, forced-choice, normative, self-report questionnaire designed to reveal basic personality preferences on four scales: extraversion-introversion (whether the person obtains energy, externally or internally), sensing-intuition (whether the person prefers to take in information in a concrete/sequential or an abstract/random way), thinking-feeling (whether the person likes to make decisions based on objective logic or on subjective values), and judging-perceiving (whether the person prefers rapid closure or a flexible life). Internal consistency split-half reliabilities average .87, and test-retest reliabilities are .70-.85 (Myers & McCaulley, 1985). Concurrent validity is documented with measures of personality, vocational preference, educational style, and management style (.40-.77). Construct validity is supported by many studies of occupational preferences and creativity.

The Type Differentiation Indicator (TDI; Saunders, 1989).

The TDI is a scoring system for a longer and more intricate 290-item form (MBTI Form J) that provides data on the following subscales for each of the four MBTI dimensions: extraversion-introversion (gregarious-intimate, enthusiastic-quiet, initiator-receptor, expressive-contained, auditory-visual), sensing-intuition (concrete-abstract, realistic-imaginative, pragmatic-intellectual, experiential-theoretical, traditional-original), thinking-feeling (critical-accepting, tough-tender, questioning-accommodating, reasonable-compassionate, logical-affective), and judging-perceiving (stress avoider-polyactive, systematic-casual, scheduled-spontaneous, planful-open-ended, methodical-emergent). The TDI includes seven additional scales indicating a sense of overall comfort and confidence vs. discomfort and anxiety (guarded-optimistic, defiant-compliant, carefree-worried, decisive-ambivalent, intrepid-inhibited, leader-follower, proactive-distractible), as well as a composite of these called "strain." Each of the comfort-discomfort subscales also loads on one of the four type dimensions, for example, proactive-distractible is also a judging-perceiving subscale. There are also scales for type-scale consistency and comfort-scale consistency. Reliability of 23 of the 27 TDI subscales is greater than .50, an acceptable result given the brevity of the subscales (Saunders, 1989).

The Modern Language Aptitude Test (MLAT; Carroll & Sapon, 1959)

This is the classic language aptitude test, with 146 items. The manual describes its five parts: I—number learning (memory, auditory alertness), II —phonetic script (association of sounds and symbols), III—spelling clues (English vocabulary, association of sounds and symbols), IV—words in sentences (grammatical structure in English), and V—paired associates (memorizing words). The MLAT was correlated .75 with the Defense Language Aptitude Battery (FSI, 1985) and .67 with the Primary Mental Abilities Test (Wesche, Edwards, & Wells, 1982)—the latter suggesting a strong general intelligence factor operating in the MLAT. Split-half reliabilities for the MLAT are .92-.97, depending on the grade or age. For college students, validity coefficients are .18-.69 for the long form of the MLAT and .21-.68 for the short form. For adult students in intensive language programs, validity coefficients are .27-.73 for the long form and .26-.69 for the short form (Carroll & Sapon, 1959). In this sample, almost all (95%) of the MLAT scores were current, that is, administered within the last 3 years. This study used the long form.

End-of-Training Learning Activity Questionnaires

Two questionnaires were distributed at the end of training. One, developed by Lucinda Hart-Gonzalez , Nikolaus Koster, Gisela Gonzales, and Madeline Ehrman at FSI, addresses various activities reported by a "snapshot" of FSI students for study on their own, without a teacher (Hart-Gonzalez, 1991). Its 36 items request the student (a) to assess the utility of the activity on a scale of "not useful, somewhat useful, very useful," and also (b) to estimate the approximate number of hours spent weekly on it. The other was developed by Madeline Ehrman and Frederick Jackson at FSI based on knowledge of frequent classroom events and on student end-of-training comments about their language learning experience. Its 70 items request students to assess on the same Likert scale as the self-study questionnaire the utility of selected classroom events in the areas of conversation, pronunciation, grammar study, listening practice, reading practice, vocabulary study, classroom structure, and the role of the teacher. Because it has taken a long time to amass a sufficient number of these two questionnaires for analysis (departing students are less likely to turn in questionnaires than those still in training that we can pursue), reliability and validity studies remain to be done. In fact, the present report is a first contribution to evaluation of their validity.

Student Learning Activities Questionnaires

At the end of training, each student in the study was asked to complete two questionnaires: "CLASSACT" (Ehrman & Jackson, 1992) on relative usefulness of a fairly detailed list of classroom activities (Likert scaled 1-3), and "SELFACT" (Hart-Gonzalez & Ehrman, 1992) on relative usefulness (1-3) of their own study activities and estimated time per week devoted to each. These questionnaires are used here for the first time. Because completion at end of training was voluntary and students were very busy with preparations for departure, the return rate was low, and Ns for a number of the items are not adequate for analysis. This and other studies using these two questionnaires are part of their validation. When there are sufficient cases, they will be subjected to reliability analysis and factor analysis.

Measures of Student Language Proficiency

At the end of training, FSI students are given proficiency assessments resulting in ratings ranging from 0 to 5 for speaking (including interactive listening comprehension) and for reading. For example, R-3 means reading proficiency level 3. S-2 means speaking proficiency level 2. The ratings are equivalent to the ILR/ACTFL/ETS guidelines that originated at FSI and have been developed over the years by government agencies. FSI usually aims at end-of-training proficiency ratings of S-3 R-3 for full-time training, comparable to ILR/ACTFL Advanced Proficiency. Reliability studies have shown that government agencies have high interrater reliability for proficiency ratings within a given agency but that the standards are not always the same at every agency; thus raters at different government agencies do not have as high an interrater reliability as raters at the same agency. Proficiency ratings are thus considered reliable indicators of the level of language performance of an individual student within an agency (Clark, 1986). Descriptive statistics for performance in terms of end-of-training proficiency are provided in Table 2. "Plus" scores (indicating, e.g., proficiency between S-2 and S-3) were coded as .5; thus, for example, a score of S-2+ was coded 2.5.

Adult second language learners usually rely on reading skills that have been built up in their native languages, unlike first language learners, who are learning reading skills, getting real world knowledge, and undergoing cognitive development, all simultaneously. Adult second language learners have many reading skills that can transfer; they have considerable world knowledge and (if well educated, and especially if they have learned another language) knowledge about how to learn. They are generally fully developed, having attained the ability to think abstractly. Their challenges as readers are more focused—particularly on skills related to foreign alphabets, on sound-symbol relationships, and on accepting the inherent ambiguity in a new cultural and linguistic system, both spoken and written. Grabe (1991) details some of these challenges.

Faculty Rating Questionnaire

After training was complete, faculty were asked to rate students on how they compared overall with other FSI students known, on observed language learning aptitude, motivation, effort, and observed anxiety. Data were collected by interview in order to get a rich texture of comments as well as quantitative data. In order to achieve reliability, interviewers were trained and asked to follow the format of the questionnaire.

Author Index

A

Abraham, R., 166, *177*
Alderson, J.C., 269, *270*
Aldrich, F., 80, *87*
Aristotle, 22, *33*
Atwell, N., 207, 223, *229*

B

Bacon, F., 22, *33*
Bartholomae, D., 108, 120, *121*
Bates, M., 43, *54* 74, 80, 86, *88*,
    154, 155, 156, 159, 160, 162,
    163, 165, 169, 173, 174, *178*,
    186, *203*, 269, *272*
Batschelet, M. 101, *103*
Baumlin, J.S., 39 *54*
Beeman, M. , 71, *87*
Berens, L.V., 80, 86, *87*
Berko, Gleason, J., xx, *xxiii*
Bernhardt, E.B., 268, 269, *270*
Berthoff, A.E., 108, 120, *121*

Bizzell, P., 22, *33*
Bloom, L., xx, *xxiii,*
Booth, W.C., 21, 27, *33*, 42, *54*
Britton, J., 97, *102*
Brown H. D., xx, xxi, xxii, *xxv*
Brown, R., xx, *xxiv*
Bruffee, K., 98, 99, *102, 103*
Burgess, T., 97, *102*
Burke, K.E., 5,*17*, 38, *54*
Burke, C., xxi, *xxiv*
Burns, M.S., 56, 58, 59, 69, 73, *87*
Burry-Stock, J.A., 159, 163, 167,
    179
Butler, L.G., 233, 234, *273*

C

Calvin, W.H., 59, 84, *87*
Campbell, G., 22, *33*
Carr, E.G., 267, *272*
Carrell, P., 237, *271*
Carroll, J., 232 *271*, 275

Carskadon, T.G., 210, *229*
Chall, J. S., xxi, xxii, *xxiv*
Chapelle, C., 166, *177*
Cherry, R.D., 42, *54*
Cheung, F., 158, *177*
Chomsky, C., xx, *xxiv*
Chomsky, N., xix, xx, *xxiv*
Clark, C.L., 98, *103*
Clark, I., 99, *103*
Clarke, M.A., 269, *271*, 276
Condon, J., 172, *178*
Connelly, C., 98, *103*
Cooper, S.A., 80, 86, *87*
Corbett, E.P.J., 22, *34*
Couture, B., 186, *203*
Cummings, J.L., 56, 58, 59, 69, 73, 87
Cunningham, D., 108, *121*

D

D'Aquili, E.G., 67, *88*
Davis, S., 61, 62, 83, 86, *87*
Day, R., 166, *178*
Deutsch, G., 56, *88*
Diamond, S., 71, *87*
DiTiberio, J.K., xv, xxi, *xxiv*, 30, 31, 32, *34*, 43, *54*, 93, 94, 96, 97, 99, *102*, 105, 107, 110, 113, 115, 118, *121*, 129, 130, 133, 139, 141, 150, *151*, 185, 194, 197, 199, 201, *203*, 208, 209, 210, 211, 222, 226, 227, 228, *229, 230*
Dong, Y.R., 158, *178*
Du Marsais, C.C., 61, *87*
Dunn, B.R., 233, 234, *271*
Dunn, K., 102, *103*
Dunn, R., 102, *103*

E

Ede, L.S., 25, 26, *34*, 42, *54*, 92, 95, 99
Ehrman, M., xxi, xxii, *xxv*, 155, 156, 159, 160, 161, 162, 163, 166, 167, 169, 169, 171, 175, *178, 179*, 230, 236, 237, 263, 264, 265, 266, 267, 269, 270, *271, 273*, 274, 276
Eimas, P.D., 58, *87*
Elbow, P., 28, *34*, 108, 119, *121*
Ellis, R., 174, *178*
Ellison, L., 87, *87*
Ely, C.M., 169, 170, *178*
Emig, J., 105, 106, 118, *121*
Eslinger, P.J., 80, *87*

F

Flower, L., 120, *121*
Fontana, D., 97, 102, *103*
Fourqurean, J., 233, *272*
Freiedman, R.B., 71, *87*
Frisbie, G.T., 107, 110, 111, 113, 114, 115, *121*
Fulkerson, R., 19, 26, *34*

G

Galaburda, A.M., 58, *87*
Gavin, F., 96, *101*
Gebhardt, R.C., 183, *203*
Geertz, C., 5, *17*
George, D., 95, 100, *103*
Giovannoni, L.C., 80, *87*
Golden, J.L., 22, *34*
Goldfield, B., xxii, *xxiv*
Gomez, M.L., 94, 95, *99*
Goodenough, D., 166, *179*
Goodman, Y., xxi, *xxiv*
Gordy, C.C., 233, 268, *272*
Goswami, D., 193, *203*
Grabe, W., 237, 272, *277*
Grafman, J., 71, *87*
Grattan, L.M., 80, *87*
Gregorc, A., 160, *178*
Guttinger, H.I., 233, *272*

H

Halliday, M. A. K., xix, *xxiv*
Halio, M.P., 211, *229*

Halper, A.S., 56, 58, 59, 69, 73 *87*
Hammer, A.L., 235, *272*
Hansen, J., 166, *178*
Hanson, J.R., 233, 234, *272*
Harshbarger, B., 157, 158, 163, 167, 171, *178*
Hawisher, G.E., 210, *230*
Hayes, J., 120, *121*
Heath, S.B., 4, *17*
Herrington, A., 193, *203*
Herzberg, B., 22, *33*
Hester, C., 233, 234, *272*
Hicks, L.E., 235, *272*
Hirsch, S., 30, *34*
Hofstede, G., 158, *178*
Hollaway, M.E., 167, 171, 172, *179*
Holsworth, T.E., 233, *272*
Horning, A.S., xxi, xxii, *xxiv*, 186, *203*
Hudson-Ross, S., 158, *178*
Hulstijn, J., 268, *272*
Hymes, D., 235, *271*

I

Infield, S., 234, *271*
Iser, W., 108, *121*

J

Jenkins, L. , xi, *xxiv*
Jensen, G.H., xv, xxi *xxiv*, 28, 30, 31, 32, *34*, 43, 54, 93, 94, 96, 97, 102, *103*, 105, 107, 110, 113, 115, 118, *121*, 129, 130, 133, 140, 141, 142, 150, *151*, 185, 194, 197, 199, 201, *203*, 208, 209, 210, 211, 222, 226, 227, 228, *230*, 236, 266
Johnson, N., 39, 40, *54*
Jones, B.F., 267, *272*
Jung, C.G., xi, *xxiv*, *xii*, 3, 5, *17*, 56, 78, *87, 88*, 95, 102, *103*
Jungeblut, A., xi, *xxiv*

K

Karis, B., 101, 102, *103*
Keirsey, D., 43, *54*, 74, 80, 86, *88*, 154, 155, 156, 159, 160, 162, 163, 165, 169, 173, 174, *178*, 186, *203*, 269, *272*
King, M.L., Jr., 44, *54*
Kirk, B.A., 171, *179*
Kirsch, I.S., xi, *xiv, xxiv*
Kolstad, A., xi, *xxiv*
Kozy, M.C., 56, 58, 59, 69, 73, *87*
Kroeger, O., 43, 45, *54*, 93, 96, *103*
Kroll, B.M., 27, 29, *34*
Kummerow, J., 30, *34*

L

Langacker, R., xix, *xxiv*
Lanham, R.A., 52, *54*
Laughlin, C.D., Jr., 67, *88*
Lavine, R., 155, 156, 159, 166, 169, 172, 175, *179*
Lawrence, G., xxii, *xxiii, xxiv*, 64, *88*, 93, *103*, 155, *178*, 210, *230*, 235, 264, *272*
Lindemann, E., 135, *151*
Lindsay, M.B., 71, *87*
Lochhead, J., 233, *272*
Locke, J., 23, *34*
Long, R.C., 25, *34*
Longstreet, E., 172, *178*
Lunsford, A., 26, *34*, 42, *54*, 92, *103*, 126, *151*

M

Maid, B.M., 31, *34*
Martin, N., 97, *102*
Martray, C.R., 234, *273*
McCarley, N.G., 210, *229*
McCaulley, M.H., xxii, xiv, xiii, *xxiv*, 20, *34*, 68, 86, *88*, 110, *121*, 154, 156, 160, 165, 169, 170, 174, *178*, 210, *229*, 232, 233, 234, 235, 240, 265, *273*, 274
McDonough, S.H., 268, *273*

McManus, J., 67, *88*
Meisgeier, C., 233, *272*
Mesulam, M.-M., 56, *88*
Miller, K.D., 43, *54*
Mitchell, R., 257, 26, 31, *34*
Moffett, J., 29, *34*
Mogil, S.I., 56, 58, 59, 69, 73, *87*
Monroe, L.B., 237, *271*
Moody, R., 237, *271*
Mulderig, G.P., 184, *203*
Murillo, D., 167, 171, 172, *179*
Murray, D.M., xxi, xxii, xiv, *xxiv*,
   108, *121*, 134, *151*
Myers, I.B., xiv, xii, xiii, xxii, *xxiv*,
   20, 30, *35*, 43, *54*, 68, 86, *88*,
   107, 109, *121*, 154, 156, 160,
   165, 169, 170, 174, *178*, 187,
   203, 219, 220, 224, 225, 227,
   230, 232, 233, 234, 235, 265,
   273, 274
Myers, K.D., 208, *230*
Myers, P.B., 208, *230*
Natter, F.L. 234, *273*

N

Nelson, G., 158, 172, *179*
Nelson, K., xxi, *xxiv*
Newman, J., 144, *151*
Nisbet, J.A., 235, *273*
Nuby, J.F., 157, 158, 163, 168, *179*

O

Odell, L., 193, *203*
Ogle, D.S., 267, *272*
Ojemann, G.A., 59, 84, *87*
Olbrechts-Tyteca, L., 41, *54*
O'Hear, M. F., xxii, *xxv*
Ong, W.J., 25, 26, *35*, 38, *54*
Ornstein, R., 56, *88*
Oxford, R.L., xxii, *xxv* ,154, 155,
   156, 157, 154, 156, 157, 158,
   159, 162, 167, 169, 170, 171,
   172, 173, 175, *178, 179*, 232,
   236, 264, 267, *271, 273*

P

Palincsar, A.S., 267, *272*
Park, D.B., 24, *35*
Pearsall, T., 108, *121*
Perelman, C., 41, *54*
Perez, E., 71, *87*
Perl, S., 125, 148, 149, *151*
Petrick, J.F., 26, *35*
Pfister, F.R., 26, *35*
Price, T., 80, *87*

Q

Quenk, N., xiv, xv, *xxv*, 187, 192,
   203

R

Raney, G., 234, *271*
Reid, J., 158, *179*
Reither, J., 98, *103*
Roberts, C., 166, *177*
Roberts, D.Y., 233, 234, 236, *273*
Robins, R. H., xix, *xxv*
Ross, T., 157, 158, 162, 167, 171,
   178
Rossi-Le, L., 159, *179*
Ruble, V.E., 235, *273*
Rymer, J., 186, *203*

S

Sapon, S.M., 232, 275, *271*
Saunders, D., 154, 174, *179, 273*,
   274
Schroeder, C., 97, *103*
Schurr, K.T., 235, *273*
Selfe, C., 207, *230*
Selinker, L., xx, *xxv*
Shaughnessy, M., xxi, *xxiv*
Sides, C., 94, 97, 102, *103*
Singer, M., 234, *273*
Skehan, P., xxii, *xxv*
Slobin, D., xx, *xxv*
Smagorinsky, P., 194, *203*
Smith, F., 194, *203*
Snow, B., xxii, *xxiv*

Sommers, N., 120, *121,* 125, 126, 145, 151, 183, *203*
Springer, S.P., 56, *88*
Stanovich, K.E., 268, *273*
Stansfield, C., 166, *178*
Sternglass M. S., xxii, *xxv*
Stewart, D., 120, *121*
Storr, A., 95, 96, *100*
Strasma, K., *98,* 105
Sudol, R.A., 210, 211, 218, 226, 227, 228, *230*
Sue, D.W., 171, *179*
Sulzby, E., xxi, *xxv*
Swank, P., 233, *272*

T

Tafoya, S., 157, 158, 162, 169, 171, *178*
Tarvin, G.A., 56, 58, 59, 69, 73, *87*
Taylor, M., 25, 26, 31, *34*
Teale, W., xxi, *xxv*
Thompson, T., 132, 139, *151*
Thorne, B.M., 233, 268, *272*

Thuesen, J.M., 43, 45, *54,* 93, 96, *103*
Trzyna, T., 101, *103*

V

VanCleave, R., 235, *271*
Vandenberg, P., 26, *35*
Via, J., 157, 158, 163, 167, 171, *178*
Vico, G., 60, 90
Vipond, D., 100, *103*

W

Wallace, B., 154, 173, *179*
Whimbey, A., 233, *272*
White, E.M., 106, *121,* 184, 202, *203*
Willing, K., 157, *179*
Witkin, H., 166, *179*
Woodruff, J., 186, *203*

Z

Zinsser, W., 211, *230*

Subject Index

A

abstract language, 59-60
African-Americans
  type and, 157-158, 163, 168,
    171,172
ambiguity tolerance, 169
anaphora, 80
anatonamasia, 62
apostrophe, 61
Arabic speakers
  type and, 157-158, 163, 171
Asians
  type and, 159, 171
assessment, 202
at-risk writers, 217, 218
audience, 148, 150
  contemporary views of, 23-29
  traditional views of, 22-23
author
  implied, 42
auxiliary type, 213, 228

B

brain hemispheres, 56-61
  right hemisphere and metaphor,
    71-73

C

case study research, 184, 218
Chinese speakers
  type and, 158-163
cognitive style
  choices of journal writing mode,
    109*t*, 111*t*
  related to type, 63*t*, 84-85
cohesion, 186
collaboration in writing,
  type and, 190
  revision and, 199
collaborative learning, 92, 96-98,
  99-102
composing process, 131
  See also writing process

computers
IBM, 211
Macintosh, 211
writing and, 208, 225
writing process and personality
preferences related to, 211,
221
writing anxiety and, 229
See also word processing
concrete language, 59-60
connectionist theory of reading,
268
core functions, *see* sensing-thinking
correctness, 126
creativity, 140, 145, 146, 147, 148,
150
cross-cultural differences
type and, 154, 156-159, 161-
163, 166-168, 170-172, 176

D

dominant type, 196, 200, 213, 228
intuition as, 253
sensing as, 253
doublespeak, 62
dramatism, 38, 42

E

editing, 133, 136, 139, 145, 183,
184, 229
e-mail, 210
ENFJ, 139, 140, 252
as persuasive leader, 43
ENFP, 16, 139, 146, 189, 190, 252
in journal writing, 114-115
in lyric writing, 68-70
storytelling, 9
use of metaphor, 71
ENTJ, 15, 142, 145, 190
hearty leadership style, 50
use of assignment sheet, 117-118
use of irony, 82
ENTP, 15, 192
in journal writing, 114-116

error, 134, 139, 141, 142, 143,
144, 145
ESFJ, 130, 136, 137, 189, 190, 191
in journal writing, 113-114
ESFP
in journal writing, 113-114
in lyric writing, 75-76
ESTJ, 15, 133, 137, 217, 252
in journal writing, 111-113
in lyric writing, 64-65, 67
revising habits, 67-68
ESTP, 15, 190, 192
in journal writing, 111-113
realism, 51
ethos, 39-42
euphemism, 62
extensive mode of response, 106
extraversion, and collaboration, 94-
96
extraversion/introversion, 49-50,
92-93, 233, 265
philosophy of writing, 20
presence of audience, 28-29
extraverted type
conflicts with introversion, 159-
160
reading in a second language,
265
responding to writing, 191
revising writing, 191
second language learning and,
156, 253, 258, 262
extraverted-feeling type
community leadership, 11
in rhetorical situations, 21
language instruction, 13-14
mimetic philosophy of
composition, 21
style, 32
extraverted-intuitive type, 252
and benefits of education, 6-7
extraverted-sensing type, 233, 252

extraverted-thinking type
  in rhetorical situations, 21
  mimetic philosophy of
    composition, 21

F

fable, 62
fantasy, 63t
  in intuitive function, 68
feeling type, 141, 184
  conflicts with thinking types,
    169-170
  emphasis on writer and
    audience, 30
  persona and audience role, 53t
  reading in a second language,
    234, 236, 237, 263, 269
  revising writing, 189, 195, 196,
    197, 198, 200, 201
  writing process of, 220, 228-229
  second language learning and,
    165, 167, 258, 260, 267, 268,
    269
  self-expression, 30
  tactful writing, 30
field independence and dependence
  second language reading and,
    237, 267-268
  type and, 166, 235
figurative language, 59-60
flexibility, 150
foreign language learning,
  definition of, 153

G

gender
  type differences and, 154
grammar, 146, 173

H

heuristics, 135, 138, 144
Hispanics
  type and, 157, 167, 171
homiletic tradition, 43

I

identification, 38
impulsive/reflective second
  language learners, 170
inferior function, 184, 186, 187,
  192, 201, 223
  extraverted sensing as, 199, 200
  extraverted thinking as, 200
INFJ, 139, 140, 142, 146, 147
  conservative values, 74-75
  in journal writing, 114-115
  in lyric writing, 68, 74
INFP, 141, 144, 147, 189, 191,
  196, 200
  easy-going idealist, 46-47
  in journal writing, 115
INTJ, 144, 146, 147, 193, 235
  in lyric writing, 79-80
  repairing a broken world, 46
  use of irony, 82
  use of repetition, 80
INTP, 143, 235
  in journal writing, 116
  in lyric writing, 79-80
  problem-solving, 49
  revising, 82
  use of pun, 81, 82
  use of repetition, 80
  versatile use of tropes, 83-84
introversion, and collaboration, 94-
  96
  conflicts with extraversion, 159-
    160
  in contrast to extraverted
    preaching, 44
  reading and, 234, 236, 265
  revising writing, 189, 195, 196,
    197, 198, 199, 200
  second language learning and,
    156, 253, 258
  with intuition and reading skill,
    234
  with sensing, 224
  writing process of, 217, 219, 226

introverted-feeling type
  in rhetorical situations, 21
  mimetic philosophy of
    composition, 121
introverted-intuitive type, 252
introverted-sensing type, 253
  and skeptical view of education,
    6
introverted-thinking type
  in rhetorical situations, 21
  mimetic philosophy of
    composition, 21
  style, 32
intuition
  use of analogy, 14
intuitive type, 127, 130, 138, 139,
    140, 141, 142, 145, 146, 148,
    186, 189
  conflicts with sensing types, 163-
    165
  IQ and, 234
  language use, 144
  performance on verbal
    measures, 233
  reading ability, 237
  reading in a second language,
    258, 263, 264
  reading proficiency and, 233,
    234, 235, 236, 237
  revision by, 142, 190, 195, 196,
    197, 198, 199
  second language learning as,
    161, 162, 232, 253, 262, 263,
    268, 269
  tolerance for ambiguity and, 267
  writing ability in a second
    language, 237
  writing process of, 220
  vocabulary ability, 234
intuitive-feeling type
  and brain domination, 57
  in journal writing, 114-115
  in lyric writing, 68-73

revising habits, 69-71
style, 33
and thinking style, 85-86
use of metaphor, 62-63, 69, 71
use of pronouns in journals, 110t
intuitive-perceiving type, 191, 234,
    252
intuitive-thinking type, 191, 252,
    264, 265·
  and brain domination, 57
  in journal writing, 115-116
  in lyric writing, 79-84
  style, 33
  temperament, 269
  and thinking style, 85-86
  use of irony, 62-63, 80-81
  use of pronouns in journals, 110t
  versatile use of tropes, 83-84
irony, 61-62
  use by intuitive-thinking type,
    80-81
ISFJ, 130, 131, 132, 136, 189, 192,
    217, 223-227
  in lyric writing, 76-78
  obligation, 45
ISFP, 217
  in journal writing, 113-114
ISTJ, 16, 130, 132, 135, 136, 138,
    219-237, 252
  checklists, 48
  in journal writing, 111-113
  language instruction, 7-8
  in lyric writing, 64, 65
  sense of duty, 44-45
  storytelling, 97
ISTP
  in journal writing, 111-113

J

Japanese speakers
  type and, 158, 163, 167, 172
journal writing, 127
  as foundation for writing
    assignments, 118-120

choices of mode by type, 109t, 111t
for reading response, 106
guidelines, 121-123
use of assignment sheet, 117-118
use of pronouns in, 110t
value of, 117
judging/perceiving, 265
judging type, 128, 136, 148
conflicts with perceiving types, 172-173
learning activities of, 261
persona and audience role, 53
reading and, 258, 265
revising writing, 189, 195
second language learning and, 169, 232, 236, 253
writing process and, 217, 226
writing in second language, 237
judgment function, 237
Jungian typology, 126, 144, 156, 157, 228, 232

K

Kiersey Temperament Sorter (KTS), 154
Korean speakers
type and, 158, 159-160, 163, 167, 171

L

language
abstract, concrete, figurative, and literal, 59-60
language learning
type and, 154
learning style, 155, 236
literal language, 59-60
literary text, response to, 106
literacy variables, 268
litotes, 61

M

MBTI, See Myers-Briggs Type Indicator
metaphor, 60-61, 140
in intuitive-feeling type, 69, 71
mixed and flawed, 71-73
in sensing-feeling type, 77-78
metonymy, 62
use by sensing-feeling type, 75-76
Modern Language Aptitude Test (MLAT), 232, 240, 241, 251, 253, 263, 275
motivation
intrinsic vs. extrinsic, 267
Myers-Briggs Type Indicator (MBTI), 37, 57-58, 85, 94, 105, 107, 154, 184, 193, 208, 210, 212, 214, 218, 219, 222, 226, 227, 228, 234, 238, 241, 269, 274
reading and, 232, 253
second language learners and, 238-239, 252, 262, 263, 264, 270

N

Native Americans
type and, 157, 163, 168, 171, 172
non-preferred writing strategies, 190, 191, 192, 198, 202, 228
North Americans
second language learning, 166, 170

O

oral interview, 193
oxymoron, 61
use by intuitive-thinking type, 81

P

parable, 62

paragram, 61
  use by intuitive-thinking type, 81
partitio, 66
perceiving, 189, 191
  conflicts with judging types,
    172-175
  learning activities of, 261
  persona and audience role, 53t
  responding to writing, 191
  second language learning and,
    169-170, 232, 236, 262
  writing process of, 217
perception function, 237
persona, 38-42
  in public documents, 52
personality preferences
  computers and, 212
  conflicts with writing process
    preferences, 222, 224
  revising writing and, 184, 202
  rhetorical roles, 53t
  second language learning and,
    231, 269,
  theory of, 227
  word processing and, 207-230
  writing process and, 211, 221
personification, 60
polyptoton, 80
portfolios, 184, 187, 202
prewriting, 132, 207, 230
Puerto Ricans
  type and, 167
pun, 61
  use by intuitive-thinking type, 81

R

reading
  proficiency correlated with
    intuition, 232
  type and second language, 173
reading response
  journal writing, 106
realism, 63t

redundancy, 186, 221, 268
reflexive mode of response, 106
research report, 130
revising
  by ESTJ, 67-68
  by intuitive-feeling type, 69-71
  by INTP, 82
  definition of, 144, 149
  editing and, 126, 139, 144, 229
  macro and micro revising, 184
  processes of, 126, 127, 129,
    133, 137, 138, 194, 221, 223,
    228
  punishment of, 142
  recursion in, 135, 139, 149
  resistance to, 125
  steps in, 135, 142, 147, 200
  strategies and type, 126, 132,
    134, 137, 146, 190
romance, 63t
rhetoric
  contemporary, 41-42
  history of, 39-41
rhetorical roles, 53t
rhetorical self, 52
rhetorical situation, 195

S

satire, 63t
  use by sensing-thinking type, 65-
    66
second-language learning
  classroom suggestions, 174-177
  definition of, 153
self
  central and rhetorical, 52-53
self-assessment, 131, 143
self-reflection, 128
sensing
  attention to detail, 129
  conflicts with intuitive types,
    163-165
  reading and, 236, 237, 263

revising and, 133, 136, 138, 190
second language learning by,
161-162, 232, 253, 262,
266, 269
second language teaching and,
168
television and, 235
writing process of, 138, 220
sensing-feeling type, 218, 226, 252,
265
and brain domination, 57
in journal writing, 113-114
in lyric writing, 64, 73-74
and metonymy, 62-63
style, 32-33
and thinking style, 85-86
use of metaphor, 77-78
use of pronouns in journals, 110*t*
sensing/intuition, 233, 237, 241,
252, 258, 265, 269
attitudes toward schooling, 8-9
contrasts between persona and
audience, 47
sensing-judging type, 219, 234,
252
conservative values, 74-75
in lyric writing, 64-65
sensing-perceiving type, 252, 253
in lyric writing, 74-75
sensing-thinking type, 223, 252,
265
brain dominance, 57, 67
in creative writing, 68
in journal writing, 111-113
practical narratives, 9
revising habits, 67
style, 32
and thinking styles, 85-86
use of pronouns in journals, 110
use of satire, 65,
use of synecdoche, 62-63, 66
simile, 60
symbolic enactment, 62
symbolic writing, 78-79

synecdoche, 61
use by sensing-thinking type, 66

T

temperament, 186
sensing-judging type, 219
thesis statements, 141, 143, 151,
188, 190
thinking, 186
conflict with feeling types, 168-
169
emphasis on subject, 30
impersonal text, 30
persona and audience role, 53*t*
reading and, 234, 236, 237, 267
reading in a second language,
263, 264
responding to writing, 190
revising writing, 195, 200
second language learning and,
165
and social challenges, 14-15
technical writing, 32
truth in writing, 30
writing in a second language,
237
writing process of, 217, 229
thinking/feeling, 236-237, 252,
263, 265
contrasts as writers, 31
contrasts in persona, 47
philosophy of writing, 20
think-aloud protocols, 192, 193,
194
tropes, 60-63
type
and teaching strategies, 97-98
type development, 227, 265
Type Differentiation Indicator (TDI),
154, 237, 239, 240, 241, 252,
253, 258, 262, 263, 264, 265,
274
type theory
culture, 4-6

U

understatement, 61

W

word processing, 222, 227, 228
writers
  at risk, 217
  experienced, 135, 222
  expert, 184, 186, 187, 192-201
  types of, 209
writing anxiety, 129, 211, 216,
  217, 224, 225, 228, 229
writing process
  approaches to, 209
  awareness of, 139
  linear, 132, 134, 145, 148

recursion and, 134, 138, 141,
  148, 149
revising as an aspect of, 183
second language, type and, 175
students and, 187
tacit knowledge of, 193
See also composing process
Writing Process Inventory (WPI),
  208, 212, 214, 218, 219, 221,
  223, 224, 226, 227
writing purpose, 132

Z

zeugma
  use by intuitive-thinking type,
  81-82